TRUTH IN THE MAKING

Is knowing a purely passive reception of something concrete outside the mind, or when we know something are we creating something too?

Spanning more than 500 years of philosophical enquiry from the Middle Ages to the present day, Robert Miner clarifies modern philosophical conceptions of knowing as making or constructing, and contrasts this view with the theological understanding of knowing as a participation in divine creation.

This study demonstrates how "creative knowledge" has its roots in the theologies of Thomas Aquinas and Nicolaus Cusanus. It explores the multiple ways in which this idea influenced the architects of the modern philosophical viewpoint, most notably Francis Bacon, René Descartes and Thomas Hobbes, despite their secular stance. Miner contends that, well in advance of Kant, one of these thinkers, Giambattista Vico, provided a remarkably succinct formulation of the metaphysical and epistemological core of modernity in his principle *verum et factum convertuntur*: "the true and the made are convertible."

In *Truth in the Making*, Robert Miner challenges the standard assumption that Kant was the first thinker to conceive of knowing as constructive activity. By tracing the development of these contrasting theological and secular theories of knowledge, Miner presents a compelling argument for contemporary theology to reclaim a concept of knowing that is both creative and participates in divine wisdom.

Robert Miner is Assistant Professor of Philosophy in the Honors College at Baylor University. He has published widely on the history of modern philosophy and is the author or *Vico, Genealogist of Modernity*.

RADICAL ORTHODOXY SERIES
Edited by John Milbank, Catherine Pickstock
and Graham Ward

Radical Orthodoxy combines a sophisticated understanding of contemporary thought, modern and postmodern, with a theological perspective that looks back to the origins of the Church. It is the most talked-about development in contemporary theology.

RADICAL ORTHODOXY
edited by
John Milbank, Catherine Pickstock
and Graham Ward

DIVINE ECONOMY
D. Stephen Long

TRUTH IN AQUINAS
John Milbank and Catherine Pickstock

CITIES OF GOD
Graham Ward

LIBERATION THEOLOGY AFTER THE END OF HISTORY
Daniel M. Bell, Jr

GENEALOGY OF NIHILISM
Conor Cunningham

SPEECH AND THEOLOGY
James K. A. Smith

CULTURE AND THE THOMIST TRADITION
Tracey Rowland

BEING RECONCILED
John Milbank

AUGUSTINE AND MODERNITY
Michael Hanby

TRUTH IN THE MAKING
Robert Miner

TRUTH IN THE MAKING

Creative knowledge in theology and philosophy

Robert Miner

First published 2004
by Routledge
29 West 35th Street, New York, NY 10001

Simultaneously published in the UK
by Routledge
11 New Fetter Lane, London EC4P 4EE

Routledge is an imprint of the Taylor & Francis Group

© 2004 Robert C. Miner

Typeset in Baskerville by
Keystroke, Jacaranda Lodge, Wolverhampton
Printed and bound in Great Britain by
TJ International Ltd, Padstow, Cornwall

All rights reserved. No part of this book may be reprinted or
reproduced or utilised in any form or by any electronic, mechanical,
or other means, now known or hereafter invented, including
photocopying and recording, or in any information storage or
retrieval system, without permission in writing from the publishers.

Library of Congress Cataloging in Publication Data
Miner, Robert C., 1970–
Truth in the making : knowledge as construction in theology and
philosophy / Robert Miner.
p. cm. – (Radical orthodoxy)
Includes bibliographical references and index.
1. Knowledge, Theory of. 2. Truth. 3. Philosophical theology.
I. Title. II. Radical orthodoxy series.
BD171.M514 2003
121–dc21
2003046529

British Library Cataloguing in Publication Data
A catalogue record for this book is available
from the British Library

ISBN 0-415-27697-7 (hbk)
ISBN 0-415-27698-5 (pbk)

"Dieu se produit, se connaît soi-même parfaitement, comme nous fabriquons et connaissons misérablement des objets hors de nous."

(S. Weil)

CONTENTS

Acknowledgments		ix
Prologue		xi
1	**Thomas Aquinas**	**1**
	Scientia Dei and creation	2
	Creation and human production	7
	Making and the "analogy of being"	11
2	**Nicolaus Cusanus**	**19**
	The dramatic setting of the *Idiota de Mente*	20
	Construction as manifestation of forms through image-making	21
	Constructions of reason	23
	The activity of *mens: vis assimilativa* and the construction of concepts	26
	Activa creatio humanitatis: making as imaging of the divine exemplar	31
3	**Francis Bacon**	**40**
	The Baconian *factum*	40
	Induction as constructive method	45
	Limits on human making: Bacon's forms	50
	For and against Bacon	55
4	**René Descartes**	**60**
	The Cartesian *factum*	60
	Representations as artifacts made from simple natures	65
	The constitution of simple natures	67
	Construction in the determination of *quaestiones*	69
	The division of the Cartesian inheritance	73

5	**Thomas Hobbes**	**78**
	The making of geometrical definitions	79
	The commonwealth as feat of technical making	85
	Science and power	92
6	**Giambattista Vico**	**96**
	Making and truth	96
	Abstraction as creation	100
	Making within metaphysics	105
	Making as imaginative mythopoesis	108
	Making as the creation of elements	113
	Making as composition from elements	119
	Epilogue	**126**
	Notes	130
	Bibliography	156
	Index	161

ACKNOWLEDGMENTS

I am grateful to John Milbank, Catherine Pickstock and Graham Ward, the editors of the Radical Orthodoxy series, for the impetus to write this book. Initial research was made possible by a Research Incentive Grant at Boston College. For this, I am pleased to thank Joseph Quinn, Dean of the College of Arts and Sciences at Boston College, and Michael Smyer, Associate Academic Vice President for Research and Graduate Studies.

During the composition of this book in Boston, many friendships sustained me. In particular, I wish to express my gratitude to my former colleagues in the Department of Philosophy at Boston College. Their (continued) friendship and support has been invaluable. Many thanks are due to other friends in Boston: Kerry Cronin, Matthew and Kelly McDonald, John Olohan, Michael and Caitlin Raiger, Elizabeth Solomon. It is a pleasure to acknowledge the students at Boston College, graduate and undergraduate, who helped to improve my thinking. Of particular assistance, both theoretical and practical, was Jason Taylor.

Work on the final chapter was greatly facilitated by Giuseppe Mazzotta's invitation to present work in progress to his seminar on Vico's poetic philosophy. I am grateful to him and to his students at Yale.

At my new academic home at Baylor University, I am pleased to have begun a conversation with my colleagues in the Department of Philosophy and the Great Texts Program. Particular acknowlegment is due to Robert Baird, Michael Beaty, Phillip Donnelly, Barry Harvey, Douglas Henry, Thomas Hibbs, David Lyle Jeffrey, Scott Moore, Margaret Tate and Ralph Wood.

Finally, I wish to give my deepest thanks to my family: Heather, Anne, Sebastian, Sophia, Emma, and Maria.

PROLOGUE

The aim of the present work is to conduct an inquiry into some influential conceptions of the relationship between knowing and making. There is no shortage of contemporary attempts to construe a wide range of phenomena as products of making. By now virtually everything has been described as a "construction." Ian Hacking provides an A–Z list of things recently said to be "socially constructed": authorship, brotherhood, the child viewer of television, danger, emotions, facts, gender, homosexual culture, illness, knowledge, literacy, the medicalized immigrant, nature, oral history, postmodernism, quarks, reality, serial homicide, technological systems, urban schooling, vital statistics, women refugees, youth homelessness, Zulu nationalism.[1] "Everything is constructed"—this might be the slogan of modernity. But do we believe in the ultimate reality or significance of our constructions? What Kierkegaard said about his own time is no less applicable to the present age: our business as makers, constructors, fabricators goes on as usual, yet there is no longer anyone who really believes in it. What is constructed can always be deconstructed. Everything that is woven seems destined to unweave. The spectre of nihilism haunts modernity.

This book is written on two assumptions. The first assumption is that we should look for some alternative to this state of affairs. There is something odd about the currently fashionable tendency to embrace the idea that modernity leads to nihilism, and yet to celebrate nihilism as if it were beneficial for thinking and doing, or somehow entertaining. The second assumption is that any meaningful articulation of an alternative to (post)-modern nihilism requires ongoing dialogue with the traditions of philosophy and theology. We are not the first to suggest that informed understanding of contemporary talk about construction and deconstruction demands historical perspective. Hacking argues that the way of thinking that underlies all contemporary social constructionist perspectives—as well as the "logical constructions" of Russell's epistemology, the *Aufbau* of Carnap's logical positivism, the worlds of Goodman's world-making, and the moral values of any number of contemporary ethicists—can be derived from Kant, whom he describes as "the great pioneer of construction."[2] Recent modes of constructivism are but "different mansions built within Kant's house."³ Even though their advocates like to "bask in the sun they call post-modernism," Hacking writes, "they are really old-fashioned."⁴

This does not go nearly far enough. Without denying the historical influence of Kant (although even here the story is more complicated than Hacking suggests), we may observe that Kant is *not* the pioneer of construction. Prior to Kant, Giambattista Vico proposed in 1710 that to verify something (*verare*) is the same as to make it (*facere*). Vico concluded that "the true is the made itself" (*verum ipsum factum esse*). F.H. Jacobi found the essence of the Kantian philosophy in Vico, whose "*verum-factum*" axiom he understood as the contention "that we can grasp an object only insofar as we can let it come into being before us in thoughts, can make or create it in the understanding."⁵ The citation of Vico may see only a minor correction to Hacking. A revised version of Hacking's position might hold that to understand "construction" as rational making we must turn to history of thought, which means primarily to Kant, but secondarily to neglected and less influential thinkers such as Vico and whoever else was fortunate enough to anticipate the Kantian standpoint.

Kant plays little role in the present work. This is not only because we reject outmoded historiographies that privilege his thought as the apex of modernity—the "historical" aspect of our study converges with others that have generally denied his status as an authentic revolutionary—but also because we doubt that his particular conception of thinking-as-making can lead anywhere except (through Hegel and Fichte) to Nietzsche. Without being able to substantiate that claim here, we may assert that both the "descriptive" goal of understanding the history of construction and the "normative" aim to articulate an alternative to the dominant modern conception of making requires an effort to think outside of Kantian categories (in loose and strict senses of the term).

But what is the dominant modern conception of making? With Heidegger, we would emphasize the notion of *techne*. Heidegger holds that philosophy as "metaphysics" generally construes thinking on the model of making, which it understands in technical or instrumental fashion. In order to find a way out of the nihilism to which the enthronement of technical making leads, we need to retrieve a radically non-technical conception of *poiesis*. Given these rather substantial agreements with Heidegger, one may legitimately wonder how the present approach differs from his.

First, our exposition of the presence of the "maker's knowledge" paradigm in the architects of modern philosophy strives for a clarity of thought and expression with which Heidegger is not customarily associated. Our reading does not try to understand Bacon, Descartes and Hobbes as specimens of "productionist metaphysics." It proceeds by paying close attention to their use of "making-language," indicated by terms like *facere, factum, operare, opus, ars, artifex*, in connection with the deployment of "knowing-language," indicated by terms like *scire, scientia, cogitare, conscientia, ratio, intelligere*. Our investigations do not approach the texts with Heideggerian preconceptions, even if there is some overlap between our concerns and his. This is not to say that our approach to texts is uninformed by any preconceptions. In a sense, our exemplar is Vico rather than Heidegger. One aspect of our reading of Bacon, Descartes, and Hobbes is the intention to unearth and isolate the sense in which modern thought as a whole embodies some version of Vico's principle: "the true and the made are convertible" (*verum et factum convertuntur*).

A second major difference from Heidegger is our conception of the alternative to making-as-technique. The alternative we propose can be summarized in a single word: *creation*. Heidegger's resolute denial that the Christian conception of creation provides a genuine alternative to technical models of making derives not so much from his profound understanding of that tradition, as from the fact that his relation to that tradition was conditioned by his early reading of Scotus. It is not that Heidegger was wrong to look for another conception of *poiesis*. The problem is that Heidegger's attempt to find a richer conception of *poiesis* in a nostalgic return to the pre-Socratics is not convincing, even to himself. Heidegger's thought culminates not in the celebration of thinking and making within a more primordial "dwelling," but in the anguished cry that "only a god can save us." The attempt to root both making-as-constructing and making-as-cultivating within "dwelling" can be exposed as an unpersuasive denial of Augustine's view that our hearts are restless until they find rest in the divine, and that no abiding "dwelling" in a world cut off from the transcendent is possible. As some critics have noticed, the Heideggerian attempt to recover an original *poiesis* leads to an affirmation of the priority of non-being (chaos) over being (order), and so to nihilism in the most primal sense. Stanley Rosen suggests that if Heidegger's abolition of metaphysics leaves everything literally valueless and without substance, "nihilism" is the most appropriate term for this state of affairs, and no application of "orientalist kitsch and Gothic etymologizing" (to use Rosen's phrase) will change this.[6]

A better (and more sober) guide to the problem of making and its relation to technique is R.G. Collingwood. Independently of Heidegger, but no less profoundly, Collingwood sees the importance of the distinction between the work of art and the artifact, between non-technical making ("art") and technical fabrication ("craft"). Greek conceptions of *poiesis*, Collingwood argues in the *Principles of Art*, are (with rare exceptions) reducible to technical or mimetic conceptions of making. The only viable alternative to technical *poiesis*, he finds, lies in the concept of *creation*. But what is creation? How is it distinguished from technical making, in either the human or the divine case? Our investigation of these questions begins with Thomas Aquinas. Thomas may seem an unlikely starting point, because he conspicuously refuses to attribute creativity to human beings. But this is just what makes him an appropriate beginning. What moderns habitually run together, Aquinas distinguishes. From the standpoint of modernity, as Lachterman suggests, it may appear evident that "construction," "making," "production," "creativity" and "*poiesis*" are "equivalent designations." Our examination of Aquinas will suggest that any such conflation is not evident.[7] In its strict sense, Aquinas argues, humans are not and cannot be "creative," even if they are makers in other respects. By denying creativity to human beings, it may appear that Aquinas is trapped within the technical conception of making, even as he articulates an alternative to that conception in the divine case. Against this appearance, we will contend that Aquinas's use of the notions of analogy and participation ensures that he does not understand human making in purely technicist terms, even as he maintains that it perpetually falls short of genuine creation.

It is only after Aquinas, in the Renaissance, that one finds a clear attribution of creativity to human beings. We will probe the sense of this attribution by focusing on the thought of Nicolaus Cusanus, particularly his *Idiota de Mente*. Our reading of that text will disclose the radical character of the Cusan emphasis on the creative power of reason and intellect. This emphasis will strike some as surprisingly "modern," although it could be argued that Cusanus is giving new expression to a conception of theurgy he finds in Proclus (mediated no doubt by Ficino, who translated Proclus into Latin). Without denying Cusanus's comparative "modernity" in relation to Aquinas, we will contend that what makes Cusanus interesting is not his role in anticipating this or that later philosopher—such views of Cusanus as merely a "transitional" thinker remain all-too-common—but his ability to elevate making to the rank of creativity while maintaining fidelity to the Thomist framework of metaphysical analogy. Our reading of Aquinas and Cusanus will suggest a theological conception of human making as "analogical creativity," as a participation in divine reason. The very existence (not to mention the viability) of such a concept remains largely invisible to those who approach the history of ideas from a narrowly philosophical perspective, for which theology is the incomprehensible other. This refusal to bracket theological discourses, and a corresponding willingness to learn from them, indicates a primary sense in which the present work may be considered an example of "radical orthodoxy."

After exploring the conception of making as analogical creativity in Aquinas and Cusanus, we will move to a close reading of texts by the architects of modernity, Bacon, Descartes, and Hobbes. We will find that these authors affirm, in ways often ignored or unsuspected, the nexus between knowing and making. Here we are pleased to acknowledge our debt to the work of David Lachterman, who clearly understands that the modern emphasis on construction precedes Kant. In his study on *The Ethics of Geometry*, Lachterman discovers "a fairly direct line" that runs from the "construction of a problem" in Descartes through the "construction of an equation" in Leibniz to the "construction of a concept" in Kant.[8] Not only in its later Kantian phase, but in its very origins, modernity must be understood as the invention and elaboration of the idea that the mind is "first and last *poietic* and only secondarily or subsidiarily *practical* and *theoretical*."[9] This radical commitment to making is what provides unity to the otherwise protean character of modernity. Thus Lachterman concludes that construction is "the mark of the modern."[10] Common to otherwise divergent philosophies is the notion that "mind is not nature's mirror; it is nature's generative or creative source."[11]

What are the origins of this idea? Lachterman thinks they are to be found within Cartesian geometry. In the strict sense, he argues (with reference to the *Géométrie*), construction is a mathematical technique. The success of this technique, according to Lachterman, encouraged practitioners of non-mathematical disciplines to adopt the constructivist paradigm in the hope that its application in other domains would prove as fruitful as it had in the mathematical case. Later modern applications of the constructionist motif remain "tributaries" to the strict mathematical sense, Lachterman argues, but enjoy the latter's "protective authority."[12]

Without wanting to deny the considerable merit of Lachterman's reading of Descartes, we may notice something odd about the emphasis on the casual role of mathematical discourses. Prior to the advent of Cartesian geometry, an exaltation of the dignity and power of human making had already occurred, as our reading of Cusanus (whom Lachterman entirely ignores) shows. Lachterman arbitrarily overlooks the possibility that what provides the notion of making with its initial prestige are theological discourses that speak of divine creation, human making, and the link between the two.

Our reading of Bacon, Descartes, and Hobbes will show just how committed the architects of radical modernity are to the motif of construction. It will bear out Lachterman's insight that construction is the mark of the modern. Beyond Lachterman, however, we argue that modernity gives rise to a *new* concept of construction—a conception of making as technical production that occurs within a domain that has been sealed off from the transcendent. We show that, with increasing clarity, Bacon, Descartes, and Hobbes inaugurate the modern secularized concept of making. This conception of making differs from the earlier concept of making found in Aquinas and Cusanus to the degree that it has been detached from the framework of *analogia entis*. Our criticism is not that secular modernity connects knowing and making—orthodox theologies of creation had *already* accomplished this linkage—but that its particular mode of connecting the two ultimately serves to deny the dignity of making itself. Alongside this "suspicious" attitude to secular modernity, however, we allow that much can be learned from reading Bacon, Descartes and Hobbes. Radical orthodoxy is not afraid to consider seriously proposals that knowing is most adequately described in relation to making. It is not bewitched by the fear that human making is inevitably arbitrary. Nor does it take up a reflexively anti-modern attitude. But it characteristically seeks to bring into the conversation the modern voices that have traditionally been suppressed by Enlightenment historiographical approaches—approaches which neglect or marginalize thinkers who resist secularism. (In this respect, Heidegger would not be a critic of modernity, but a collaborator—his uncritical acceptance of the antithesis between faith and reason suggests the extent to which he remains within the Enlightenment paradigm.)

That the dominant modern concept of construction is not the only possible option, but merely constitutes one way of construing the nature of human making, can be gathered from the contrast that will emerge between Aquinas and Cusanus, on the one hand, and Bacon, Descartes and Hobbes on the other. But the thinker who most profoundly understands the nature of modern secular construction, as we will argue in the final chapter of our exposition, is Giambattista Vico. The reduction of Vico to a pre-Kantian transcendentalist cannot be supported by a careful reading of his texts. We will show that Vico understands with striking clarity the modern secular concept of making as an activity that occurs within a domain that is governed by an impersonal agency ("fate" or "chance"). We will show how Vico elaborates an alternative notion of making as a creative participation in divine Providence. This is what lies at the heart of Vico's *verum-factum* principle, and what separates him from his secular counterparts, to whom Vico is often assimilated by those with a second-hand knowledge of his texts. In its main lines, Vico's *verum-factum* is continuous with the perspective of Aquinas and Cusanus, but his novel and powerful application of the principle to the domain of history enables him to re-express, and not merely restate, the notion of making as participation.

Not all observers will endorse the standpoint which privileges the "alternative modernity" of Vico over the secular modernity of Bacon, Descartes, and Hobbes. We do not pretend to have written a value-free history of a concept, as if such a thing were either possible or desirable. But we do hope that our exposition is sufficiently thorough to convince occupants of other standpoints that the paradigm of making is present within modern thought in a way rarely understood by standard approaches, especially those that reduce modern thought to a sterile contest between "rationalism" and "empiricism."

Are theological conceptions of making as analogical creative participation more worthy of appropriation than secularized conceptions of making? Does the modern separation of making from the sacred implicitly contain or inexorably lead to nihilism? These are questions which inform the expository chapters, and will be faced directly in the conclusion.

1

THOMAS AQUINAS

For the classical tradition, knowing is first and foremost a seeing. The demiurge of Plato's *Timaeus* looks to forms or ideas, and molds raw material on the basis of what he sees, with the aim of embodying these forms in matter. Human craftsmen, insofar as they are craftsmen, do the same. Following the analysis of R.G. Collingwood, we may summarize the primary features of craft, or technical making:[1]

1. Craft involves a distinction between means and end.
2. Craft involves a distinction between planning and execution, where "planning" means precise foreknowledge of what is to be made, before the making is executed. In the order of planning, the end is prior to the means; in the order of execution, the means come before the end.
3. Craft involves a distinction between raw material and finished product or artifact. "A craft is always exercised upon something, and aims at the transformation of this into something different. That upon which it works begins as raw material and ends as finished product. The raw material is found ready made before the special work of the craft begins."[2]
4. Craft involves a distinction between matter and form. "The matter is what is identical in the raw material and the finished product; the form is what is different, what the exercise of the craft changes."[3]
5. Crafts are hierarchically related; the finished product of one is the raw material of another. (This also holds for means and parts.)

Is there a type of making that is not an exercise in craft? There is—the making of the incompetent pseudo-craftsman. Collingwood imagines a person who sets out to make a table, but conceives the table vaguely, "as somewhere between two by four feet and three by six, and between two and three feet high."[4] Such a person may produce something resembling a table, but he is no craftsman. He lacks the precise, explicit foreknowledge of what he wants to make, a knowledge whose possession is the hallmark of the person with the intellectual virtue of *techne* (*ars*). It is this knowledge of the formal cause of an artifact, together with the ability to impose the form onto matter, that defines the craftsman.

The paradigm of craft entails a particular conception of the relation between knowing and making. The relationship is one of dependence: making (understood as the execution of the means through the transformation of matter) depends upon an antecedent knowledge of the form. The activity of making does not provide knowledge of the formal cause of the artifact, but presupposes this knowledge. Is there another conception of the relation between knowing and making, according to which the activity of making does not merely devise means for the sake of giving material embodiment to what is already known, but actually contributes to our knowledge? A positive answer to this question requires a concept of making other than either the incompetent bungling of the pseudo-craftsman or the proficient fabrication of the technical maker. The name for this alternative concept of making is "creation." Creation is a type of making, but it is not technical making. Aquinas's significance for the present inquiry is that he is among the first theologians to have a clear grasp of how creation differs from technical making. A proper appreciation of this point will cast doubt on any treatment of Aquinas that would interpret his theology of creation as little more than the application of a technicist paradigm to God's making.[5] It will question the value of histories of philosophy according to which Western metaphysics construes all knowing, even divine knowing, as a kind of technical manipulation. It will, finally, raise the question of the relation between divine creation and the human activities of knowing and making.

Scientia Dei and creation

Aquinas himself seems to invite the charge that he reduces divine creation to technical making, in precisely the sense described by Collingwood. But this cannot be because (1) creation involves a distinction between means and end. It is impossible to identify any implements or instruments that God uses to create the world. The apparent affinity between divine creation and human craft would derive from the fact that (2) craft involves a distinction between planning and execution, where "planning" means precise foreknowledge of what is to be made. When Aquinas argues that *scientia Dei est causa rerum*, he introduces an analogy to technical making. "For the *scientia Dei* is to all *res creata* as the knowledge of the craftsman (*artifex*) is to artificial things (*artificiata*)."[6] Both God and the craftsman make works *per intellectum*. In both cases, there is a distinction between ideas in the intellect and works that embody those ideas. To bring about such works involves the action of will. God's knowledge is the cause of things, Aquinas concludes, insofar as the operation of the will is joined to it.

Aquinas uses the analogy to human art not because he wants to downgrade divine creation by reducing it to technical making, but because he wants to emphasize that, like the competent craftsman, God knows what he wants to make. This becomes important in the discussion of how God knows singular things (*singularia*). God cannot know singulars merely as instances of a type, as an astronomer might be able to predict all future eclipses on the basis of universal knowledge. To know "singulars in their singularity" (*singularia in sua singularitate*)[7], God's knowledge must be more than the application of universal principles to particular effects. Thomas holds that his exhaustive knowledge of particulars is related to the fact that he produces them. "Since God is the cause of things by His knowledge, as said above, His knowledge extends as far as His causality extends."[8] If the "active power of God" (*virtus activa Dei*) extends not only to forms, but also to matter, then the knowledge of God must also extend to singular things. It cannot be confined to universals.

The analogy between the knowledge of the human craftsman and the knowledge of the divine creator thus gives way to a disanalogy. The housebuilder knows the form of a house, and works to embody that form in matter. But he does not create the entire form/matter composite, since he does not create the matter out of which he makes the house. Thus, whereas God's knowledge of singulars is "productive of the whole thing, and not only of the form,"[9] human knowledge of singulars must always stop short of knowing a thing in its full particularity. It is limited to a knowledge of form in matter, since it can only produce a house through the transformation of matter. This means that although God possesses a precise knowledge of what he makes, his creation cannot involve (3) a distinction between raw material and finished product or artifact. There is no raw material that creation transforms. Aquinas makes this clear in the *prima pars* of the *Summa theologiae*: creation is the emanation of all being from the not-being which is nothing.[10] Even if it is correct (and in fact necessary) to describe creation as a product which exists separately from its producer, this product has not been made from a raw material, and so cannot be a product of craft. As Collingwood observes, "a craft is always exercised upon something, and aims at the transformation of this into something different."[11] In the case of creation, there is no "something" upon which divine will is exercised. The craftsman works from natural things such as wood and brass, "which are caused not by the action of art, but by the action of nature."[12] Divine creation, by contrast, presupposes no raw materials from which to work. The notion of a *natura creatrix* (as in Lucretius) would be a contradiction in terms, since "nature itself causes natural things as regards their form, but presupposes matter."[13] Because creation presupposes no matter, it cannot essentially (4) involve a distinction between matter and form. Aquinas's insistence that both matter and form are created ensures the impossibility of collapsing creation into the technical transformation of matter. It is, finally, impossible that creation should participate in (5) the hierarchical relations among crafts. Creation is not a member of the hierarchy among crafts, whether with respect to materials, to means, or to parts. As the cause of the most universal of effects, being itself, it is what makes the hierarchical relations among crafts possible.

That creation should possess only *one* of the characteristics of craft as enumerated by Collingwood seems to support the view that Aquinas's view of creation is a genuine alternative to technical making. One might object, however, that the possession of precise foreknowledge of what one wants to make is *the* essential characteristic of craft, and to the extent that Aquinas's theory of creation insists that God makes from ideas, he is beholden to the paradigm of *techne*. In response to this objection, one may begin by observing that Aquinas's use of the analogy to the craftsman does not so much reduce divine creation to technical making, as it elevates the gnoseological value of human art. Both God and the *artifex* have a superior knowledge of what they make; they have *scientia practica* and not merely *scientia speculativa* of things they make. With respect to natural things, Aquinas holds that humans are limited to speculative knowledge, which is determined and measured by things. But with respect to *res artificiales*, humans possess both practical and speculative knowledge. Aquinas contrasts the knowledge of the craftsman who builds a house with that of the person who is forced to take (*capit*) his knowledge "from a thing already made" (*ex ipsa iam facta*).[14] The latter has only speculative knowledge; the former has both practical and speculative knowledge, in the same way that God has both practical and speculative knowledge of *res creata*. Aquinas thus provides a muted but unmistakable formulation of the thesis that we know better what we make than what we do not make. When we make something, we know not only the effect, but also the cause by which it is made. With regard to natural things, however, we are restricted to contemplating them from without and conjecturing about their causes.

It remains, however, that Aquinas's use of the analogy between God and the craftsman confirms the sense that all competent human making is an instance of craft. Our claim, however, is that despite his apparent construal of all human making as craft, Aquinas does possess a genuine alternative to craft because he thinks of divine making—creation—as something radically other than craft. The view that Aquinas's notion of creation is not radically other than *techne*, but a hyperbolic instance of it, seems to derive from the sense that any God who creates according to archetypes is nothing but a variation on the Platonic demiurge, who is only "half a god." The fear is that Aquinas's affirmation of archetypes to which God looks compromise his divinity, and makes him into a kind of super-technician. This fear seems to be motivated by the notion that *any* analogy between human craftsmanship and divine creation will collapse the latter into the former. But this inference is arbitrary: one can equally argue, as Aquinas would, that the ability of the craftsman to make artifacts with intelligence, is the precise point at which human making bears an analogy with divine art. But it does not follow from this that divine making is essentially technical. Creation involves no distinction between means and end, no distinction between raw material and finished product and artifact, no distinction between matter and form. Although it does involve a knowledge of forms, it is not the case, as for craft, that this knowledge temporally precedes making. This is because creation is not a temporal process or motion. There are no discrete stages, no "before" and "after" in creation. Creation involves a harmony between God's knowledge and God's will, but this does not entail that God knows the form of a created being, and then wills it to be. The "joining" of the will to practical knowledge (*necesse est quod scientia sit causa rerum, secundum quod habet voluntatem coniunctam*[15]) does not involve a temporal succession.

Another reason for rejecting the suggestion that God's use of ideas makes him into a divine super-technician is that the process whereby God knows ideas is entirely different from the way in which a human craftsman knows a form. More precisely, there is no "process" by which God knows ideas. The ideas are part of God's non-discursive self-knowledge. When God knows the ideas, he knows the multiple ways in which His essence can be imitated by creatures. This knowledge, in the first instance, is a speculative knowledge. Divine self-knowledge is necessarily speculative, because God does not make or cause himself. But this knowledge, although speculative, is not sterile. It gives rise to divine practical knowledge, which is distinct but not separate from God's speculative knowledge of Himself. Aquinas considers that knowledge of the ideas is speculative if it considers the form without it directing it to operation, and practical if it is used to make something. Thus God's knowledge of ideas may be either entirely speculative, or both speculative and practical. When they are known speculatively, as principles of knowledge, they are "types" (*rationes*).[16] When they are not only known speculatively, but also directed to the making of something, they attain the status of an *exemplar*, that is, the "principle of the making of things" (*principium factionis rerum*).[17] A distinction between speculative and practical knowledge of ideas is necessary, because Aquinas allows that God knows some types of created things but chooses not to actualize them. But he does not sever practical knowledge of exemplars from speculative self-knowledge. "In speculative knowledge of Himself, He possesses both speculative and practical knowledge of all other things," Aquinas concludes the final article of Question 14.[18] Thus God's knowledge of exemplars is essentially different from the craftsman's knowledge of forms, because the former is a function of perfect self-knowledge, and the latter is not: "whatever we know speculatively in things by defining and dividing, God knows all this much more perfectly."[19] Yet even here there may be some analogy between God and the poet. Distinguishing between the poet and the craftsman, Maritain argues that the "creative intuition" of the former "is an obscure grasping of his own Self and of things in a knowledge through union or through connaturality which is born in the spiritual unconscious, and which fructifies only in the work."[20] This "free creativity of the spirit," Maritain holds, makes the poet like a god, although he adds that that the poet is a "poor god" because he does not know himself.²¹

The absence of a temporal dimension in creation, conjoined with the fact that God does not acquire knowledge of forms by abstracting from something outside himself, ensure that the possession of knowledge as a requirement of making—that is, the respect in which Thomist creation comes closest to the craft paradigm—cannot be univocally ascribed to God and human craftsmen. Unlike either human fabricators or the Platonic demiurge, God has no recourse to intelligible entities that are, in any sense, external to himself. The conception of principles of production is not a work of divine imagination or will, but part of God's self-knowledge that occurs within the life of the Trinitarian Persons, through the utterance of His *Verbum*. This utterance cannot be reduced to the technical paradigm: it is neither creation nor technical making, but generation. Aquinas follows the precedent of the Nicean rejection of *poiesis* for generation within the Godhead.²² The ideas generated within the *Verbum* are not distinct from the generator (as any *factum* is distinct from its *factor*), but co-equal with him, one in substance. A *genitum* comes from the substance of the generator, whereas a *factum* is always made from a substance that is contrary in some respect. The contrariness is absolute in the extreme case of creation, where being is made from nothing. Hence Aquinas speaks both of *creatio ex nihilo* and *facere ex nihilo*, but never *generatio ex nihilo*.²³

Aquinas does not detach creation from generation, because he thinks that creation presupposes the generative conception of exemplars. Any misunderstanding of generation will have adverse consequences for one's understanding of creation. Aquinas explicitly says that to attain the "right view of the creation of things" (*recte sentiendum de creatione rerum*), it is necessary to have knowledge of the divine persons.²⁴ The denial of any role for ideas in creation produces the error that God made the world by chance. The mislocation of these ideas outside the generated *Verbum* produces the error that God made the world out of necessity. "The fact of saying that God made all things by His Word excludes the error of those who say that God produced things by necessity."²⁵ Aquinas does not think that God creates because he is unable to escape the demand of unity to diffuse itself into multiplicity. "When we say that in Him there is a procession of love, we show that God produced creatures not because He needed them, nor because of any other extrinsic reason, but on account of the love of His own goodness."²⁶ Unless one attends to the processions of the divine Persons, one will fail to grasp that creation is a free and intentional act, motivated by love rather than need. This conceptual truth about the nature of creation is confirmed by Scripture: "So Moses, when he had said, 'In the beginning God created heaven and earth,' subjoined, 'God said, Let there be light,' to manifest the divine Word; and then said, 'God saw the light that it was good,' to show proof of the divine love."²⁷

The unity of generation and creation is underscored by Aquinas's use of *emanatio* to describe both. In both the first Question on the Trinity and the first Question on Creation, Thomas uses the term *emanatio* to describe the *processio divinarum personarum* and the *processio creaturarum a Deo*.[28] The processions of Persons within the divine Trinity are not motions. They are "to be understood by way of intelligible *emanatio*, for example, of the intelligible word which proceeds from the speaker, yet remains in him."[29] Creation, too, is an *emanatio*, although as a *facere*, it is "transitive," giving rise to a *factum* that is distinct from its maker. Thus the distinction between generation and creation, necessary to draw in order to preserve to co-equality of the Son, co-exists with a profound continuity between them. Both are *emanationes*. The *emanatio* that is *generatio* functions as the *ratio* of creation; it is the source of the exemplars that are the principles of making. Thomas explicitly conceives creation as the work of the Trinity. The processions of the divine Persons are "the type of the productions of creatures inasmuch as they include the essential attributes, knowledge and will."[30] Order within the created world, far from being disconnected from the triune God, is a refraction of the order within the Trinity.

The intrinsic relation between generation and creation serves to further establish that the divine *facere*, while it involves exemplars in a manner analogous to the use of forms by the human craftsman, cannot be rightly construed as an instance of technical making. Aquinas's model of generation and creation—interior conception of exemplars via processual self-knowledge accompanied by the production of being from no raw material—is a decisive moment in the articulation of a concept of making that is not technical making.

Creation and human production

Does Aquinas ever apply the model of creative non-technical making to human beings? *Videtur quod non*. Aquinas denies that human beings are able to create anything, in the proper sense of the term. He recognizes an equivocal use of the word, as when we say that a bishop is created. But "to create can be the action of God alone," because only God can produce being absolutely.[31] Humans are able only to produce this or that being through the transformation of matter, which is to say, through the exercise of craft.

But is there another sense in which humans cause something to be, without making it by craft? As we have seen, technical making presupposes a form that the craftsman holds in mind as he attempts to embody that form in matter. But how does the craftsman acquire knowledge of the form? He cannot create the form, properly speaking, since he cannot create anything. It is possible that he obtains the form by abstraction. With respect to trees, for example, the painter of a tree may abstract the form of a tree from particular form/matter composites, that is, from individual trees. But it is an error to push the abstractive model too far in this domain, if the craftsman's idea is, as Maritain contends "in no way a *concept*, for it is neither cognitive nor representative."[32] This is a useful corrective to some recent accounts which suppose that Aquinas equates the craftsman's form with a "picture." Against such accounts, Maritain writes that the "craftsman's creative idea is an intellectual form, or a spiritual matrix, containing implicitly, in its complex unity, the thing which, perhaps for the first time, will be brought into actual existence."[33]

Our question remains: by what process does the craftsman derive the exemplar from which he works? Certainly with respect to *res artificiales*, for which there is no counterpart in nature, the abstractive model would be lacking. Consider a bridge, to use Collingwood's example. The engineer who constructs a bridge is making the bridge, where "to make" means to impose the form of the bridge upon matter. But where does he obtain the plan (the principle of production, or the exemplar) for the bridge? Collingwood answers this question in a manner foreign to Aquinas, but which may nonetheless be helpful for understanding him. According to Collingwood, the making of the plan itself (as opposed to making the bridge from the plan) is "not imposing a certain form on a certain matter; it is a making that is not transforming, that is to say, it is a creation."[34] This answer is non-Thomistic, because it conflates the *conception* of the plan with the activity of creation. For Thomas, a human being may conceive a plan, but he does not create it. Would Aquinas acknowledge that conception is productive in any sense, even if it not well described as either creation (*pace* Collingwood) or technical making? Or would he insist that all conception is ultimately a passive seeing or beholding?

An answer to this question is suggested by the analysis of the craftsman in Question 44, Article 3 of the *Prima Pars* of the *Summa theologiae*. If effects are to receive determinate forms, Thomas contends, they require exemplars. In support of this conclusion, Thomas cites the example of the human craftsman, "who produces a determinate form in matter by reason of the exemplar before him, whether it is the exemplar beheld externally, or the exemplar interiorly conceived in the mind (*extra intuetur, sive sit exemplar interius mente conceptum*)."[35] As God conceives exemplars through the knowledge He has of His essence, humans are able to generate exemplars within the mind, without beholding external objects. In this sense, a Thomist perspective may save the appearance of Collingwood's doctrine that humans can create, while denying that humans are able to create in the strict sense. Humans are able to conceive exemplary forms, in a manner that is analogous not to creation, but to generation.

Why does Aquinas prefer the analogy of generation to creation? One answer to this question is that in conceiving exemplars, the mind is engaged in an activity that is more like speaking than any *facere*, whether *facere ex nihilo* or the *facere* that presupposes matter.[36] The conception of an exemplar in the mind is like the utterance of an inner word, a *verbum* which proceeds from the mind, but is not distinct from the mind. Maritain notes the importance of the *verbum mentis* doctrine for Aquinas's account of making: "before the work of art passes from art into the matter, by a transitive action, the very conception of the art has had to emerge from within the soul, by an immanent and vital action, like the emergence of the mental word."[37] He quotes a pertinent text from Aquinas's commentary on the *Sentences*: "the procession of art is twofold, that is, from the soul of the artificer to his art, and from his art to his artifacts."[38] If Aquinas were to describe conception of an exemplar as making or creating, he would have to make a distinction between the mind and what it conceives. His unwillingness to make this distinction is the ground of his decision to analogize human interior conception with utterance of the *verbum mentis* rather than the production of an artifact. Thus Aquinas understands the distinction Collingwood makes between the activity of making a bridge from a plan, and making the plans themselves, but refrains from describing the latter in a way that would confuse it with any instance of transitive making.

Aquinas construes human making as analogous to the divine in two major senses. First, humans imitate God in their capacity to make things freely and intelligently, rather than by necessity or by chance. Second, humans are able to engage in an interior conception of exemplars from which they transitively make. It still appears, however, that although divine making cannot be reduced to technical making, Aquinas considers all competent human making to fall under the paradigm of craft. This appearance is not entirely wrong. Nonetheless, following Pieper's suggestion that creation "determines and characterizes the interior structure of nearly all the basic concepts in St. Thomas's philosophy of Being,"[39] we may hazard that Aquinas's transcendence of the craft paradigm through his theory of creation has important consequences for his understanding of human making, consequences which tend to "elevate" it.

Perhaps the clearest example of this elevation is the treatment of the human participation in divine providence. Although there are no intermediaries in creation proper, "there are certain intermediaries of God's providence, for he governs things inferior by superior . . . not on account of any defect in His power, but by reason of the abundance of His goodness; so that the dignity of causality is imparted even to creatures."[40] Providence ensures that creaturely causality will always be something more than it is for an Aristotelian or modern naturalist. All things are created at an instant, through God's knowledge of his own essence and the diverse modes in which it can be imitated. But things *also* "come to be in time," as Thomas says.[41] Humans do not create in the strict sense, but they are not denied a role in the temporal achievement or realization of the idea. This lends creaturely causality a dignity that it would otherwise lack, as Maritain recognizes in his observation that "artistic creation does not copy God's creation, it continues it."[42]

Another domain in which Aquinas accords human making a certain dignity is the natural law. The definition of natural law as the rational creature's participation in the eternal law is not merely the apprehension of that which does not change. When considering whether the natural law is the same for all persons, Thomas holds that the principles of natural law, which are called the *communes conceptiones*, are invariant across individuals and cultures.[43] But he adds that as soon as the natural law is applied to matters of action, truth will not be the same for all. Thomas does *not* confine the sense of *lex naturalis* to the part of law that is immune to cultural or circumstantial modification. The variability of practical reason does not render it unnatural; Thomas resists any simple identification of "the natural" and "the unchangeable."

This resistance is evident in the gap between the *sed contra* and the *respondeo* of Question 95, Article 5 of the *Prima Secundae* of the *Summa theologiae*. The *sed contra* reproduces a quotation from the Decretals: "The natural law dates from the creation of the rational creature. It does not vary according to time, but remains unchangeable." Thomas's response shows that his understanding of natural law is not confined to this model. The *respondeo*'s opening declaration that "a change in the natural law may be understood in two ways" presupposes that the natural law can in fact be changed. The two ways of understanding change in the natural law are "addition" and "subtraction." By "subtraction," Aquinas refers to the rare instances in which the natural law ceases to command something that it ordinarily commands. More significant alterations occur in the cases of "addition," where "nothing hinders the natural from being changed: since many things for the benefit of human life have been added over and above by the natural law, both by the Divine law and by human laws."[44] Although the first principles of the natural law are engraved on the human heart, immune to change, the natural law *as a whole* is a cultural artifact that humans actively shape and modify over time. Thomas specifically invokes the parallel between the human legislator and the craftsman who "needs to determine the general form of a house to some particular shape."[45]

In the strict sense of the term, the specification or determination of the natural law by human beings is not creative. But—perhaps going beyond Aquinas—one may wonder whether the craftsman analogy holds in every respect. The craftsman model implies that the competent law-maker, *qua* law-maker, has a precise knowledge of the human good, which is presupposed in his craftsman-like activity of legislation. But does the law-maker, even the law-maker whose knowledge of general principles is irreproachable, actually have this precise knowledge? Or does his activity require not only craft, but also prudence, such that the acquisition of true knowledge about particulars is not anterior to the process of law-making, but is acquired through the very performance of the activity? It is at this point that Aquinas most visibly leaves room for the idea that intelligent human making may not only require antecedent knowledge, but itself plays a role in contributing to true understanding. Maritain sees this point clearly, recognizing the "altogether particular knowledge by which the poet, the painter and the musician perceive in things forms and secrets that are hidden to others and which are expressible only in the work—a knowledge which may be called *poetic knowledge*."[46] Aquinas thus opens the way for the idea, more fully elaborated by Cusanus and Vico, that truth, far from being transparently present to the mind at the beginning of making, is something that emerges within constructive activity, such that we not only see before making, but also that we see *through* making.[47]

With respect to creation, Thomas transcends the technical paradigm, although he leaves human beings ambiguously within it. Nonetheless, even technical making is transfigured and elevated when situated within the framework of divine generation and creation. The artist becomes, as Maritain notes, "an associate of God in the making of beautiful works."[48] We have located significant points of intersection in Thomas's account between the divine and human, for example, freedom from necessity or chance, the use of exemplars in operation, the derivation of exemplars from the non-technical activity of generation, the relation of making to providential design, the human ability to know and even construct the natural law. Aquinas's use of the craftsman analogy may encourage the impression that divine creation is a hypertrophic form of technical making. But this cannot be the final verdict. As Mark Jordan observes, "human artistry is, *secundum ordinem rerum*, a truncated version of creation, just as form is a truncated version of *esse*."[49] As important as they are, the disanalogies between human and divine making are finally (as Jordan puts it) "sublated by the prior ontological dependence, by the analogical unity of being itself," a unity suggesting that "the analogy reverses direction and the limited, disanalogous form-making of human art is seen as the enigma, as what must be explicated by reference to a more integral making, the making of being."[50] What entitles Aquinas both to assert the radical difference between human making and divine creation, and to explicate the former as a truncated version of the latter, is the "analogy of being."

Making and the "analogy of being"

But is there a doctrine of "metaphysical analogy" in Thomas? As more than one commentator has pointed out, Aquinas did not write a treatise on analogy. Although particular uses of *analogia* are dispersed throughout Thomas's writings, it is not clear that these amount to a coherent and unified treatment of the topic. Later commentators have tended to perceive this possibility as a lacuna that demands filling. Undoubtedly the most influential of such commentators is Cajetan. In his work *De nominum analogia*, Cajetan attempts to elaborate and systematize what Thomas leaves implicit. Taking his cue from a passage in Thomas's *Sentences* commentary, Cajetan distinguishes three kinds of analogy: (1) the "analogy of inequality," or analogy *secundum esse et non secundum intentionem*. The analogy of inequality is the unequal participation of diverse species in a common genus; (2) the "analogy of attribution," or analogy *secundum intentionem tantum, et non secundum esse*. The analogy of attribution corresponds to what Aristotle means by *pros hen* predication, or what a contemporary interpreter (following G.E.L. Owen) might call "focal meaning." As Cajetan observes, Aristotle did not use *analogia* to denote *pros hen* predication; (3) the "analogy of proper proportionality," or analogy *secundum intentionem et secundum esse*. The analogy of proper proportionality is a four-term proportion of the form "A is to B as C is to D." It expresses a relationship not between things, but between ratios.

Which of these various modes of analogy does Aquinas consider to most aptly express the bond between creatures and their Creator? The question presupposes that Aquinas would recognize Cajetan's tripartite distinction as adequate for a sound teaching on analogy, and that analogy is genuinely metaphysical. Both of these presuppositions have received much criticism. Let us for now accept the presuppositions and examine Cajetan's particular answer to the question. Cajetan, and much of the Thomist tradition in his wake, privileges the third type of analogy, the analogy of proper proportionality. To see why, we must consider the motives of the Cajetanist tradition for rejecting the other modes of analogy as illicit or improper. The rejection of analogy of inequality is simple enough. As the participation of different species in the same genus, the analogy of inequality requires that diverse species have something generically in common. This commonality is shared in unequal degrees, but it is present univocally according to the same *ratio*. Hence the "analogy of inequality" can exist only within a more basic univocity. This prompts Cajetan to declare that it is not true analogy, indeed that it is "entirely alien to analogy" (*alienus ab analogia omnino sit*).[51]

More complex are the grounds for rejecting the analogy of attribution. One may detect a whiff of Renaissance philological purism. Cajetan does not hesitate to point out that from a Greek standpoint, "*analogia*" used of any relation "to one or in one or from one" (*ad unum vel in uno aut ab uno*)—an essential characteristic of the analogy of attribution—is just "what we call 'analogy' abusively" (*quae nos abusive vocamus analoga*).[52] But philological scruples are not the primary motive. The Cajetanist tradition finds that the analogy of attribution fails to represent the tie between creatures and God, because it cannot do justice to "being" in the "analogy of being." It is analogy only "according to intention, not according to *esse*." To use the Aristotelian example familiar from Thomas's texts, "healthy" is said of animal, urine, and medicine, but in different ways. Health has being only in the animal. It has no being in the other things denoted by the analogous predication of "healthy," since there is no health, properly speaking, in urine or medicine.

Urine and medicine are related to health (as sign and cause), but there is no health that actually exists in urine or medicine. Hence "health" is "extrinsically denominated" of urine and medicine. Cajetan argues that *all* analogy of attribution is characterized by extrinsic denomination. There is unity of concept or intention—"health" does not change its meaning across the different cases—but a diversity of relations between the secondary analogates and the prime analogate.

What is true of the *sanitas* example holds, according to Cajetan, for *all* cases of the analogy of attribution. Consider, for example, the proper application of "being" to substance and the analogous or equivocal application of "being" to accidents. "Being" is primarily said of substances. In Cajetan's language, "only substance is being formally."[53] It is secondarily said of accidents, which are termed beings "because they are properties or becomings of being, etc."[54] Although they are intrinsically related to substances, accidents do not "formally" realize the notion of being. Hence they are termed "beings" only by extrinsic denomination, just as medicine and urine are termed "healthy" by extrinsic denomination. In neither case do the secondary analogates formally realize the notion that is formally realized by the prime analogate. Whence the essential characteristic of the analogy of attribution: it occurs only according to intention, not according to *esse*.

We can now see why, from a Cajetanist perspective, the analogy of attribution is unfit to serve as the paradigm for the "analogy of being." If attribution were the appropriate paradigm, then God would be the prime analogate in whom is *uniquely* realized the notion of being. It is true, of course, that God realizes being in a singular manner, since his *esse* cannot be distinguished from his *essentia*. But it can hardly be the case that creatures simply fail to realize the notion of *esse*. Taken rigorously, the analogy of attribution entails the absence of any being proper to creatures. "Being" would be extrinsically denominated of creatures, who would be related to God as mere accidents or modes of the one infinite substance. Such a "degradation of the finite," as one Cajetanist interpreter puts it, is hardly compatible with Aquinas.[55] Hence the analogy of attribution cannot be the fundamental way of expressing the Thomist analogy of being.

From the conviction there must be *some* analogy of being, supplemented by arguments that the first two of the three available modes of analogy fail to express it, the Cajetanist tradition concludes that the analogy of proper proportionality is what best captures the analogy of being. The "classic proportion," as James Anderson terms it, is that God is to His *esse* as the creature is to its *esse*.[56] Unlike attribution, proper proportionality does not deprive creatures of being by reserving *esse* to God, the prime analogate. Rather, God and creatures alike have *esse*, but this *esse* is not numerically or specifically one—as it cannot be, if one seeks to avoid univocity of being. As Anderson writes, "the analogy of proper proportionality involves an intrinsic participation, the proportional sharing of diverse things in a common perfection." Similarity between creatures and God is inscribed within difference, since God's *esse* is essentially diverse from the *esse* of creatures. The appeal of proper proportionality can be put thus: it appears to safeguard both likeness of being—it is authentically *secundum esse*, and not merely *secundum intentionem*—and difference of being—divine *esse* and creaturely *esse* are proportionally related, but not numerically one. Although in practice there may be some room for the attribution analogy, since creatures are in fact ordered to God as "a principal term on which they depend," it must nonetheless be rigorously subordinated to the analogy of proper proportionality. Anderson supplies the rationale for this subordination: proper proportionality "is alone properly analogical, if for no other reason than that this analogy alone has to do with a concept which is analogical in itself, in the sense that it can be realized intrinsically and formally (though proportionately) in each and every one of the subjects of which it is predicated."[57]

Given the case for the analogy of proportionality, made so ably by Cajetan, Anderson, and Maritain, why has it come under such severe criticism from recent Thomists? Part of the criticism is exegetical. Ralph McInerny has argued (persuasively, in my view) that the division between attribution and proportionality, at least as Cajetan construes it, is foreign to the Thomistic texts.[58] From another angle, the coherence of its basic notion, viz. proportional unity, may be questioned. What keeps the analogy of proper proportionality from sliding into univocity is its insistence that the similarity between the compared ratios is not absolute, but proportional. But what does this mean? In the mathematical case, on which proportionality seems to be modelled, there is always a literal equality. "To say 2 is to 4 as 8 is to 16" is to say "$2/4 = 8/16$," where the equal sign denotes univocal sameness. Advocates of proper proportionality will counter that the essence of their preferred analogy is not mathematical, and that mathematical proportion merely offers a convenient illustration of what is in itself a metaphysical concept. But this reply is beside the point, because it fails to clarify what kind of relationship does obtain between the ratios. To merely say that the relationship is "proportional" leaves us no wiser than we were before. Burrell poses the vital question: "Can we honestly invite a term like proportional to carry the burden of a new and unique usage when we have severed its mathematical spine?" If one says that "x is similar to y," one must be prepared to add "in respect z." It appears, as Burrell suggests, that Cajetanist attempts to speak of a "proportional similitude" that "in its very nature includes . . . diversity" amount to a case of language on holiday.[59]

Another, related problem with the decision to make proper proportionality paradigmatic for the analogy of being is that it leads (quite against the intentions of those who privilege it) to an unacceptable agnosticism about the divine nature. An example from the (unjustly neglected) treatment of analogy in Eric Mascall's *Existence and Analogy* makes the point clearly.

Although we may use "life" of both a cabbage and a man, we do not want to assert the equality "life of cabbage = life of man." To avoid this, we may have recourse to an analogy of proportionality: the life of cabbage is to the essence of cabbage as the life of man is to the essence of man. If only some type of similarity, and no equality, exists among the two proportions, and if attempts to specify the type of similarity lead only to further weakened iterations of the analogy (e.g., "the way in which the life of cabbage is determined by the essence of the cabbage is to the essence of cabbage, as the way in which the life of man is determined by the essence of man"), *ad infinitum*, then, as Mascall writes, "our proportionality has completely collapsed, and all we are left with is the fact that cabbages have nothing in common with men except the fact that, for no valid reason, men have described them both as being alive."[60] Mascall adds that even if this objection can be evaded, it remains that the analogy of proper proportionality still leads to total agnosticism about the divine nature. Even if it is correct to say that "the life of man is to the essence of man as the life of God is to the essence of God," the analogy "will not in fact tell us in what sense life is to be predicated of God." Rephrasing the analogy as "the essence of man is to the existential act of man as the essence of God is to the existential act of God" gets us no further, since both terms of the latter proportion are unknown. Hence "sheer agnosticism seems to be the outcome."[61] Milbank concurs with this verdict, finding that proportionality, "if formally dogmatic, is substantively agnostic."[62]

How, then, ought one to understand the analogy of being? The analogy of attribution (as understood by Cajetan) seems problematic because it leaves no room for predicating *esse* of creatures, except through extrinsic denomination. But is there another way of understanding the analogy of attribution, such that it might allow *esse* to be *intrinsically* denominated of both God and creatures? Suarez's "analogy of intrinsic attribution" represents one answer to this question. In our judgment, this solution has some promise, although it cannot be taken exactly as it stands in Suarez. This is because Suarez appears to hold that both the divine *esse* and the *esse* intrinsically attributed to human beings can be expressed by a uniform concept. If this be the case, then, whatever his intentions, Suarez has moved from analogy to univocity.[63] The task is to find a mode of analogy that is neither sheer extrinsic denomination nor the intrinsic attribution of something that is essentially identical in both God and creatures. Some (e.g., Garrigou-Lagrange) suggest a mixture of the analogies of attribution and proper proportionality. This may be formally correct, but the question of which analogy in the compound is to be regarded as fundamental inevitably resurfaces.

One may be tempted to simply dismiss the doctrine of *analogia entis*, perhaps because the *verba ipsissima* do not appear in Thomas, or perhaps because one agrees with Barth that *analogia entis* is "the invention of anti-Christ."[64] Against either of these extreme solutions, we may suggest the following. Whatever else it may be, the analogy of creatures to God is the analogy of effect to cause. But the relationship between effect and cause is, according to Aquinas, that of participation. Hence the analogy of being is, in its most basic form, a participation of the *esse* of creatures in the *esse* of God, considered as their efficient, exemplary and final cause.

Human *esse* is participation in divine *esse*. This does not mean, of course, that humans share in the divine *esse* as a species partakes of its genus. This notion of participation is simply the "analogy of inequality," which leads directly to univocity, or a notion of being common to God and creatures. The implication of univocity, as Mascall writes, is that being is "some kind of cosmic material, a metaphysical modelling-clay appearing now in this shape and now in that."[65] But does not the affirmation that creatures are what they are by participation deprive creatures of the possibility of being in their own right. It is certainly true that the denial of *any* substantiality to creatures leads to an obliteration of the ontological difference, as most clearly seen in the philosophy of Spinoza. In the face of this problem, many Thomists have wanted to read Aquinas as emphasizing substantiality as the primary fact about human beings, ignoring or minimizing the loci where Thomas speaks of participation. Hence we find, for example, Anderson characteristically asserting that "being is ontologically prior to relation: things are things before they are *related* things."[66] This may well be the case with respect to ordinary relations. But is it true of the relation of dependence that is creation? Or does createdness enter into the very *esse* of a creature? If Aquinas's answer to the question is ultimately negative, the accusation that he inaugurates the fateful severing of being from gift, which eventuates in modern atheism, becomes plausible. But if Thomas's deepest teaching is that creatures do not have being simply and solely in themselves, but exist by participating in the divine *esse*, then the force of the charge disappears entirely. In multiple guises, Thomas holds that "all beings apart from God are not their own being, but are beings by participation."[67] Yet he does not associate the affirmation of participation with the denial of substantiality. His position is that creatures have being *both* by way of substance and by way of participation. As Rudi te Velde shows in detail, Thomas consistently strives to overcome the antinomy that he inherits from Boethius, in the interest of affirming both substantiality and participation.[68]

Thomas's willingness to hold substantiality and participation together has deep roots in his relational conception of the Trinitian persons. As Olivier Boulnois has suggested, shifts away from relational readings of the Trinity lead to the notion that being is univocal. This notion is correctly associated with John Duns Scotus, but, as the recent work of Anne Davenport demonstrates, one cannot ignore the fundamental importance of Scotus's Franciscan predecessor, Peter Olivi. Denying that the divine persons are distinct *per relationes*, Olivi holds that they are distinguished *per modos essendi*, or (as William of Ware summarized Olivi's position) that the "three persons are nothing but one substance posited three times" (*tres personae non sunt nisi substantia posita ter*). The implication is that *productio* occurs within the Trinity. Against productionist modalism, Olivi's Franciscan brothers declared that "in the divine, no producing or produced essence is to be posited, and to hold the contrary is an error" (*in divinis non est ponere essentiam producentem et productam, et contrarium est error*).

Scotus seems to accept this condemnation. His official position is that one may speak of the Word as a *productio*, as long as one understands the term of production as a Person rather than an essence. But Davenport argues that Scotus secretly has a strong interest "in vindicating key aspects of Olivi's censored doctrine."[69] On her view, Scotus deprives himself of the conceptual resources that would enable him to reject Olivi's notion that production in the divine is the production of one essence by another essence. Beneath his pretense of neutrality with respect to the *per relationes* theory, Scotus destroys the possibility that the Persons could be relations. Davenport's understanding of Scotus's argument may be cast as a *reductio ad absurdum*, using the first Person as an example:

1. The Father is the self-subsistent relation of paternity (assumption for *reductio*).
2. God is *essentially* infinite, that is, infinite apart from any relation (core Scotist premise).
3. Paternity is not formally infinite, because infinity does not belong to a relation as such (corollary of 2).
4. The Father is not infinite (1,3).
5. The Father is not God (2,4).
6. The Father is God (assumption).

Because 5 and 6 are contradictory, the assumption that a divine Person could be a self-subsistent relation has been reduced to absurdity. As Davenport writes, "divine persons *cannot be self-subsistent relations, since relations, as such, are not formally infinite, and are therefore not God.*"[70] Davenport concludes that Scotus's analysis suggests "a vast effort to establish a dynamic doctrine of the Trinity as three divine *modi essendi* without provoking censorship," adding that the "exasperating technicity of Scotus's discussion simply tesifies to his extreme caution."[71]

The modalism of Scotus's Trinitarian theology, as Davenport also shows, can be correlated with both univocity and epistemological representation. The Father, as infinite, is a productive *ens quantum*; the Son, as infinite, is a produced *ens quantum*. Both Persons are understood not as relations, but as unlimited quantified being. They are infinite essences that exist in two contrasting modes, as producing and produced. Against those (e.g., Aquinas) who would hold that the Word is communicated but not produced, Scotus's position is that the Word is *communicatum per productionem*. But if Davenport's Olivian reading of Scotus is correct, this is merely a dodge, since production of univocist being has usurped the older notion of *communicatio*. The commitment to representation can be understood as a transfer of the divine *producere* to the human production of *esse*, which though finite is essentially the same quantifiable stuff. Against any "carnal" Aristotelianism, Olivi strives to conceive the human person as the *vir spiritualis*. Because the *vir spiritualis* is not essentially embodied, his most godlike production is intellectual. Like God, he is able to make ideas of things (concepts, representations, essences). Thus Olivi and Scotus, in the name of the *vir spiritualis*, inaugurate the turn toward knowing as mirroring or representation. Although this turn is promoted for theological reasons, it occurs in a secular space. Depending only on the natural light, the epistemological production of ideal being is not constrained by anything outside itself, since (as Olivi and Scotus agree) there is no necessity in the world that would constrain it. Thus, as Davenport concludes, the modalism, univocity, and representationalism adumbrated by Olivi and more clearly articulated by Scotus anticipate key features of the "modern scientific project."[72]

In contrast to Scotus, Thomas thinks of human making as distinct but not separate from divine creation. This conception is embedded in a doctrine which affirms the analogical participation of human *esse* in divine *esse*. This elevates the status of human making beyond a merely technical transformation of matter within an autonomous realm. Aquinas clearly rejects the idea that either human beings or nature act in a space sealed off from creation: "the operation of nature takes place only on the presupposition of created principles."[73] It follows that human art also takes place on the presupposition of created principles; *ars imitatur naturam in sua operatione*.[74] Because Aquinas does not imagine human making to occur within a desacralized, sheerly human territory, but understands it rather as a mode of participation in the divine, it may be said that human construction acquires a significance that is difficult for modern secular perspectives to appreciate. It becomes a privileged site where God speaks through the creature, the agent of divine providence. Yet the making proper to finite beings remains different in kind from that proper to the Creator. The doctrine of metaphysical analogy ensures that humans can never create as God does. But does it altogether prohibit the imputation of genuine creativity to human beings? In the next chapter, we will consider Nicolaus Cusanus's attempt to maintain substantial continuity with Thomas on the question of analogical participation, but to move beyond Aquinas in the direction of attributing creative power to rational finite agents.

2

NICOLAUS CUSANUS

In her treatment of *The Mind of the Maker*, Dorothy Sayers writes:

> Looking at man, [the author of Genesis] sees in him something essentially divine, but when we turn back to see what he says about the original upon which the "image" of God was modeled, we find only the single assertion, "God created." The characteristic common to God and man is apparently that: the desire and the ability to make things.[1]

Sayers writes as if this understanding of the *imago Dei* is (or ought to be) self-evident to any thinking Christian. The ancient and medieval traditions do not, however, explicitly understand the *imago Dei* in this manner.[2] Although the texts of Aquinas decisively transcend the paradigm of craft in the divine case, and serve to "dignify" human making by relating it to divine Providence, Aquinas does not take "making" as the primary sense in which the human being is made *ad imaginem Dei*. He maintains grave reservations about the idea that one ought to ascribe any form of the power of creation to human beings. When he considers man as the image of God, he most explicitly stresses *ratio* and *voluntas*, with no adversion to the "desire and ability to make things," let alone create them.

Sayers is not wrong, however, to connect human creativity with the first chapter of Genesis. The thinker after Aquinas who takes a decisive step in articulating the notion that humans can be authentically creative—while maintaining profound continuity with the Thomist conception of human *esse* as participation in divine *esse*—is the fifteenth century thinker and mystic Nicolaus Cusanus.[3]

This chapter does not pretend to offer a complete interpretation of the Cusan corpus. Our approach is to focus on the Cusan text that provides the most thorough articulation of his concept of making (*facere*) over the widest range of topics. That text is the *Idiota de Mente*, a dialogue Nicolaus composed in the middle of his career in 1450.

The dramatic setting of the *Idiota de Mente*

In the *Idiota de Sapientia*, which dramatically and chronologically precedes the *Idiota de Mente*, we encounter a meeting between an educated orator and an untutored layman, which may represent an encounter between "a knowing in pride and a knowing in humility and charity."[4] Cusanus begins the *Idiota de Mente* with a conversation that does not involve an *idiota* at all. Instead, an orator approaches a philosopher. Having spent a lifetime on the Delphic quest, the philosopher finds himself in Rome. Standing on a bridge, the philosopher is able to admire the simple folk crossing the bridge in transit to the Jubilee, without being able or willing to cross the bridge himself. The orator seeks knowledge from the philosopher, who in turn asks the orator for help in procuring some writings of the wise that are located in the temple of the Capitol dedicated to Mens. It is not clear, the orator says, whether the temple contains the writings on mind. He suggests instead that the philosopher speak with an *idiota* of his recent acquaintance, a layman whom he judges to be most wonderful. Having just confessed his own wonder about the faith of simple laymen, the philosopher has no choice; he agrees to follow the orator. In small compass, then, Cusanus suggests an inversion of a standard way of relating faith, rhetoric, and philosophy. The order complacently assumed by the philosopher has been turned upside-down: the philosopher will follow the orator, who in turn has bowed to the superiority of the layman.

As if to underscore the humiliation that the philosopher must undergo, Cusanus has him descend from the area near the Temple of Eternity into a small underground cave. There he finds the *idiota* making an artifact, a spoon. Blushing because the *idiota* is engaged in a rustic task, the orator warns him that the philosopher will scarcely believe him capable of theorizing. A master of commonplaces, the orator supposes that the activity of making and the activity of contemplation are essentially foreign to one other. The layman, however, assumes the philosopher's capacity to see past the scorn of the orator. In response, the philosopher rewards the layman's trust. Against the facile certitude of the orator, the philosopher recalls a rumor that Plato painted once a while, and suggests that he would never have done such a thing if art and contemplation were simply opposed. Ever wanting the philosopher's approval, the orator interjects that Plato used painting as a source of illustrations to make great things easy. From his standpoint, the function of art can only be to illustrate truths known to the wise by some other means. The layman's reply suggests a superficial agreement with the orator: "indeed in my art I seek symbolically what I want, and feed my mind. I sell the spoons to replenish the body."[5] The agreement is superficial, because the layman's art is not useful for the mind in the way that the orator thinks. The function of his art is not merely to provide examples of what he knows by other means. It is the food of his mind. The connection between the act of making and the function of the mind is stronger than the orator can imagine.

But what is the connection? How is the power of mind related to making? These questions will recur in one form or another throughout the dialogue. Though not as convention-bound as the orator, the philosopher is hesitant. He does not know how to approach someone as unconventional as the layman. It seems that Cusanus has deliberately placed the learned philosopher in an extraordinarily strange situation. He is stuck in a cave, subject to free conversation with an *idiota* not bound by ordinary academic standards. Yet the connection with intellectual tradition has not been severed altogether: the three men are seated in a triangle. Despite his obvious hesitance, generated in part because he cannot follow his usual procedure of quizzing his interlocutor by reference to his writings, the philosopher appears ready to begin the inquiry. Before he can begin, the orator makes yet another slighting reference to the layman's simplicity, remarking that the *idiota* lacks the decency required for addressing someone as important as the philosopher. The orator adds that he hopes not to have led the philosopher to the layman in vain.

At this point, the philosopher shows his impatience with sycophantic windiness. He demands the orator's silence for the duration and turns to the layman directly, asking him to state his "conjecture" (*coniectura*) about the mind.[6] The layman's conjecture is that "mind is that from which comes the limit and measure of all things" and that *mens* is derived from *mensurando*, measuring.[7] The layman adds that some distinction obtains between the *mens* and the *anima*—the *mens* subsists in itself, and is either infinite or the image of the infinite. But minds of the latter class may also serve to animate the body. When they perform this function, they may be called *animae*. Thus the layman agrees with the philosopher that "the mind is the same as the soul of a human being: what as such is mind is soul by its function."[8]

Construction as manifestation of forms through image-making

To his suggestion that *mens*, mind, is named from *mensurando*, measuring, the layman adds that no human name can precisely reflect the nature of its object. When the philosopher interprets this as an expression of linguistic conventionalism, the layman implores him to understand him "more deeply" (*profundius*).[9] The philosopher superficially assumes that names are either natural or conventional. Against this, the layman contends that names carry both an element of arbitrariness and an aptitude for reflecting the essence of a thing, although never with full precision. What holds for the naming activity will be true of human art generally. Thus the layman turns to a more overtly "artistic" example, his own craft of spoon-making.

The layman wants to elucidate his thesis that "all human arts are images, as it were, of the infinite and divine art."[10] After telling the puzzled philosopher that this idea is both obvious and the common property of all philosophers, the layman claims that all human arts are mutually distinct and, therefore, finite. Distinct human arts have their own principles; the principles themselves stem from an infinite art, a "unique absolute eternity" (*unica absoluta aeternitas*).[11] This single infinity does not have a principle (else it would be finite), but simply *is* the absolute principle. As such, it is the precondition and source for all other arts. "Therefore every finite art comes from the infinite art. In this way the infinite art must be the paradigm (*exemplar*) of all arts, their beginning, middle and end, their rule, measure, truth, exactness and perfection."[12] From the layman's perspective, it makes no sense to conceive of autonomous human arts that exist in a space separate from the divine art. (The layman is historically accurate, moreover, in suggesting no philosopher has yet clearly thought the notion of "secular space" that would be the necessary condition of denying his thesis.)

Sensing that the philosopher understands the argument, or at least assents to it verbally, the layman proceeds to illustrate it with the art of spoonmaking. Here we see the first clear sign of an ascription of creativity to human beings. The layman insists that in making spoons, he does not imitate the figure (*figura*) of any natural thing. The spoon has no exemplar outside our mind (*extra mentis nostrae*).[13] There are mimetic crafts that look to exemplars in nature, existing outside the mind. The layman's art, however, is not one of them. Rather than imitate nature, it "aims more to perfect than to imitate the figures of created things, and in this regard is more like the infinite art."[14] Here "perfection" should be taken in its literal sense—"to bring to completion" or "to make more thoroughly." The layman's making does not imitate things that are already found within nature. It brings into being created forms that have never existed naturally.

What does the layman construct when he makes a spoon? The form, the artifact (the physical spoon), or both? The most radical attribution of creativity would hold that the layman makes the very form of the spoon from scratch. This cannot be the case, because the layman has already declared that all forms employed by any particular human art have their origin in the infinite divine art. One may therefore be led to suppose that if the layman cannot make the form of the spoon *ex nihilo*, he does not make it at all. He merely finds it pre-existing in his mind. Yet the layman's whole point is to reject this antithesis. When the layman makes a spoon, he not only produces a physical artifact, but also "makes sensible" (*sensibilem facere*) the form of "spoonness." In making a spoon, the artist uses instruments to arrange matter until it exists in certain proportions. These proportions are those in which "the form of being a spoon fittingly appears" (*convenienter resplendeat*), in which it can be known by the measuring mind. The artifact is that in which the form "shines forth" (*resplendere*).¹⁵ Thus it is the "image" of the spoon, since it manifests the form, enabling it to shine forth. (It is not, however, a mere copy, since copies cannot be made without full access to the original.) Thus the layman concludes that forms are known and manifested through the making of images. Image-making is not inferior to the contemplation of originals. It is the closest approximation to the divine art.

Yet the ability of any constructed image to manifest its form is limited. No particular spoon exhausts the form of spoonness. "The truth and precision of a spoon (which cannot be multiplied or communicated), cannot be made perfectly sensible whatever the tools or craftsman employed."¹⁶ All instances of spoon-making are reflections of the utterly simple ideal spoon. Some images shine more brightly than others; not all images are equally apt to manifest the form. No image, however, can do so exactly: one can always speak of "more and less." With this analysis in mind, the layman returns to the naming activity. The name "spoon" is joined to particular spoons in a manner that is indeed arbitrary, yet "not alien or totally separate from the natural name joined to the form."¹⁷ Just as all material spoons reflect the form of spoonness, so all conventional names for spoon reflect the natural name. Both naming and artifact-constructing are human arts whose practitioners must be understood as constructing images that "make sensible" and therefore provide knowledge of forms that in themselves are non-sensible. To impose a name on an object is to create a linguistic space in which the nature of the thing can shine forth. Cusanus thinks of artifice as the medium in which the natural shines forth. What from one standpoint seems extraneous to nature appears from another perspective as the medium for its expression.

Making, in its first sense as *facere sensibilem*, is required for any cognitive progress beyond an implicit or virtual knowledge of form. The layman does not exempt his own self-understanding from this necessity. He expressly engages in an *explicare* of his own *ars* by making it sensible—in this case, by giving it outward verbal expression.¹⁸

Constructions of reason

A complication of the *Idiota*'s second chapter is that the layman considers two apparently distinct accounts of the relation between making and naming, only to suggest their ultimate harmony. First, the layman gives what might be considered an "Aristotelian" account. The imposition of names is an activity of reason (*motus rationis*). The object of this activity is that which falls under the senses (*sub sensum cadut*). Thus it follows that "nothing is in the reason except what was first in the senses."¹⁹ So far, so conventional. But just before he affirms the Aristotelian axiom, the layman says that "reason *makes*" (*ratio facit*) the relations that obtain among things perceived by the senses—"discretion, likeness, and difference" (*discretio, concordatia &*

differentia).²⁰ That the use of *facere* is precise, rather than somehow accidental or metaphorical, is confirmed a few sentences later. Since *ratio* cannot attain the true form of its objects, it settles for "conjecture and opinion."²¹ But how does it form conjectures or arrive at opinions? By *constructing* its own beings, the *entia rationis*, which the layman identifies as genus and species. These are precisely the beings that, from the likeness and difference of sensible things, "reason has made for itself" (*ratio fecit*).²²

Genera and species are doubly constructed, as it were—they are made from the foundation of "likeness and difference" which itself, according to the layman, is made by reason. The "Aristotelian" account entails that, from the standpoint of intelligibility, "a thing has no being unless it falls under a name."²³ Because it involves a genuine *motus rationis*, philosophical logicians of this stripe enjoy the activity of approaching things through names, and deepening their knowledge of names. However, the layman adds, they deprive themselves of the ability to know forms "in themselves and in their truth" (*in se & in sua veritate*).²⁴ Forms, according to them, are nothing other than *entia rationis*. The constructive capacity of *ratio* is affirmed at the price of denying the mind's ability to apprehend real essences. Human reason can know only what is contained in nominal definitions.

The layman appears to think that the "Aristotelian" position slides inexorably into terminism. He proposes to consider a second, "Platonic" account, affirmed by "those who admit that something is present to the mind's understanding which was not present to sense nor to reason, namely the exemplary and incommunicable truth of the forms which shine forth (*relucet*) in sensible things."²⁵ Unlike the *entia rationis*, exemplars do not depend on sensible things. The converse is true: sensible things depend upon intelligible exemplars. "Exemplars precede sensible things by nature, just as truth precedes its image."²⁶ If all particular human beings were destroyed, the *ens rationis* "human being" would also be destroyed. The exemplar, however, would remain, because its existence does not causally depend upon particular human beings. Against the "Aristotelian" position, the "Platonic" account denies the legitimacy of reducing a thing to its appearance under the constructed classifications of genus and species. Appearances are images and can be destroyed, but the exemplary truth would remain. It is not that logical taxonomies can or should be discarded. But knowing them is not an end in itself, since "reason and logic deal only with the images of forms."²⁷ Rather than remain satisfied with knowing the meaning of terms, adherents of this position "strive to see things theologically (*theologice intueri conantur*), turning to exemplars and ideas."²⁸

Must one choose between the two accounts? The layman and philosopher agree that they exhaust the options supplied by the "sects of philosophers, Aristotelians and Platonists."²⁹ What distinguishes the layman from the philosopher is his desire to transcend sectarian differences and harmonize the two accounts. Rather than straightforwardly identify himself with the

"Platonic" description of knowing, the layman asserts that the two accounts may be reconciled "once the mind lifts itself to infinity."[30] The "Aristotelian" account is correct in at least two respects. First, it rightly denies the independent existence of multiple separate forms, since all forms, insofar as they are plural, are but images of the one and simple infinite form. It is also correct to insist upon the constructedness of *entia rationis*. Genus and species are indeed images made by reason. But in order to exist *as* images, they must be images of something, viz. the infinite form that is not a product of the human mind.

Thus the layman can affirm both the constructive character of the naming activity and its subordination to an infinite *ars* that humans do not make, which is equivalent to the "name beyond speech" (*ineffabile nomen*).[31] Human names are images of the infinite *nominalitas*. Thus the layman returns to his initial contention. Names are made by human beings, but they are not merely arbitrary inventions. All *facta* disclose something of the infinite art: "every name is an image of the precise name."[32] Yet no image is adequate to its original. Thus making is always conjectural, pointing toward a truth that it can never fully attain. The activity of making necessarily falsifies what it wants to know: the "specific differences formed by our reason (*per rationem nostram formatas*) from the exemplifications" cause the "one and utterly simple exemplar" to appear as "multiple exemplars."[33]

The layman can harmonize the conflicting sects of philosophy, but only because he "speaks theologically." Implicit in the dialogue is a judgment on philosophy. The philosopher is depicted as one who tries to say what the layman has said, but not as well. Comparisons between Leibniz and Cusanus are understandable; both proclaim the ambition to reconcile divisions between sects. Cusanus, however, differs dramatically from Leibniz in his rejection of the ability of philosophical discourses to bring about any such reconciliation. Only the unlettered layman, who has not merely heard about wisdom but has actually tasted it, can approach this task.[34] The philosopher comes to recognize this: "as I listen I cannot but agree with you that all the philosophers wanted to say nothing else but what you said."[35] Philosophy is incomplete, but not therefore useless. By emphasizing the philosopher's openness toward truth and endowing him with the ability to ask the right questions, Cusanus is able to suggest *both* the utility of academic philosophical discourses and their ultimate insufficiency.

What Cusanus thinks about rhetoric (or at least the rhetoric of his own time) is suggested by the fact that silence was imposed upon the orator in the first chapter. The silence is broken in chapter 3, when the orator asks the layman to explain what he has said about the precision of a name. Once again, the layman begins his explanation with a reference to the constructive power of mind. "You are aware, orator, how we bring forth from the power of mind (*exerimus ex vi mentis*) mathematical figures."[36] The layman explains that when he wants to "make visible" (*visibilem facere*) the form of triangularity, he begins with construction. "I make a figure (*figura facio*) in which I establish three angles, so that in a figure thus disposed and proportioned, triangularity may shine forth (*reluceat*)."[37] As with the spoon, so with the triangle. Both are artifacts whose construction is the indispensable condition of the form's shining forth.

The activity of *mens: vis assimilativa* and the construction of concepts

To emphasize the link between *ratio* and *facere* may seem to warrant the ascription of only a weak constructivism to Cusanus. Standing above *ratio* is *mens*. Is *mens* constructive or creative? In several places, the layman speaks of *mens* as a faculty that intuits or contemplates truth. An important text in chapter 3 seems to support this reading. When the philosopher asks the layman what he means by *mens*, the layman replies with a contrast between the "mind of God" (*divina mens*) and "our mind" (*nostra mens*).

> If you call divine mind the totality of truth about things, you will call ours the totality of the assimilation of things, so that it is the totality of notions (*notiones*). Conception (*conceptio*) for the divine mind is the production (*productio*) of things; conception for our mind is the notional knowledge (*notio*) of things. If the divine mind is absolute thingness, then its conception is the creation (*creatio*) of things, whereas conception for our mind is the assimilation (*assimiliatio*) of things.[38]

The layman adds that whereas God knows things in their exact and proper truth, we only know them in their image or likeness (*similitudo*), which is to know them "notionally" (*notionaliter*). God knows things, because he makes them; we know only their likenesses, because we do not make them. Yet this does not destroy the analogy between the divine mind and human mind. "All things are in God, but there as exemplars of things; all things are in our mind, but here as likenesses of things."[39] But the analogy between the objects of divine mind and the objects of human mind entails a more basic connection between the minds themselves. The connection is between exemplar and image. Thus the layman declares that mind is the "image of God (*imago dei*) and of all God's images following upon the exemplar itself."[40]

What does it mean to say that the mind is the *imago dei*? Before we examine Cusanus's answer to the question, we should note the contrast the layman has emphasized—the contrast between the *productio/creatio* of divine *mens*, and the *conceptio/notio* of human *mens*. The philosopher interprets this contrast as another way of making a distinction with which he is already familiar, namely, that between an "absolute formative power" and a "conformative or configurative power."[41] The divine mind creates; the human mind conforms to what has been created. But things are not quite this simple. The layman begins his answer to the philosopher with the declaration "since what ought to be said cannot be properly expressed, a multiplication of discourse is most useful."[42] It may be true to speak of the mind as conformative. But this cannot be taken to imply sheer passivity. As the "most simple image of the divine mind amid all the images of the divine enfolding," the mind is something more than an inert unfolding (*explicatio*).[43] It is a "living substance," the layman says at the beginning of chapter 5, a genuine image appropriately described as possessing godlike power.[44] Thus the layman proceeds to speak of the "power of our mind that must be admired" (*admiranda mentis nostrae virtute*).[45]

This power, in the first instance, is what the layman calls the *vis assimilativa*. The assimilative power denotes the ability of the mind to grasp every magnitude, multitude, time, motion, composition, diversity, inequality, and disjunction. These are all "unfoldings" of elements that the mind possesses within itself, and thus can assimilate itself to. The layman concludes: "By being the image of the absolute enfolding which is the infinite mind, mind has the power to assimilate itself to every unfolding."[46] What enables the mind to assimilate itself to an infinite number of objects is its infinite simplicity. But the mind cannot assimilate itself unless it is stimulated by the senses. Cusanus argues this explicitly in chapter 4, but the argument has been prepared by the earlier insistence upon the necessity of "making sensible" for knowledge of intelligible form. Here again one detects Cusanus's willingness to weave an Aristotelian strand into his account, even if the layman rejects membership in any school of philosophers as unbefitting to one who has tasted wisdom.

What sort of mental activity is assimilation? Earlier it was associated with *conceptio*, in a context where *conceptio* was set off in antithesis to *productio* and *creatio*. But the layman proceeds to weaken this antithesis. Assimilation is now linked to making. The mind is a power which, "even if it lacks every conceptual form, once stimulated, can assimilate itself to every form and make notions of all things" (*omnium rerum notiones facere*).[47] The distinction between *productio* and *conceptio* has given way to their connection. To conceive is to assimilate, and assimilation is related to the construction of *notiones*. The layman illustrates with the example of a person who comes from darkness into light. In the darkness, prior to sensory stimulus, he has no idea of visible things. When he comes into the light, his mind is able to possess notions of visible things. This occurs not through passive reception, but through active construction. "Once the mind comes into the light and is stimulated, it assimilates itself to the visible so that it may construct a notion (*ut notionem faciat*)."[48]

The vision example may be generalized: "the mind assimilates things in the same way it assimilates visible things in seeing, audible things in hearing, the flavorful in taste, what has odor in smell, what is touchable in touch, what is sensible in sense, the imaginable in imagination, and what can be reasoned about in reason."[49] Assimilation is not identified with construction, but depicted as its natural prelude. The *vis assimilativa* is what enables the mind to make *notiones* of things. Chapter 5 amplifies the comparison of *mens* to vision. The layman asserts the analogy between *discretio/visio* and *mens/ratio*. Just as vision requires discretion in order to focus, the syllogizing of *ratio* requires the judgment of *mens*. Ratio "does not know what it syllogizes without *mens*."[50] But why should *mens* have a superior knowledge of the *notiones* disposed by *ratio*? Here we may discern a positive use of the maker's knowledge paradigm. *Ratio* looks upon its notions, but *mens* originates them, and therefore knows them exhaustively. "Just as if the forms of all things were reflected in the simplest indivisible point at the angle of a highly polished diamond that was alive, it would find by looking within itself the likenesses of all things and through them be able to make notions of everything" (*de omnibus notiones facere posset*).[51] The power of mind is specifically described as its aptitude to make. Its productive power is tied to its simplicity, as Cusanus suggests both through comparing *mens* to the simplest point of the diamond's angle and through the simplicity of the layman himself.

After the layman describes the "mirroring power" (*vis specularis*) of *mens* that is "prior to all quantity," the philosopher makes a request: "Can you apply your own art paradigmatically to the creation of mind?"[52] The Latin is ambiguous: *in mentis creatione* may be understood as signifying *both* "to the way mind was created" and "to the creative activity of mind." The layman honors the philosopher's request by recalling the spoon example. When he makes a spoon, he elicits the proportion in which the form of the spoon perfectly shines forth. He now proceeds to polish the spoon until it comes to have the form of a mirror; he has added the mirror form to the spoon form. Is the layman creating a new form? Strictly speaking, it would seem that he is not. The initial presentation of the spoon example suggests that he is engaged in the disposition of matter which enables the manifestation of a form already existing in the divine *ars*. But when Cusanus has the layman declare that "the form of mirror had no temporal existence (*temporale esse*) before the spoon," he opens the possibility that human makers are able to create forms, where "to create" means precisely the bestowal of *esse*.[53]

However this may be, the layman's elucidation of his art provides a twofold analogy to God's creation of humanity. First, it suggests that as the craftsman disposes his material until spoonness shines forth, so God disposes an appropriate matter until animality shines forth. Second, as the mirror form is added to the spoon form, the form of *mens* is added to *animalitas*. The illustration serves to emphasize the non-passive character of mirroring. Rorty and those influenced by his treatment of noetic mirroring tend to assume, unreflectively, that mirroring is essentially passive. But the layman provides a significantly different picture of mirroring. When he describes *mens* as a "living mirror" (*vivum speculum*), he means to connect its "aliveness" with its creative capacity, its ability to construct its own *notiones*.[54]

After probing the sense in which the mind is analogous to number, the layman asserts that anyone who examines his own mind will find that "the mind fabricates (*fabricare*) notions from itself."[55] This inspires the philosopher to report that others have also found a nexus between the divine mind and the human mind. Commenting on the philosopher's report, the layman states what is literally the central teaching of *Idiota de Mente*:

> The difference between God's mind and ours is the difference between making (*facere*) and seeing (*videre*). In conceiving, the divine mind creates. Our mind, in conceiving notions or in making intellectual visions (*concipiendo notiones seu intellectuales faciendo visiones*), assimilates. The divine mind is the power of giving being (*vis entificativa*); our mind is power of assimilating (*vis assimilativa*).[56]

Notice how Cusanus invokes a contrast between making and seeing, but proceeds immediately to undermine the contrast by describing human seeing as itself a matter of "making intellectual visions." Both divine creation and human seeing are described by recourse to *facere*. One may hazard that any author who asserts a polarity between *x* and *y*, but includes *x* in the description of both *x* and *y*, is not principally concerned to keep the poles apart.[57] The mind not only constructs *notiones*, but then uses *notiones* as material from which "to make mechanical arts and physics and logical conjectures" (*facit mechanicas artes & physicas ac logicas coniecturas*).[58] Although the layman does not go into detail, he suggests the existence of a domain in which the *mens* assimilates itself to sensible things and proceeds to make notions of them. These notions do not unproblematically "represent" things as they are. In fact, the layman emphasizes the opposite. "All such notions are more conjectures than truth," he says, because they are obtained through the medium of "rational assimilations."[59] Notions are made from assimilations; *ratio* makes assimilations from sensible things; sensible things depend upon intelligible exemplars. The chain of dependencies ensures that the *notiones* made by *mens* in the domain of sensible things are uncertain and conjectural, since they are "more in accord with images of forms than with truths."[60]

There is another domain, however, in which *mens* operates *per se*, rather than as immersed in a body. In this domain, the layman credits *mens* with the ability to grasp immutable quiddities (*immutabiles quidditates*).[61] Here one might expect Cusanus to abandon the language of construction for that of direct intuition into essences. In fact, however, the layman reaffirms the commitment to construction. The assimilations made by *mens* are of a higher quality than those made by *ratio*, but they are still related to *facere*. Operating *per se*, the mind "makes (*facit*) assimilations of forms not as immersed in matter but as they are in themselves and through themselves."[62] *Mens* constructs the ideal circle, the figure from whose center all lines drawn from the circle are precisely equal. Here it is not imitating sensible things, since nature provides no examples of precisely equal lines. The mind is able to conceive such abstractions as the ideal of the circle "because it makes the assimilations in itself and separated from matter" (*quia mens ut in se & a materia abstracta has facit assimilationes*).[63] There is no priority of conceiving to making. To conceive the ideal circle *is* to make it. Once again, the mind is able to use its assimilations to continue the task of constructing *scientiae* and *notiones*. "In accord with this power it produces (*exerit*) certain mathematical sciences and discovers that it has the power to assimilate itself to things insofar as they exist in the necessity of connection (*in necessitate complexionis*) and to make notions (*notiones faciendi*)."[64] The contrast is between the domain where *mens* operates in conjunction with the body, seeing only the contingent relations between sensible things, and the domain where *mens* operates *per se*, where it sees things in the necessity of connection. But notice that such necessities are apprehended *only* through the "making of *notiones*," which are derived from assimilations that are also the result of the productive power of *mens*. In each domain, the mind knows its objects by making them.

The cognition of mathematical things is the penultimate region of *Republic* VI's "divided line." Like Plato, the layman proceeds to imagine a higher region in which *mens* grasps things neither as contingently related, nor as mutually bound in the "necessity of connection," but rather as existing "in absolute necessity," with no tinge of "otherness" (*alteritas*).[65] In this region, *mens* would not assimilate itself to sensible things or intelligible mathematical realities. It would bypass these assimilations in favor of turning towards its exemplar. Through such an effort, "it would intuit everything as one and itself as the assimilation of that one."[66] Construction has finally given way to self-contemplation, it would appear. But the layman does not break the pattern of introducing *assimilatio* for the sake of *facere*. Instead, he repeats it by using *facere* twice in rapid succession, as if to emphasize that mind's deepest imitation of its exemplar is coeval with the highest pitch of its creative power. Having made the effort of self-assimilation, *mens* proceeds "to make notions concerning the one which is all: and thus make theological speculations" (*notiones facit de uno quod omnia: & sic facit theologicas speculationes*).[67] The mind is primordially creative, at every level, in every domain. Such is the truth about mens said "briefly and awkwardly" (*curiose & rustice*) not by a professional thinker, but by an *idiota* whose own competence lies in making.[68]

Has the philosopher understood the *idiota*? It would seem not, because he immediately asks the layman when the mind is said to conceive. The *idiota* replies, "when it makes likenesses" (*facit similitudines*), which may be called either *notiones* or genera, differences, species, properties and accident. "God creates in the soul the power of conceiving; the mind makes the things I have mentioned."[69] *Deus creavit, mens facit*—the analogy between divine and human action appears secure. The heading of chapter 8 condenses the teaching of chapter 7: the layman finds no difference between *concipere* and *intelligere*, on the one hand, and *notiones & assimilationes facere* on the other. Under questioning from the philosopher, the layman does acknowledge a distinction between *concipere* and *intelligere*. The former is an *imitatio*, knowing things in the mode of form, matter, or the composite, whereas the latter is perfective. *Concipere* is imitative and thereby less than creative, but it is only the starting point (*initus*) of the mind's activity. Its "perfection" (*perfectio*) is *intelligere*. The *imitatio/perfectio* contrast recalls the initial presentation of the spoon example, where the layman described his own art as a *perfectio* rather an *imitatio*. The identification of *intelligere* with the terminal act of *mens*, conjoined with its link to *perfectio*, confirms our sense that the layman regards the highest act of *mens* as constructive.

Is such understanding of possibilities, or of what actually exists? The question bears on how contemporary readers might understand Cusanus. If *intelligere* is the highest act of *mens*, and if it refers to the construction of possibilities, then the objects of constructive understanding would be something like "possible worlds." Existence would be irrelevant to the objects of understanding; neither their essence nor their ability to be constructed would depend on what is actual. If this is correct, then Cusanus would accurately be seen as following the path of Scotus and Ockham, as well as anticipating Leibniz and others who affirm the "priority of the possible." The layman's words in chapter 8 of *Idiota de Mente*, however, preclude any such interpretation. Insofar as they are distinct, *intelligere* is prior to *concipere*. *Concipere* may traffic in mere possibilities, but the layman emphasizes that "what is actual is understood and not conceived" (*actuale intelligitur & non concipitur*).[70] From the perspective of understanding, the highest act of *mens*, the possible is parasitic on the actual. The layman's affirmation of the priority of the actual over the possible places Cusanus in line with Aquinas rather than Scotus or Ockham. Like Aquinas, Cusanus thinks that the possibility of things is determined by their actuality, even if he adds that actuality is never manifest all at once, but must be regarded as emerging through an infinite *explicatio*.

Activa creatio humanitatis: making as imaging of the divine exemplar

Each of the *Idiota de Mente*'s fifteen chapters begins with an observation from the philosopher. *Video noctem accedere*, the philosopher remarks at the beginning of chapter 9.[71] Before the sun sets, the philosopher wants the layman to explain once again how the mind is able to measure everything.

At this point, the layman is able to connect explicitly the mind's measuring ability with its constructive capacity. *Mens* is able to measure things only because it constructs measures: *facit mensuras variarum rerum*.[72] The measures it makes are the point, line, and surface. At the request of the philosopher, the layman serially explains how *mens* makes the point, line and surface. It does so by a two-step process of abstraction. The mind begins by imagining (*considerando*) a thing *x*; then, it subtracts an essential feature of *x* to make another thing *y*. In any such case, *y* is the limit (*terminus*) of *x*. For example, the mind imagines a surface, but then subtracts its width to make a line. The line is thus the limit of surface. Generally stated: "the mind makes (*facit*) the point to be the limit of line, and it makes (*facit*) the line to be the limit of surface. It makes (*facit*) surface as the limit of body. It makes (*facit*) number, whence multitude and magnitude are from the mind: and thus it measures everything."[73] The mind's *mensurando* is grounded in its *faciendo*.

If point, line, surface, and number are things made by this abstractive process, is there anything outside the human mind that it does not make? There is: "outside the mind only solidity (*soliditas*) actually exists."[74] From the perspective of human *mens*, solidity appears as what is given, unintelligible until the mind operates on it. But in a universe ruled by the creative power of God, there is nothing that is sheerly given: "Wood and stones indeed have a fixed measure and limit beyond our minds, but these come from the uncreated mind, from which every limit in things descends."[75] As the human mind creates its measures, so the uncreated mind makes the things that are measured. "Man therefore is God, but not absolutely, since he is man. Hence he is a human god."[76] He is divine, because he is able to construct the measures of all things. He is not absolutely divine, because he is unable to construct what is measured—the world of *soliditas* that exists outside the human mind, but not the divine mind. (The layman denies that any finite thing can be outside mind, since its limits always derive from mind.)

Through the construction of measures, the mind discovers something about itself. In taking the surface as the limit of body, the line as the limit of surface, and the point as the limit of the line, it finds that it cannot proceed *ad infinitum*. Construction begins with *soliditas*, makes quantitative measures through abstraction, and arrives at a limit that is not itself quantitative, the "terminal point" which is "indivisible."[77] The *punctum*, in this sense, is not merely a very short line, but a thing that has no quantitative features: "a point is not a quantum and quantity cannot be constituted (*constitui*) from points since composite things cannot stem from what is without quantity."[78] The *punctum* is one: "there are neither many points nor many unities."[79] As the limit of a line, the point is present in the line, but without division. "In any line there is nothing but one point, which having been extended is the line."[80] Because the point can be undividedly present in the line, it constitutes the line's "totality and perfection" (*eius totalitas ac perfectio*). Thus the point "enfolds the line in itself", while the line is the unfolding of the point. The layman puts the matter succinctly: "the line unfolds what is enfolded in the point" (*linea explicat complicationem puncti*).[81]

Apprehending the relation between *complicatio* and *explicatio* is the key to understanding the nature of *mens*, since "*mens* is the first image of the enfolding of infinite simplicity."[82] As an image of the divine *complicatio*, *mens* contains the limits of what it unfolds through its *explicatio*. Referring back to *Idiota*, chapter 4, one may tabulate the mind's enfoldings and unfoldings as shown.[83] The table could be expanded, as the layman suggests.

Enfoldings (*Complicationes*)	*Unfoldings* (*Explicationes*)
Unity	Number
Rest	Motion
Eternity	Time
Simplicity	Composition
Present	Time
Point	Magnitude
Equality	Inequality
Identity	Diversity

As we have seen from the layman's use of *facere* and cognate terms, the *explicationes* are things made. One might conclude that Cusanus's concept of human making is substantially equivalent to his concept of human *explicatio*. If this were the case, however, the enfoldings necessarily presupposed by the unfoldings would not be a function of human making. They would exist within the mind as seeds implanted by God prior to and independent of human construction. Such an account has some initial plausibility: it seems unlikely that eternity (for example) would be made by the mind. If we have an idea of eternity, it must already be present within the mind, rather than having been constructed by it (or so one might contend in the spirit of Descartes's *Third Meditation*). Such a "Cartesian" reading of Cusanus, however, is not adequate to the text. We have seen that Cusanus describes one of the unfoldings—the point—as a thing made by mind (*mens facit punctum*). This suggests that the human *mens* makes not only the *explicationes*, but also the *complicationes*. It is true that the *realities* of unity, rest, eternity, the point, and so on cannot be made by the human mind. But Cusanus does not think that the human mind literally possesses the realities. The layman's contention is not that the human mind contains the seminal elements of all things, but that it has their likenesses or images. This is because human mind itself "is the first image of the divine enfolding which comprises in its simplicity and power every image of enfolding. As God is the enfolding of enfoldings, so the mind, God's image, is the image of the enfolding of enfoldings."[84] The mind possesses images of the *complicationes*, but it does so because it has made them through the abstractive process that the layman describes in chapter 9. (Here one may anticipate Vico's contention that mind makes the "geometrical point," but not the original of which it is an image, the "metaphysical point.")

As impressive as the creative power of the human mind is—and Cusanus certainly makes *mens* creative in a way that Aquinas did not—it remains the case that for Cusanus the mind makes neither the original elements of things, nor the world created from those elements. Humans construct *notiones* and *mensurae* in a way that images the divine creative power without usurping it. Cusanus's insistence on the constructive character of the human mind and its proper objects co-exists with a basic realism about the world created by God. The layman holds that things exist outside the mind, but he also thinks that they are fundamentally unintelligible until the mind constructs things to measure them. One must say "things to measure them," rather than "their measures," because the layman insists that the proper measures of things—their "limits"—come from God. Thus human knowledge/construction is always an approximate affair, admitting not of *precisa veritas* but involving the "more or less" characteristic of conjectures.

The end of the mind's *mensurando* is not simply to construct a realm of entities that it uses to conjecture about the world. Rather, the layman adds, "everything the mind does (*agit*) is to come to know itself."[85] The mind comes to know itself not by a self-reflexive turn, but through its own distinctive activity. What is this activity? The layman's punning example confirms our analysis: the mind makes itself a measure *modo quo absoluta facies omnium facierum se faceret mensuram*.[86] In the activity of *facere*, the mind discovers itself to be an image of the divine. Its constructive power indicates its status as an absolute measure, not restricted to any quantity. In this sense, Cusanus affirms the power of the mind to create, although he adds that the world it creates depends on a world not of its own making. Access to this world, however, cannot be had through unmediated contemplation. Contemplation is possible only by looking through the prism (genera, species, assimilations, notions, points, lines, surface, number) that the mind constructs.

The possibility of a Kantian reading of Cusanus is evident. Such a reading would translate Cusanus into the contention that we know what we make, the world of appearances, but that we do not know (or at least know scientifically) the world of noumena, since we do not make it. Thus Cusanus affirms the autonomy of the human mind, and its sovereignty over its own constructions. Ernst Cassirer proposes such a reading of Cusanus: "although man's being is completely derived from God, there is nevertheless a sphere in which he functions as a free creator and in which he reigns autonomously."[87]

Cassirer's view, along with more recent interpretations that differ from his only superficially, is immediately called into question by chapter 10 of the *Idiota*. There the layman declares: "knowledge of God and of all things comes before the knowledge of each thing."[88] In this chapter the layman recurs, for the last time, to his art of spoon-making. Spoon-making is creative. It is not merely the copying of a template that the artist looks to before he makes. But it is not thereby disconnected from the divine, occurring in a supposedly autonomous sphere. On the contrary, the layman says that he cannot make any part of a spoon unless he has an implicit knowledge of the spoon as a whole. In order to dispose the parts in their proper proportion, he must refer to an idea of the whole, which he holds before his mind. But where did this idea come from? Not, as we have seen, from the contemplation of nature. It is creatively conceived by the spoon-maker himself. But is this creation autonomous? The layman argues that it cannot be. The idea of a whole spoon is itself something finite, and thereby a part of a totality. Can it be conceived with no prior knowledge of that totality? Consistent application of Cusanus's principle that "knowledge of the whole and its parts come prior to knowledge of a single thing"[89] suggests not. If humans are to create spoons (or any other cultural artifact), they must *already* possess some knowledge of the whole. Therefore, the layman declares, "if God who is the exemplar of the totality of things is unknown, nothing of the totality is known. If the totality of things is not known, obviously no one of its parts can be known."[90] Thus *scientia dei & omnium* comes before the knowledge of any particular thing. Cusanus does not merely neglect to mention the possibility of free creation occurring in a sealed-off secular space. He specifically rules it out.

Cusanus's persistent interest in construing the world as the likeness of the divine and thereby refusing "secular space" is particularly evident in chapter 11 of *Idiota*. The layman considers the possibility of a theologically neutral description of mind, such as might be drawn from Aristotle's ten categories. He insinuates that the philosopher and others like him ("*vos philosophi*") aspire to such a thing, and cajoles the philosopher into confessing his belief that the ten categories "embrace everything."[91] Against this, the layman seeks to expose the non-ultimacy of the categories, applying the principle *ante omne divisione connexio*.[92] There must be something prior to the ten categories. The layman tells the philosopher that the *connexio* prior to *every* division is "the most simple eternity, which is God."[93] But the assertion of absolute unity also requires the layman to speak about trinitarian difference. Thus the philosopher asks the layman how everything exists in a trinitarian way. The layman proceeds to supply a rendering of how created things exist *in trinitate* according to the master concept of *facere*. He begins by asking the philosopher "to consider the universe of things in time."[94] The set of things that exist in time corresponds precisely to the set of things that can be made. Thus "mentally you see all things in their power to be made (*posse fieri*)."⁹⁵ *Posse fieri* is the first mark of the universe. The layman's next claim is that passive power to be made entails an active power to make. If things "have the power to be made, there was necessarily the power to make them (*posse facere*) before they existed."⁹⁶ Thus the second mark: *posse facere*. Is there a third mark? The layman invites the philosopher to "see in the eye of his mind" the universe of temporal things as implying both *posse fieri* and *posse facere*. But if the universe contemplated is to be more than a picture—if things are to actually exist—then a connection (*nexus*) must exist between the power of something to be made and the power of an agent to make it. The *nexus* between passive power and active power is the third trinitarian mark. Thus *posse fieri*, *posse facere* and the *nexus* proceeding from both are the "three absolutes" (*tria absoluta*) that characterize the divine, which is nevertheless a simple eternity.⁹⁷

The layman speaks of the *tria absoluta* not because he wants to speculate in detail on the divine trinity, but because he wants to speak about things as they are in *mens*. This requires a delineation of the structure of *mens*. The layman begins with the declaration: "all subordinate effects (*principiata*) have in themselves a likeness (*similitudo*) to their principle (*principia*)."⁹⁸ As the likeness of the eternal mind, human *mens* will exhibit a trinitarian structure corresponding to the *tria absoluta* of the simple eternity. But since the correspondence is one of likeness, the layman substitutes *assimilare* for *facere*. The three ways of knowing that comprise the mind, its three "modes of comprehending" (*modi compraehendi*), are the power to be assimilated (*posse assimilari*), the power to assimilate (*posse assimilare*), and the connection between the two (*nexus utrium*).⁹⁹ Once again, Cusanus presents us with a contrast that he quickly proceeds to undermine. Although *facere* is properly said of the divine, and *assimilare* of the human, assimilation also turns out to be a matter of making. Thus the layman does not hesitate to use *facere* to describe the three modes of comprehension.

The connection between *facere* and the modes of comprehension may be summarized as follows: (1) The first way of knowing is to presuppose something *in similitudine posse fieri*, which means to think of it as indeterminate matter (*materia*). "When the mind comprehends according to the way of matter (*modo materiae*), it makes genera (*genera facit*)"; (2) The second way of knowing is to consider an object *in similitudine posse facere*. This refers to the power of determining a thing by thinking of it under a form. "When the mind comprehends a thing under the mode of form (*modo formae*), it makes differentiae (*facit differentias*)"; (3) To understand a thing, it is not enough for the mind to think matter and form separately. The thing is fully intelligible only when the connection between the two is perceived. "When the mind comprehends a thing under the mode of the composite (*modo compositi*), it makes a species or an individual (*species facit vel individua*)."¹⁰⁰

The layman thinks that each of the three *modi compraehendi* of the mind are well described as proficiencies in making. To comprehend an object is to make the genus, difference, and species under which it becomes intelligible. The layman's intent is not merely to reproduce an Aristotelian account, but to suggest that hylomorphic epistemologies must be situated within the context of the trinitarian *facere*. He addresses the philosopher: "you see that our mind understands (*intelligere*) after the likeness (*similitudo*) of the eternal mind."[101] To see this does not require a denial of the ten categories—to describe them as human constructions is not to say they are false—but it does require their rigorous subordination to the three modes of comprehension, which are fully intelligible only in light of their divine originals. The layman expects the philosopher to be disturbed by his contention that "mind constructs (*facit*) the ten most general categories as first principles."[102] By way of reassurance, he tells the philosopher that the mind does not construct them out of a common genus. Since the mind is creative, it does not require a pre-existing matter out of which to construct the categories. It creates them solely through its capacity to consider anything according to diverse modes, the likenesses of the modes of *facere* that constitute the divine mind.

But what justifies the movement from the description of things as most intelligible to human *mens* when conceived in trinitarian fashion to the assertion that things actually exist *in trinitate*? The layman does not recognize any grounds for a sharp distinction between how-things-are-according-to-mind and how-things-are-in-themselves. He acknowledges no primacy of mind over things: "all things, as they actually are (*ut actu sunt*) exist in matter, form and their connection."[103] One can say *either* that things exist in a threefold manner because the mind perceives them to exist that way, or that mind perceives things to exist in a threefold manner because they actually are that way. Since Cusanus considers both *mens* and *res* to have their common root in God, and therefore thinks of each as essentially trinitarian, both of the above statements are equally possible. Although such a position may seem hopelessly naive from a Kantian perspective, it suggests an alternative for those who are sceptical of any attempt to draw a firm line between phenomena and noumena. Rather than argue for the absolute priority of mind over being, or vice versa, Cusanus is content to assert their kinship: "there is a very explicit likeness between the mode of being of all things as they exist in reality (*ut sunt actu*), and as they exist in the mind (*ut sunt in mente*)."[104]

Attention to the text of the *Idiota* suggests that one should beware of any facile assimilation of Cusanus to Kant. Cusanus does not link human creativity to the idea that we have complete power within a clearly demarcated sphere. The closing chapters of *Idiota* explicitly interpret human making as a privileged activity that is capable of leading the *imago Dei* ever closer to its original. There is no possibility that human art can ever attain the preciseness or the productivity of the *absoluta ars creativa*, where *ars* and *artifex* perfectly coincide. But there is some analogy between the divine force that creates through spirit, and the human force that constructs through motion, since "there is no motion without spirit" (*motus sine spiritu non est*).[105] To say that the mind is the *imago Dei* is to say that it is the *imago artis divinae*.[106] What does it mean for something to be an image of the divine art? The layman considers a painter who wants to paint a self-portrait. Which of two paintings would be a better likeness, he asks: a painting whose outward features are very much like those of the painter, or a painting of a person who looks less like the painter, but happens to be alive and can imitate the activity of the painter by painting himself? The second is a "more perfect" (*perfectior*) likeness, the layman answers.[107] The example illustrates the core contention of the *Idiota*: "static" conceptions of the *imago Dei* must be rejected because "an image, however perfect, if it cannot be more perfect and more conformed to its model" is always inferior to "any imperfect image which has the power of corresponding more and more without limit to its unreachable original."[108] Through dynamic creative endeavor—what the *De coniecturis* terms the *activa creatio humanitatis*—the human image draws closer to its original by becoming more like its divine exemplar.[109] Any attempt to detach the Cusan conception of making from its telos in asymptotic *theosis* will inevitably distort and falsify it.

What group stands in danger of disrupting the delicate equilibrium involved in affirming the genuinely creative power of the human mind, without forgetting the ontological difference between the divine and its participations? The answer is plain enough. It is the group whom the layman addresses as "you philosophers." The *idiota* does not suppose that philosophers are uneducable. In fact, the philosopher seems to be an indispensable instrument for the layman's own *explicatio*. But the *Idiota* does reject the pretensions of philosophers who take their own categories (whether Aristotelian or not) to embrace everything. Wisdom cries out in the streets.[110] Thus both the "religion natural to men" and the "common undoubted assertion of all people" testify in favor of the immortality of the soul.[111] The subordination of philosophy to another type of discourse that is informed by the traditions of theology, and learns from the *sensus communis* without being imprisoned by it, will also be found in the later work of Vico.

Although Vico never explicitly mentions Cusanus, one can read his work as an original development of the *Idiota*'s claim that "mind is the image of eternity, but time is its unfolding, though an unfolding always less than the image of the eternal enfolding."[112] Of the modern thinkers who succeed Cusanus, it is Vico who places the most obvious stress on the role of the *factum* in human cognition.[113] But, as we shall see in the following pages, Vico is hardly the only post-Renaissance thinker to privilege the nexus between knowing and making. On the contrary, each of the three primary architects of secular modernity—Bacon, Descartes and Hobbes—accord the *factum* a far greater prominence than standard treatments recognize. In this way, they clearly continue the trend represented by Cusanus's willingness to ascribe creativity to human beings. But they just as clearly represent a decisive break from the perspective of the *Idiota*. In different ways, Bacon, Descartes and Hobbes will reject the notion that making is or can be the human creature's mode of participation in divine truth. They will thus inaugurate what may be considered the canonically modern concept of making.

3

FRANCIS BACON

The Baconian *factum*

In the *Novum Organum*, Bacon considers at least three types of things as essentially made or constructed by human beings: (1) instruments for making new discoveries, both theoretical and practical; (2) axioms that express theoretical discoveries, which Bacon regards as "like new creations, imitations of divine handiwork"[1]; (3) works that flow from the axioms.

In the *Distributio*'s summary of part 2 of the *Instauratio Magna*, Bacon holds that to purge the mind of its idols is to prepare and adorn the "bridal chamber of the mind and the universe."[2] The marriage cannot occur, let alone bear useful children (the prayer of Bacon's nuptial hymn), without the assistance of human artifice. The absence of any natural concord between the human mind and the universe it seeks to understand ensures that the two will not come together spontaneously. Any hope for a union between the two requires a clear perception of the mind's natural weakness and a corresponding appreciation for the necessity of what Bacon calls "the aid of instruments or machines."[3]

This point has puzzled some readers of Bacon. C.S. Peirce attributes to Bacon the view "that there are irremediable defects in human intellect, which can nevertheless be nullified by an artificial contrivance, somewhat like a method of bookkeeping."[4] Bacon is not, however, committed to this self-contradictory formulation of his view. His doctrine is that, while the defects of the human intellect in its original condition are deep and indeed "natural," they are susceptible to treatment. Bacon does not claim that the defects are "irremediable"; he thinks that remedy is difficult, but not impossible. The cure for the natural debility of the intellect is not to be sought in nature. Its remedy is art.

The function of Bacon's speech about the "subtlety of nature" is to persuade the reader that, in the absence of an equally subtle *ars*, nature will continue to dominate man, as it has since the Fall.[5] Without the fortification of arts, the mind will remain at the mercy of nature. Bacon compares those who use their "bare understanding" against nature to a man or group of men who attempt to move an obelisk with their bare hands.[6] Artificial helps are necessary if this job is to be done. Only by the "art and intervention of man" can nature be "forced out of her natural state and pressed and molded." Nature is subtle, but will yield under the pressure of artifice. "The nature of things betrays itself more readily under the vexations of art, than in its natural freedom."[7] Men begin as servants and interpreters of nature, forced to acknowledge her initial dominance, but end by recognizing themselves as engaged in a contest between art and nature. Only one party can win. The fortifications that Bacon provides to the mind give him confidence to "stake all on the victory of art over Nature in the race."[8]

Bacon does not consider himself to be the first to discern the necessity for human artifice in the contest with nature. The ancients invented dialectic because they were "obviously looking for intellectual props, not being entirely confident in the natural unassisted working of the mind."[9] Dialectic and the syllogism are inadequate tools, from Bacon's standpoint, but not because they are artificial. All weapons against nature are fashioned by human beings. The problem with the syllogism is not that it is an artificial creation, but that it is "unequal to the subtlety of Nature" and "the subtlety of nature is far greater than that of argument." The syllogism may be able to command assent, and so has limited utility in matters of disputation, but it is utterly unable to take hold of things themselves.[10] When applied to nature, it is dull and demands to be replaced by a sharper tool. Bacon names the new tool *induction*.

Almost invariably, Bacon pairs speech about induction with critique of the syllogism. For example, in the *Distributio* he writes:[11]

> I concede to the syllogism and famed and vaunted demonstrations of that kind their jurisdiction over arts that are popular and based on opinion (which I leave undisturbed), yet in regard to the nature of things, I use induction throughout, both for minor and for major propositions. I consider Induction to be that form of demonstration which upholds the sense, presses down upon Nature and is intent on and closely bound up with works.[12]

Like the syllogism, induction is a man-made tool. Unlike the syllogism, induction has the ability to put nature to the torture and make it yield up its secrets. As the creator of the *novum organum*, Bacon displays a certain pride of possession. He repeatedly speaks of induction as "my method" (37) and emphasizes its total novelty, arguing that it cannot be judged by the old ways.[13] One might wonder, however, whether Baconian induction is a true artifact. Even if we say that it is *like* an artifact, as Bacon does, might it not be more plausible to view it as something natural? In what precise sense is induction an artificial tool? Michel Malherbe characterizes induction as an "intellectual behavior and a logical procedure."[14] Considered strictly as a behavior or procedure, induction might be understood as a practice that has no existence separable from its practitioner, and would thus differ from artificial products that can exist independently of their producers.

Such objections against the construal of induction as essentially artificial are useful to the degree that they warn against attributing to Bacon the notion that induction is arbitrary. Bacon links induction with "the inner recesses of the mind" and "the very bowels of Nature"; it differs from common logic in that it addresses "not only the operations and discourse of the mind, but the nature of things as well."[15] Malherbe characterizes induction as an "artificial device of method," but not without adding that its proper use "gives way to reality" and that "the power of men over nature is artificial so long as it is imperfect."[16] An implication of this reading, which Malherbe fails to note, is that human power over nature will always be artificial, because it will never be perfect. The concluding aphorism of *Novum Organum* holds that the twin losses of innocence and dominion over creation "can even in this life be *in some part* repaired." Malherbe cites this passage in support of his own reading, but does not recognize that Bacon is expressing not only an optimism about the power of human sciences, but also a doubt about their ability to attain perfection. If we attend to the note of pessimism in Bacon's conclusion—muted, to be sure, but unmistakably there—it follows that on Malherbe's own assumptions, the power of men over nature will *always* be artificial.

Bacon stakes all on the victory of art over nature. Induction is the tool whose proper use will enable victory. It is not found just lying about; it is a device contrived by man. (In Aphorisms 61 and 122, Bacon compares it to a compass.)[17] Like all tools, its ultimate justification is whether it works or not. Any other justification would be irrelevant. Induction is applied to a recalcitrant matter which it must actively dissect, to use Bacon's own term.[18] Since it is dissective, it is anything but a passive process of observation or fact accumulation. It is not that Bacon considers himself to have made the tool from nothing. Bacon recognizes the existence of two forms of induction prior to himself: that which "proceeds through simple enumeration" and is therefore useless for invention, and that which can "analyze nature" and was used by Plato "to some extent in examining definitions and ideas."[19] This "Platonic" form of induction constitutes the material out of which Bacon will construct his own tool, using "very many things which no mortal has yet thought of." The result will be a device which gives men the power to "analyze experience and take it apart, and through due exclusion and rejections necessarily come to a conclusion."[20] The relation between induction in its prior forms and induction as Bacon's artificial method is well captured by an image later employed by Descartes. It is the relation between a stone with a sharp point and an anvil used by a competent blacksmith. Because it is artificially constructed, that is, more than a simple development of the mind in its natural state, the tool gives Bacon the confidence to imagine a world "most carefully dissected and anatomized."[21] "Rather than turn Nature into abstractions, it is better to dissect her."[22] Bacon's persistent use of the dissective motif strongly suggests that the primary function of the tool is to cut.

But to cut what? What is the thing made by the new method? This brings us to the second type of Baconian *factum*, the axiom. At first, it seems strange to think that Bacon would conceive of axioms as things that are made. Bacon's favorite image for axioms is "light." Is not light seen rather than made? Bacon does think that light is seen. But he also thinks that we make our own light. Axioms are not, in the first instance, gazed upon by a scientific contemplator, or found lying about ready-made. They are achievements of human construction.

The question "How are axioms made?" must wait until the next section. In this section, our aim is simply to show *that* Bacon regards the axiom as a *factum*. In doing so, there is no need to deny that Bacon speaks of the light cast by axioms as "seen." Contrary to popular ideas, Bacon does not characterize his natural philosophy as anti-contemplative. He considers prior philosophy to fail not because it is too contemplative, but because it lacks "a true model of the world, as it is found to be." To the degree that it realizes "how great a difference there is between the idols of the human mind and the ideas of the divine mind,"[23] Bacon regards his own philosophy as the most contemplative. He writes that "actually seeing the light is more beautiful than all its manifold uses; in the same way, surely, the very contemplation of things as they are, without superstition or imposture, error or confusion is in itself more praiseworthy than all the fruit of inventions."[24]

The "false philosophy" common to what Bacon labels as the sophistical, empirical, and superstitious approaches err in a variety of ways, which Bacon diagnoses in some detail, but not primarily because they are too contemplative.[25] False philosophy is barren in results, but its sterility derives from its lack of adequate knowledge of Nature. This is true especially of empirical philosophers who bypass the contemplative moment of philosophy because they are motivated by a "premature and childish desire to snatch up hastily some kind of pledges of new works."[26] (It is significant that Aphorism 62 charges the empirical school with responsibility for creating *more* error than the rational).[27] Those who seek works too quickly will fare no better than Atalanta, "interrupting their run and letting the victory slip from their hands."[28]

How is this condition to be remedied? Bacon's answer is that the human natural philosopher must imitate the divine procedure. In Aphorism 70, Bacon declares:

> In the true course of experience, one that will bring new works, divine wisdom and order should be the pattern before us. For God on the first day of creation created light only, devoting to that task an entire day, in which he created no material substance. In the

same way and from experience of every kind, we should first of all
discover causes and elicit true axioms; and seek experiments that
bring light, not fruit.

An obvious meaning of the analogy between human procedure and the divine pattern is that the pursuit of light must assume temporal priority over the production of fruit, even if the latter constitutes the *telos* of natural philosophy. To stop with this evident meaning, however, is to read Bacon superficially. The parallel to divine creation suggests not only the priority of light to works, but more deeply that human knowers are to imitate God by *making* the light required for the eventual production of works.[29] Just as God creates light which issues in fruit, so humans are to create light which, if the making is successful, will "bring hosts and troops of works in their train."[30] The key to Bacon's thought is to recognize that he is capable of associating the notion of light with *both* contemplation ("seeing the light is more beautiful than its uses") and construction (light is not simply there for the seeing, but must be actively generated through human artifice). Thus Bacon finds that "discoveries, in fact, are like new creations, imitations of divine handiwork."[31] The practice of the human natural philosopher engaged in *inventio* is analogous to the creative activity of God. Any interpretation of Bacon that assumes a strong dissociation between "discovering" and "making" necessarily overlooks this parallel.

There is another consideration in favor of attributing to Bacon the view that humans make their own light. Bacon seems to regard light as given neither by God nor by nature. God, according to Bacon, is the omnipotent instigator of a cosmic game of hide and seek. The divine glory is to conceal, not to reveal.[32] God may be the ultimate source of light, but this theological datum is irrelevant for the scientist who follows Bacon's admonition to rigorously separate human things from divine things.[33] Nature, likewise, does not disclose itself. It is a source of darkness to be overcome.[34] Insofar as it is present within the human mind, it constitutes a barrier to understanding. Bacon is constantly skeptical about the power of "native human reason"[35] and indicts those who trust to the "natural unassisted workings of the human mind" as guilty of nothing less than idolatry.[36] Those who rely on the "uncertain light of the sense"[37] are equally helpless, since the sense "either forsakes us, or it deceives us."[38]

Baconian science requires artificial light that is made before it can be seen. In the next section, we will consider more precisely how humans are able to engage in the construction of light, that is, the skillful making of axioms. The third major Baconian *factum* is the *opus*, the "work" that is produced through the use of axioms. It may not be clear at first that Bacon thinks of the human being as the principal agent that produces works. Aphorism 4 declares that "with respect to works, man can only bring natural objects together or separate them; Nature does the rest by her internal operations." It would be a mistake, however, to hold that Bacon's consistent doctrine is that humans do no more than enable natural generation, without constructing anything themselves. Bacon more characteristically regards the works that flow from the application of his method as genuinely new things. Far from being reproductions of nature, they are "effects that have never been produced before, such as neither the vicissitudes of Nature, nor tireless experimenting nor mere chance would have ever brought into being, and which men would never have thought of."[39]

As *facta*, works are produced by an activity that Bacon does not hesitate to describe as magical. Owing to its "broad paths and greater command over Nature," a physics fecund in works is nothing less than "magic (in the purified sense of the word)."[40] Attainment of the true metaphysics will result in a power so creative, so fruitful, so god-like that it deserves the name of magic. The habit of attending to nature and natural generation is a necessary preliminary to overcoming the rationalist or sophistical approach, which encourages humans to confuse their own verbal constructions with true creation. Ultimately, however, attentiveness to nature must give way to a new condition—a state where humans have the power to make works.

It would be a waste of time to belabor the point that *opera* are things made, in part if not in whole, by human activity. We must turn to the questions that naturally arise. How does Bacon understand the constructive or creative process by which humans are able to make axioms and works? What is the nature of the "making" involved in the production of Baconian *facta*?

Induction as constructive method

To name the activity by which Bacon considers discoveries to be made is simple. One need only to mention "induction." A more difficult task is to describe the operation of induction. As we have seen, Bacon proclaims that "discoveries, in fact, are like new creations, imitations of divine handiwork." To understand better the sense in which Bacon perceives the activity of the inductive scientist to be creative, recall the set of images used in Aphorism 95.

> Those who have handled the sciences have been either Empiricists or Rationalists. Empiricists, like ants, merely collect things and use them. The Rationalists, like spiders, spin webs out of themselves. The middle way is that of the bee, which gathers its materials from the flowers of the garden and field, but then transforms and digests it by a power of its own. And the true business of philosophy is much the same, for it does not rely only or chiefly on the powers of the mind, nor does it store the material supplied by natural history and practical experiments untouched in its memory, but lays it up in the understanding changed and refined. Thus from a closer and purer

alliance of the two faculties—the experimental and the rational, such as has never yet been made—we have good reason for hope.

The ant does not construct. He merely finds what has already been made and stores it for his own use, without transforming it. The spider is constructive, but what she makes is worthless, because the materials come only from her own entrails.[41] Her making is a 'making up.' Such fabrication involves a remarkable degree of ingenuity, but is worthless because it bears little or no relation to anything outside itself. Bacon recognizes a sense of construction as purely arbitrary, and associates it significantly with the schools.[42] His real critique of scholastic thought is not that it is hyper-contemplative, *pace* historiographical mythology, but that it is hyper-constructionist. Its making is sterile, because it is either insufficiently attentive to how the materials are gathered or insufficiently diligent in gathering enough of them.[43] The problem is not making as such, but the particular form of making endemic to the "sophistical or rationalist approach," which Bacon finds embodied most strikingly in Aristotle, who "constructed the world out of categories."[44] Bacon's solution is to emulate the bee. This means not to eschew construction in favor of ant-like accumulation, but to construct new sciences that are weightier and more enduring than flimsy spider webs.[45] For all their talk about Being, scholastic systems have little relation to it.[46] Bacon's science, by contrast, will arrive at a genuine knowledge derived from things themselves, since knowledge is the image of being.[47]

The new logic of induction aims to construct new sciences. It will replace "the logic we now have," which "is of no use in inventing sciences."[48] But if sciences consist of axioms, then it follows that axioms are the proximate end of construction. Hence Bacon speaks of "the formation of notions and axioms by true induction"[49] and "establishing axioms by means of this induction."[50] The axioms are not generalities of any kind, but "axioms properly and methodically derived from particulars", which will ultimately "point to and indicate new particulars again, and so render the sciences active."[51] These are the axioms invented by light-bearing experiments: at Aphorism 103 Bacon explicitly speaks of "the new light of axioms derived from those particulars by a certain course and rule, which in turn will point to new particulars."

The process begins with experience. But which experience? Bacon recognizes the force of this question, which must be engaged if one is not to accumulate mindlessly like the ant or arbitrarily like the spider. To avoid "a mere groping in the dark,"[52] we must pay heed to "the right order of experience." This means "first to kindle a light, then with that light to show the way, beginning with experience ordered and arranged, not irregular or erratic, and from that deriving axioms, and from the axioms thus established deriving again new experiments, just as the word of God operated in an orderly way on the unformed matter of creation."[53] The comparison of the process to *creation*—once again—reaffirms the sense that Bacon is anything but a positivist who thinks that scientific activity consists simply in fact collection.[54]

In Aphorism 10 of Book 2 of *Novum Organum*, Bacon divides the process of axiom-construction into three stages corresponding to sense, memory, and reason. Ultimately it will be difficult to separate these stages, since they are actually moments of a single process, but it is helpful to comment upon them serially before considering their unity. The first stage is the compilation of "natural and experimental history," an *inventio* whose results are not products of imagination or supposition, but truthful indications of how Nature acts and is acted upon. This corresponds to the first activity of the bee, who gathers its materials from the flowers of the garden and field—that is, from Nature.[55] *Inventio* has to be followed by a second stage, which as Bacon well knows involves *dispositio* or *iudicio*. The crude facts gathered by *inventio* are useless unless they are "set out and presented in a suitable order"; otherwise, they are merely "an army so scattered and diffuse as to distract and confuse the understanding."[56] Imposition of order among particulars corresponds to the second activity of the bee, which is to digest what it has gathered.[57] Digestion assumes the form of tabulation; the particulars gathered must be "disposed and arranged by appropriate tables of discovery."[58] Bacon specifically links the tabulative activity to digestion, referring to his tables as "well-prepared and digested assistance" for the mind.[59] The tabulating activity involves a measure of construction, since order cannot simply be "read off" from the data. The tables have to be actively "drawn up and put together in such a manner and order as to enable the understanding to deal with them."[60] Such tables, if they are to be useful, are necessarily written, or perhaps better, rewritten, since Bacon emphasizes that such tables, including his own, can always contain mistakes and stand in need of correction. Writing makes the tables transparent; their deficiencies will be as evident "as if in writing or printing, one or two letters perhaps were wrong or misplaced, which does not impede the reader much, since the mistakes are easily corrected from the reading."[61] Bacon considers the relative lack of writing in prior investigations of nature—"up to now thinking has played a greater part than writing in the business of invention"—to have contributed to their sterility.[62] The ancients wrongly thought it "unnecessary and inconvenient to publish their summaries of particulars and memoranda and notebooks, like builders removing all scaffolding and ladders out of sight, once the building is up."[63] They did not sufficiently appreciate that effective memory requires the conversion of crude facts gathered by *inventio* into written tables. The task requires a judicious degree of subtlety, although not the subtlety of the scholastics.[64] Bacon's term for experience tabulated, arranged, put into writing is "literate experience." Literate experience is an artifact produced by the constructive activity of tabulation.[65]

Literate experience is superior to illiterate experience, "yet we cannot hope for very much" from literate experience on its own.[66] More hope is to be had from the "new light of axioms"[67] constructed from literate experience. To understand the sense in which Bacon conceives the derivation of axioms from literate experience as essentially constructive, consider the third activity of the bee. This is neither gathering from Nature, nor the digestion of what has been gathered, but the "transformation" of nectar into honey. Honey is what the bee makes; axioms are what the natural philosopher constructs. The "work of forming axioms" is accomplished by the employment of "a legitimate and true induction, which is the very key of interpretation."[68] It is striking that induction in its highest sense corresponds to the *most constructive* stage of the process, the stage which has the most claim to be a true making, because its result is a product that is separable from the producer. In this sense, Bacon affirms the "construction of light," although insofar as it provides a "true model of the world,"[69] it is a fit object for contemplation. He is entirely faithful to his analogy between human invention of axioms and divine creation of light.

There is an important sense in which any stage-by-stage delineation of the process whose employment leads to axioms (including Bacon's own description) tends to distort what Bacon has in mind. A serial model implies that *first* the natural philosopher collects the facts, and *then* arranges them according to some theory holding how data ought to be ordered. Such a model, one might argue in the spirit of Popper and others, is untrue to the actual operation of the working scientist, whose selection and observation of facts is always theory laden. This may be true, but as a criticism of Bacon, it is entirely ineffective. Bacon himself recognizes that the natural philosopher inevitably brings presuppositions to experience. If he did not recognize this, his contrast between "a natural history compiled for its own sake" and "one collected in an organized way with the aim of informing the intellect and building a philosophy"[70] would have little meaning. The compilation of the natural history is itself informed by particular aims; this fact alone distinguishes it from uncritical accumulation of data. Hence Bacon differentiates "experience that is aimless and takes it own course" from "experience [that] proceeds in accordance with a definite rule, in due order and without interruption."[71] The aphorisms that exhort the natural philosopher to discard his preconceptions are not a call to divest ourselves of hypotheses. As Brian Vickers points out, the Popperian assumption that "preconceptions" means "hypotheses" entirely lacks textual warrant.[72] Bacon's intention is not to have us abandon theory and think ourselves into a blank slate, but to say that many of our current preconceptions represent serious failures of imagination. His pronouncement "it is surely better to know what one needs to know, and yet to think one does not know everything, than to think one knows everything and yet know nothing of what is needed to be known"[73] makes no sense unless one has some idea in advance of what one "needs to know." This point is well understood by R.G. Collingwood, who attributes to Bacon what he terms the "the principle of the limited objective." This principle calls upon the scientist to "[a]im at interpreting, not as the Greeks did, any and every fact about the natural world, but only those which you think need be interpreted, or can be interpreted (the two things are not, after all, so very different)."[74] Whatever the accuracy of his portrayal of ancient Greek science, Collingwood's use of Bacon in arguing that some presuppositions must be brought to any profitable investigation of nature is a salutary counter-example to the Popperian habit of reading Bacon as a naive empiricist.[75]

Let us return to the construction of axioms. Bacon declares that the lowest axioms, the first to be invented and the least potent, are "little different from bare experience."[76] As knowledge progresses, natural philosophers will construct axioms that are more general, but still well anchored in particulars. These are the "intermediate axioms" which are "the true and solid and living ones, on which the affairs and fortunes of mankind are built."[77] Above these are the "most general axioms." Bacon distinguishes between two types of general axioms: those we currently have, "conceptual and abstract, without any solidity," and those constructed by his science, which are "not abstract but are really limited" by the intermediate axioms.[78]

But how can the natural philosopher judge the quality of the axioms he constructs? What assurance does he possess that his axioms are superior to different axioms constructed by, say, a user of the Aristotelian syllogism? Part of the answer to this question involves the fecundity of the axiom—if the axiom proves fruitful in producing what Bacon calls works, there is a presumption in its favor. An axiom that explains only the things that we already knew it would explain when we constructed it, but fails to "indicate new particulars,"[79] is an axiom with a presumption against it. Negative presumption may be justifiably hardened into outright rejection when "new particulars and examples" can be adduced which conflict with the constructed axiom.[80] Precisely because they are human constructs, Baconian axioms are never incorrigible; they are provisional without being arbitrary. Bacon thinks that the natural philosopher can have more or less assurance as to whether or not they are worthy constructions. To qualify as worthy constructions, they should (1) indicate new particulars, (2) resist falsification by contrary instances.[81]

But in what does the process culminate? Which kind of axioms constitute the goal of Bacon's science? How do we know that we have found what we are looking for?[82] There may be different strains in Bacon's thought on this point. Sometimes he strongly suggests that intermediate axioms are the proper goal, and that the search for general axioms is a will-o'-the-wisp. The ancient philosophies concerned themselves with "the first principles of things and the ultimate parts of Nature," but in the wrong manner, because "everything of practical utility depends on things intermediate."[83] Although

Bacon makes frequent use of the "dissection of nature" motif, he also thinks that dissection beyond a certain point is useless. Atomism may well arrive at the ultimate constituents of nature, but its generalities are such that "even if true, can be of little help to the welfare of mankind."[84] Bacon countenances the possibility that many theories may differ on the most general principles and yet all agree with the phenomena. "I do not think it matters much to the fortunes of mankind what abstract views about Nature and the first principles of things a man may hold," Bacon says, adding that he has "nothing to do with such unprofitable conjectures."[85] Yet Bacon also suggests that general axioms of a sort—viz. the kind that are "really limited" by intermediate axioms—are eminently worth attaining. In Aphorism 1.19, Bacon describes his method as one that "calls forth axioms from the senses and particulars by a gradual and continuous ascent, to arrive at the most general axioms last of all." This implies that general axioms are the proper goal of science, provided that one does not fly to them with undue haste but is patient enough to pass through all the intermediate steps. The issue is not so much whether the most general axioms are to be sought, as it is the mode of their pursuit.

Limits on human making: Bacon's forms

Bacon is optimistic about the power of human artifice to produce, and thereby know, the intermediate axioms. His attitude about the general axioms, however, is markedly different. Bacon fears that the most general axioms about nature cannot be attained by human making, but only conjectured about. This is not to say, however, that we cannot acquire some knowledge of them.

To search for the most general axioms is to aim for the invention of forms, which Bacon takes to be the "worthiest to be sought, if it be possible to be found."[86] Bacon invokes a Platonic precedent: "Plato, in his opinion of Ideas, as one that had a wit of elevation situate as upon a cliff, did descry, *that Forms were the true object of knowledge.*"[87] Bacon does not want to credit Plato with actually understanding forms. He erred by considering them "as absolutely abstracted from matter, and not confined and determined by matter."[88]

Form belongs to the set of "current notions" that Bacon condemns as "ill-defined" and "fantastical."[89] The notion of form bequeathed by tradition is an idol of the marketplace. Bacon distinguishes two species of marketplace idols: words that denote things which simply do not exist, and names of objects "which do exist but are muddled and vague, and hastily and unjustly derived from things."[90] The latter type of marketplace idol is subdivided— in order of increasing error—into substance-names, action-names, and quality-names. The quality-names are "heavy, light, rare, dense, etc." We know that *forma* is included in the *et cetera*, because Bacon has already given a list of the most erroneous notions that begins identically but proceeds to name "form."[91] Since form belongs to the class of idols that is most infected by error, one might expect Bacon to abandon the notion altogether. And yet among this class, Bacon says, "there are inevitably some notions that are slightly better than others, depending on how many things strike the human sense."[92] If *forma* can be rehabilitated, we ought to expect Bacon to provide an alternative notion of form that is not "ill-defined" and "fantastical," but well-defined and grounded in reality.

The conventional assumption is that Bacon fails miserably at this task. One consequence of this assumption, as Pérez-Ramos writes, is that "the Baconian Forms seem to have attracted a purely historical (or antiquarian) interest" and so have been regarded "as a totally useless tool in the construction of modern science."[93] Our task is to show that Bacon's account of form, if not perfectly coherent, is vital to a proper understanding of his philosophy. It marks the outer limit of human making.

Bacon begins the second part of the *Novum Organum* by polemically distinguishing his notion of *forma* from that of Aristotle. Aristotle is right to define true knowledge as knowledge through causes and to divide the causes into four kinds. What needs revision are the Aristotelian notions of what these causes are. Final causes exist, but are relevant only for sciences concerned with human actions.[94] Emphasis upon them has only corrupted natural philosophy—a view Bacon explains more fully in *The Advancement of Learning*. The other three causes may be admitted into natural philosophy, as long as they are redefined. Commonly accepted efficient and natural causes are "perfunctory and superficial," because they are "remote and removed from the *latent process* leading to the form."[95] Formal causes, in the Aristotelian sense, must be rejected: their discovery is but a desperate hope. *Formae* are not "primary essences": "Nothing truly exists in Nature except separate bodies performing separate pure actions, in conformity with a law."[96] If nature does not act randomly or arbitrarily, but in a law-governed manner, philosophy may continue its Platonic quest to attain knowledge of forms—provided that forms are understood as laws which govern the motions of natural bodies. If this is properly understood, we may continue to use the term *form* and engage in the "search for, discovery, and explanation" of such laws, which "are the foundation of knowledge as well as of operation."[97]

These laws are not man-made. They are not *facta*. The route to their discovery, however, does not lie in detached contemplation. Bacon denies that the inquirer should try to gaze upon forms prior to or independent of operation. It is "much safer to begin and raise up sciences from those foundations that relate to the active part, and let that part indicate and determine the contemplative part."[98] The discovery of forms is to be sought in the midst of pursuing the primary task of *operatio*. The primary task of *operatio* is to generate and superinduce a nature onto a given body, for example, gold onto silver. To do this reliably and predictably is to do it in accordance with some determinate procedure, expressed by a precept. Precepts that are "true and complete" will lend themselves to experimental verification, suggest a multiplicity of means for generating the desired effect, and enjoin a course of action that is within the power of the operator. The scientist with the ability to state a precept of operation that meets these conditions is *ipso facto* able to discover the true form, since "the form of any nature is such that when it is there, the given nature infallibly follows."[99] One has a form of a particular nature when one has the ability to generate that nature by following a certain rule.

Bacon does not, however, collapse the very idea of *forma* into either the power to generate a nature in accordance with a rule or the rule itself. The form is the basic nature out of which other natures are reliably generated in a rule-governed manner. It is the "nature-engendering nature," or the "source of emanation."[100] Although Bacon does consider operational precepts as the gateway that leads to forms, he does not reduce the object of *scientia* to heuristic directives. Thus Pérez-Ramos is wrong to identify forms as "recipes for successful action," although it is certainly correct to see a connection between our possession of such recipes and our ability to apprehend forms.

Further evidence that Bacon did not mean to collapse ontological natures into rules for operation may be had in Aphorism 2.5. Here Bacon distinguishes two kinds of precepts that relate to *operatio* and its intention of transforming bodies. Of the first kind, Bacon holds that it

> regards a body as a troop or collection of simple natures; thus in gold the following occur together: that which is yellow; that which is heavy, up to a certain weight; that which is malleable or ductile, to a certain extent; that which is not volatile, and is not consumed by fire; that which becomes fluid, to a certain degree; that which can be separated and dissolved by certain means; and so on, through all the natures that are united in gold. An axiom of this kind therefore derives the thing from the forms of simple natures.[101]

In describing this kind of rule for operation, Bacon considers it to be a directive that begins with simple natures (yellowness, heaviness, malleability, etc.) and manipulates them in a controlled fashion to produce a complex nature. Bacon is not saying that the rule *is* the form. What he holds is that the rule *makes use of* the form in order to generate.[102] The form itself belongs to "those things that in Nature are immutable and eternal and universal." As immutable, eternal and universal, it is not a human *factum*. It is the non-constructed *conditio sine qua non* for the most potent sort of human construction, which promises to "open up for human power broad paths, such as the comprehension of man (as things now stand) can scarcely grasp or imagine." The main benefit of the method of operation that looks at simple natures is precisely the benefit that Bacon attributes to the method practiced by the person who "knows forms" and "embraces the unity of Nature in substances utterly different from one another."[103] There can be little doubt: whatever the hesitations of earlier texts, forms in *Novum Organum* are simple natures, things existing apart from human endeavor.

As simple natures—immutable, eternal, universal—forms are not themselves human constructs. They are, rather, the elements employed in human construction. They cannot, in any sense, be made; they can only be apprehended. Precisely because they lie outside the realm of full human control, Bacon proceeds to name a "second kind of axiom" pertaining to the transformation of bodies which he thinks can prove more immediately useful. This kind of axiom is directed to "Nature's particular, special patterns of behaviour, not to her fundamental, general laws, which constitute forms."[104] Its goal is discovery of the *latent process*, which "does not proceed through simple natures but through concrete bodies, as they are found in the ordinary course of Nature."[105] Here Bacon's idea is not for the scientist to attempt the daunting task of constructing complex natures out of simple forms, but rather to conceive of nature herself as an agent who generates bodies out of primary elements. Bacon again uses the example of gold: the discovery of latent process would entail finding "from what beginnings it came, how and by what process, from its first seeds or earliest rudiments down to the perfect material."[106] Discovery of the latent process is the secondary and subordinate task assigned to *scientia*. It seems "quicker and nearer at hand, and to offer better hope" than the primary task of discovering forms.[107] Ultimately, however, latent processes are sought for the sake of investigating forms: Bacon consistently characterizes latent processes as "leading to" or "resulting in" forms.[108] Success in the secondary task will offer greater hope in accomplishing the primary.

Despite Aphorism 2.5's "confession" that the primary task of attaining *scientia* of forms is difficult, the unfinished second book of *Novum Organum* is far from abandoning it. Aphorism 2.6 distinguishes Bacon's notion of latent process from anything currently "entangled in the most stupid and downright useless web of so-called learning."[109] Aphorism 2.7 suggests that, just as invention of forms requires discovery of latent process, so the discovery of latent process and the form requires the investigation of latent schematism. A "schematism," in Bacon's sense, is the structure of a compound. Contemporary anatomy, according to Bacon, has rightly taken the dissective approach to compounds, but errs by restricting its focus to what can be perceived by sense. The true schematism is latent, hidden, more subtle and exact than what can be discerned by the naked eye, Bacon says, without suggesting that it will be non-material. Discovery of schematisms will then enable derivation of "the rule governing every proper alteration and transformation"—the rule that, as we have established, is the route leading to the knowledge of form.[110]

Bacon tacitly acknowledges that his emphasis on the dissection of complex natures into simple elements might lead some to confuse his own view with atomism. Against such conflations, he declares "we shall be led, not to the atom, which presupposes a vacuum and immutable substance (both of which are false) but to real particles, such as are found."[111] He counsels those worried by the subtlety of the inquiry not to be alarmed: "the closer the inquiry comes to simple natures, the more intelligible and clear will everything become."[112] Many commentators have rushed to attribute an anti-mathematical animus to Bacon.[113] They seem to have missed his proclamation that "the study of Nature proceeds best when physics is bounded by mathematics."[114] Bacon invokes the stability of mathematical discourse in order to assuage those worried by the possibility of excessive subtlety in the inquiry. Mathematics will keep science well grounded: "no one should be afraid of large numbers or of fractions. For in things that are dealt with by number, it is as easy to posit or conceive a thousand as one, or a thousandth part of one as the whole number one."[115]

The first eight aphorisms of Book Two of the *Novum Organum* culminate in the ninth. This climactic aphorism draws upon what has been argued to match the sciences with their proper objects. Knowledge of forms constitutes the proper object of metaphysics. Inquiry into latent process and latent schematism is the proper object of physics. Metaphysics is superior to physics because, as Bacon reminds us, the inquiry proper to the latter concerns "only the common or ordinary course of Nature, not fundamental and eternal laws."[116] The contemplative sciences have their practical counterparts. Knowledge of true material and efficient causes in physics will yield an improvement in the mechanical arts. The practical counterpart of metaphysics, given its "broad paths and greater command over Nature," is nothing less than "magic (in the purified sense of the word)."[117]

What provides the limits on the scope and power of human making are Bacon's concepts of Nature and form. Nature is dissected, manipulated, shaped, tortured, but its originative elements are not constructed. As the necessary template for "superinduction," Nature exists independently of the human will. It is not something posited by it. Attempts to elide the basic realism about Nature in Bacon lead only to confusions that cannot be reconciled with the texts. To attribute the strongest possible form of constructivism to Bacon would suggest not only that he envisages the constructive power of humans to create new works from *scientia* of forms, but also that he ascribes to human power the capacity to generate forms themselves. This he plainly does not do. We may construct the apparatus of knowledge that permits ascent to *scientia* of forms. We may also construct new *opera* on the basis of forms. But we do not construct the forms.

The idea that humans create the forms themselves would strike Bacon as a type of idolatry. Hence "there is a great difference between the idols of the human mind and the ideas of the divine mind; that is to say, between certain empty opinions and the genuine signatures and marks impressed on created things, as they are found to be."[118] Contemplation serves the end of construction, but effective construction returns us to the contemplation of divine ideas. Hence "works themselves are of greater value as pledges of truth than as comforts of life."[119]

For and against Bacon

Bacon's high valuation of the work, the *opus* or the *factum*, must be connected to his emphasis on the necessity of *charity* in science and in life. Like Nietzsche, Bacon believes that all philosophy, especially natural philosophy, must serve life. The Baconian formulation of this point is that all knowledge must be infused with charity. In *The Advancement of Learning*, Bacon's "small globe of the intellectual world,"[120] charity appears as the "corrective spice" that must be added to any knowledge that contains "some nature of venom or malignity, and some effects of that venom, which is ventosity or swelling."[121] If human discourse is "severed from charity, and not referred to the good of men and mankind, it hath rather a sounding and unworthy glory, than a meriting and substantial virtue."[122] Without charity, the ideal of fruitful knowledge will degenerate into mere power, technical proficiency unguided by moral virtue. Bacon is sometimes criticized for wanting to make humanity into something divine or Promethean. He explicitly rejects, however, the desire to have as much knowledge or power as God. Only "by aspiring to a similitude of God in goodness or love, neither man nor angel ever transgressed, or shall transgress."[123] The augmentation of knowledge and power will turn out to be a disaster, unless it is tied to the aspiration to emulate the divine goodness. This is possible only through the possession and exercise of charity.

Charity is not just one virtue among others. It is the highest virtue, singular in that it admits of no excess. Bacon's homage to charity recalls both the Bernardine maxim that "charity knows no limits" and the Thomist claim that charity is the "form of the virtues."[124] One may be surprised to find such a striking affinity between Bacon and scholasticism. The implication is not that Bacon is something other than the vociferous critic of scholasticism which he in fact is. Rather, Bacon's polemic against medieval thought ought to be understood as the charge that, whatever its pretensions, scholasticism lacks charity. Part of the problem lies in its debt to Aristotle. Against Book X of the *Nicomachean Ethics*, Bacon counters: "For contemplation which should be finished in itself, without casting beams upon society, assuredly divinity knoweth it not."[125] This is the familiar allegation that pure contemplation is unworthy because it is sterile. Bacon's position is not, as we have seen, to be confused with the notion that contemplation is not a good. Rather (much like Aquinas, whether he knows it or not) he takes the highest form of contemplation to be that which begets, naturally and profusively, works of charity.

Bacon locates the flaw of scholasticism not only in its sterility, but also in its disunity, which he considers to be the primary effect of charity's absence. Charity is the remedy to the natural condition in which desirable qualities of mind "seldom meet, and commonly sever."[126] It is the virtue that ensures cohesion, the "bond of perfection, because it comprehendeth and fasteneth all virtues together."[127] Scholasticism lacks the charitable bond, on Bacon's view, because in multiplying distinction upon distinction, it forgets that "the strength of all sciences is, as the strength of the old man's fagot, in the band."[128] Lacking generosity of spirit, the schoolmen frequently succumb to the temptation to cavil. When you "descend into their distinctions and decisions, instead of a fruitful womb for the use and benefit of man's life, they end in monstrous altercations and barking questions."[129] If the mind is not informed by charity, it will become infected by pride. Bacon does not hesitate to deploy this Christian *topos* against the schoolmen: "pride inclined them to leave the oracle of God's word, and to vanish in the mixture of their own inventions."[130] Such inventions are bound "to putrify and dissolve into a number of subtle, idle, unwholesome, and, as I may term them, vermiculate questions."[131]

Against interpretations that take Bacon to reduce knowledge to power, one must take due account of the role of charity in Bacon's writing. Bacon manages to conceive a real connection between knowledge and power, while maintaining their distinction and referring them to something higher. He may be read as offering an alternative both to ideologies that collapse truth into power and to conceptions that entirely dissociate the two.

But is not Baconian charity always in danger of sliding into an amorphous benevolence? Does Bacon's charity fail to distinguish itself from contentless notions of "public service" or "doing good"—notions which, owing to their vacuity, lend themselves to exploitation by those who seek power as the ultimate end? Bacon himself cannot be accused of understanding charity in such a formal manner. "But it may be truly affirmed that there was never any philosophy, religion, or other discipline, which did not so plainly and highly exalt the good which is communicative, and depress the good which is private and particular, as the Holy Faith."[132] When Bacon invokes charity, he means to invoke a virtue that he recognizes as historically specific, the proper understanding of which settles disputes about the Good at a single stroke. It "inflames the mind" in order to perfect the human being more thoroughly than "all the doctrine of morality."[133] Once "set down and strongly planted, [it] doth judge and determine most of the controversies wherein moral philosophy is conversant."[134]

And yet, as a matter of historical fact, one must acknowledge the gradual secularization of Bacon's ideal. "Perfection in charity, for the benefit and use of life," as the Preface to the Instauration urges, comes to be seen in terms that are radically desacralized.[135] Charles Taylor makes this point, quoting an anonymous unbeliever on the moral power of the Godless universe: "the moment one loses confidence in God, or immortality in the universe," one becomes "more self-reliant, more courageous, and the more solicitous to aid where only human aid is possible."[136] Is there something in Baconian thought, despite its express formulations, that lends itself to a radically secular conception of charity and its *factum*?

Bacon's stress on the universal need for the virtue of charity coexists with a division of human knowledge into two realms. "The knowledge of man is as the waters, some descending from above, and some springing from beneath; the one informed by the light of nature, the other inspired by divine revelation."[137] Despite the harmony implied by this chiasmus, where both nature and grace are conceived as sources of knowledge, "two differing illuminations"[138] of a single reality, Bacon proceeds to construct a drastic separation between faith and reason. The structure of Book II of the *Advancement of Learning* embodies Bacon's sharp distinction between human learning and divine learning. Within human learning, Bacon distinguishes three parts that correspond to three faculties: history (memory), poetry (imagination), and philosophy (reason). "Reason" is Bacon's term for whatever can be known apart from revelation. Divine learning is relegated to an appendix, reduced to a list of beliefs that do not admit of rational understanding. It is true that Bacon recognizes a use of reason in religion. The manner of this recognition, however, only confirms the split between faith and reason. Reason can be used in religion, but only to draw inferences from principles that Bacon understands as the *posita* or *placita* of God, utterly beyond rational understanding.[139]

Occasionally Bacon acknowledges areas in which rational understanding might profitably be guided by revelation, for example, the immortality of the soul. But even here, he is quick to remind the reader that "in probation of the dignity of knowledge of learning, I did in the beginning separate divine testimony from human, which method I have pursued, and so handled them both apart."[140] The structure of the text precludes any conception of divine learning as the embracing context from which human learning is to take its bearings and receive guidance, while maintaining a degree of intellectual freedom.

The most important branch of human learning for Bacon is "natural philosophy." Natural philosophy is and must be essentially secular, because its object is the understanding of secondary causes that are intelligible entirely apart from divine activity. Scripture is a poor guide to secondary causes, and hence useless for natural philosophy. Only the light of nature can be employed. One may sympathize with Bacon's insistence on keeping natural science independent of the detailed interpretation of Scripture. This is especially true if the alternative is what Bacon associates with "the school of Paracelsus, and some others, that have pretended to find the truth of all natural philosophy in the Scriptures; scandalizing and traducing all other philosophy as heathenish and profane."[141] This type of view may be opposed on theological grounds, which Bacon gives himself: "there is no such enmity between God's word and His works; neither do they give honour to the Scriptures, as they suppose, but much imbase them."[142] One thinks of Augustine's contrast between the Manicheans, who thought their sacred texts told them everything about the physical world, and the Catholics who would impress him as credible seekers of truth because they were not afraid to confess their ignorance of natural phenomena.[143]

With good reason, Bacon wants "to condemn that interpretation of the Scripture which is only after the manner as men use to interpret a profane book."[144] He does not, however, stop with this salutary distinction between Scriptural hermeneutics and the interpretation of nature. He insists that to find *any* marks of the sacred in the world of nature "is to seek the living amongst the dead."[145] One may contrast this desacralizing tendency with later admirers of Bacon, including not only Vico and Coleridge, but the Calvinist theologian William Ames. In his *Technometria*, published in 1643, Ames relates the human mind to the divine in a way that recalls the Thomist and Cusan concept of human making as analogical participation in the divine. Though Ames holds that the "archetypal" understanding of God must never be conflated with the "ectypal" understanding of man, he thinks that we know something of the divine through the human. This is because the divine understanding "expresses itself as if it were through a certain refraction in created and governed things that are our understanding's type, from which human understanding is gathered."[146] Divine and human understanding are united in the concept of type, which Ames understands as "that in which all art shines."[147] Type is "primarily things created and governed by God but secondarily things made or conceived in a similar manner by man."[148] The analogy suggests that human understanding of created things as refractions of divine exemplars will provide a glimpse into their source. Ames writes that God reveals himself "more clearly" in the book of Scripture, and "more obscurely in the book of nature," but he thinks that he reveals himself in both books.[149] The comprehensive application of reason to the book of nature is technometria. Because technometria is always an imitation of divine creation, it may be called "theology." Because it is always operative, not unlike Bacon's *scientia activa*, it may equivalently be called "art."[150]

Unlike Ames, Bacon does not conceive an intrinsic relationship between art and theology. He tends to deny that nature can tell us anything significant about its maker, even if he officially construes nature as a work of God. The "book of God's word" and the "book of God's works" are not meant to be read as sources of mutual illumination.[151] The *lumen siccum*, the dry light, can shine only when it is rigorously kept from being watered down by anything alien to it, especially revelation. Bacon explicitly ties the prospect of a new science to its radical separation from discourses that draw inspiration from revelation. His name for this new science is "natural philosophy," which he promotes as the new queen of the sciences.[152]

Bacon's dethronement of theology does not prompt us to question the sincerity of his faith. We have no reason to conclude that Bacon did not hold the religious convictions that he always claimed to hold, even if his admonition "to keep a sober mind and give to faith only that which is faith's"[153] ultimately implies the enslavement of theology to other discourses and the destruction of religion itself. The point is that in divorcing reason from revelation, Bacon paves the way for his successors to understand the secular in its modern sense, as a realm that can be transparently and exhaustively known without reference to its donating source.

Our conclusion is not simply that Bacon offers us a desacralized world. It is true, as Charles Whitney remarks, that "in science Bacon posits a mundane order that will be explicable purely in natural and human terms."[154] The construction of such a secular space is deeply problematic—and not only from a standpoint external to the *Novum Organum*. Its radical instability may be seen from Bacon's own perspective. Bacon wants *both* to insist upon the sovereignty of a theological concept—charity—over natural philosophy, *and* to exclude theological concepts as such from the domain of rational discourse. Bacon's secular successors have responded to this incoherence—expressed by the skeptical queries "*Why* should natural philosophy serve charity? *Why* should charity be allowed to direct or limit natural philosophy?"—in two ways. The first is the denial that charity is a properly theological concept, accompanied by its conversion into thinner notions like "public service" and "benevolence." The second is the position that natural philosophy and other cognitive enterprises are to be guided by a conception of the good which cannot be rationally justified, but only fideistically asserted. The failure of both strategies is instructive. It suggests that the charitable science of the very kind which Bacon espouses is not possible in a desacralized world.

4
RENÉ DESCARTES

The Cartesian *factum*

Innate ideas, the corporeal imagination, the rules for deduction—these items are just the beginning of a list of Cartesian entities that seem to lie well outside the territory of the *factum*. The notion of reading Descartes as any kind of constructivist is bound to strike many readers as perverse. If construction is somehow a mark of modernity, it must be present in Descartes, in more than a marginal sense. But is it so present? David Lachterman attempts to argue for the importance of construction to Descartes in two main ways. First, he has sought to read the *Discours de la Méthode* as an exercise in willful self-making.[1] On Lachterman's account, the Cartesian ego is not simply discovered through introspection. It is also and more primarily constructed in a narrative that Descartes deliberately understands to be a fable rather than an accurate history. Second, Lachterman tries to show that Descartes rigorously and explicitly conceives the procedures used in the *Géométrie* as constructivist.[2] On Lachterman's reading, although the primary *factum* of Cartesian geometry is the problem, any entity that is mathematically intelligible can be constructed, in the sense of "able to be graphically imaged."

Lachterman's work compellingly shows that "construction" and cognate concepts are not nearly as alien to Descartes as traditional readings might suppose. His suggestion, however, that the technical concept of construction, as it functions in Cartesian geometry, pervades the whole of Cartesian thought remains largely undeveloped. We will proceed by offering an answer somewhat different from that of Lachterman to the question: "What is the Cartesian *factum*?"

There are three things of cognitive value—things bearing a close relation to the *verum*—which the Cartesian philosophy also regards as a *factum*. These are as follows: (1) the universal method; (2) representations constructed by the method; (3) problems or questions (*quaestiones*) that have to be constructed before they can be solved.

Let us begin with the method. Against the Aristotelian tradition, which holds that diverse subjects require different methods, Descartes tries to furnish a single method that "extends to everything."³ Where does the method come from? Is it found lying about, ready-made and waiting to be tripped upon? The *Discours* may seem to suggest that Descartes discovered the method through a feat of introspection. As is so often the case, however, what is obscurely gestured at in the *Discours* (a text addressed to a popular audience) is more clearly indicated in the *Regulae ad directionem ingenii*. In *Rule VIII*, Descartes proclaims that "our method in fact resembles the procedures in the mechanical crafts, which have no need of methods other than their own, and which supply their own instructions for making their own tools."⁴ Descartes draws a parallel between himself and a blacksmith who recognizes that before he can make swords and helmets for others, he must devise "hammers, an anvil, tongs and other tools for his own use."⁵ The manufacture of these tools requires some pre-existing elements. The blacksmith modifies the tools he is "forced" to use "at first," for example, a "hard stone or rough lump of iron" as an anvil, a rock as an hammer, wood as a pair of tongs. Similarly, the method begins with "some rough precepts which appear to be innate in our minds rather than the product of any skill."⁶ The finished method, however, will *not* be innate, but an artifact that is made by technique. One may note, moreover, that Descartes is careful to say not that the rough precepts *are* innate, but rather that they *appear* to be innate. His language leaves open the possibility that even the most basic precepts are constructed by mind.

Like Bacon, Descartes thinks that progress in knowledge requires the invention of a new instrument, and that the instrument is to be humanly made. But what is the method to make? The short answer to this question is: "the representation." We make or construct representations. In the next section, we will consider in some detail the questions "What is the process or activity by which the representation is made? What, if any, are the constraints on this making?" Let us establish the sense in which for Descartes the representation is authentically a *factum*.

A representation is an idea, although not all ideas are representations. Descartes occasionally uses the term "representation" as a noun (the French translator of the *Meditationes* frequently uses the adverbial form). His characteristic procedure is to use the verbal form: an idea in the intellect represents something that exists outside the intellect. For example, in responding to Gassendi, Descartes asserts that "the idea which we have of the infinite does not merely represent (*repraesentare*) one part of it, but actually the entire infinite, in the mode by which it ought to be represented (*repraesentari*) through a human idea (*per humanam ideam*)."⁷ We may follow the habit of speaking of substantive "representations," as long as we bear in mind that a representation is "an idea that represents."

The example of a representation cited above—the idea of the infinite—is particularly helpful—because it liberates us from the error of ascribing to Descartes the view that *all* representations are constructed.⁸ There is an entire class of representations that are not made by human endeavor. These are the "innate ideas" that are born from within. There is another class of ideas that are neither innate nor any kind of representation. These are the "adventitious ideas" of which Descartes speaks in *Meditatio III* and elsewhere. Because these ideas "come to" us from the outside, they cannot re-present reality. They merely present it, in a confused and obscure manner. The remaining type of idea is that whose genesis Descartes frequently describes by the verb *facere*. These are the ideas that "seem to be made by me" (*a me ipso factae mihi videntur*), rather than being found to exist within.[9] That such *facta* exist, and cannot be reduced to either innate or adventitious ideas, Descartes explicitly maintains against Gassendi: "I am amazed at the lines of reasoning by which you try to prove that all our ideas are adventitious, and that none of them are made by us (*a nobis factas*)."[10]

It may seem that Descartes takes chimeras, hippogriffs, sirens, and similar items as exemplary cases of humanly constructed ideas. Is this not a way of suggesting that the ideas that we make are false? Descartes answers this question negatively: the idea of a chimera "cannot strictly speaking be false."[11] Both the idea of a chimera and the idea of a goat exist in the mind. Error enters only at the level of judgment, that is, when the will judges that "the ideas which are in me resemble, or conform to, things located outside me."[12] The idea of a chimera does not represent anything outside the mind. Descartes never infers, however, that all humanly made ideas are non-representative. On the contrary, he insists that such ideas are to be divided into those which represent and those which do not. Consider his distinction between the sensible idea of the sun and the astronomical idea of the sun. The sensible idea of the sun is an adventitious idea, but radically false, since it makes the sun appear very small. The astronomical idea of the sun, by contrast, is not adventitious: it does not simply come to us from experience. It is, therefore, either innate or made by us. That it is not innate can be seen from Descartes' avowal that "it is derived from certain notions which are innate in me (or else it is constructed by me in some other way)."[13] Although the astronomical idea of the sun may be constructed from a base of innate ideas, it cannot itself be an innate idea. It is a *factum* which, unlike the sensible idea of the sun, has a claim to be *verum*, because it correctly "shows the sun to be several times larger than the earth."

The Cartesian representation, then, is either an innate idea (e.g., the idea of God that represents God to us, the idea of the self that represents the self to us) or a *factum* that bears some positive relation to something outside the knower. We have acquiesced in the habit of identifying Cartesian ideas as "representations." Although our main point has been to establish that Descartes regards at least some ideas—and not merely fictional ideas like chimera—as *facta*, more needs to be said about the Cartesian concept of representation. Richard Rorty's influential reading of seventeenth-century epistemology attributes to Descartes the aim of "accurate representation," where knowledge consists in gathering "an assemblage of representations in a Mirror of Nature."[14] Charles Taylor puts forward a similar view, asserting that for Descartes "knowledge is to be seen as correct representation of an independent reality," an "inner depiction" that matches an outer reality.[15] It is easy enough to see why one would be tempted to ascribe the "mirroring" concept of representation to Descartes. If non-representative ideas such as sirens or hippogriffs are those which do not "resemble, or conform to, things located outside me" (as Descartes clearly says), then it appears to follow that representative ideas are simply those which *do* resemble or conform to things outside me.

This appearance is deceptive. As John Yolton has pointed out, there is no textual evidence for Rorty's claim that "in the Cartesian model, the intellect *inspects* entities modelled on retinal images."[16] Yolton suggests that the function of the Cartesian representation is not to "look like" the things they represent, but to make things intelligible, to exhibit them to us in a manner bearing some analogy to how words stand for things. Dennis Sepper makes a similar point. Descartes is not concerned, at least in his early writings, with "whether the shape that consciousness registers in looking at a star is the star's shape in reality, but rather with how the mind can take a figure and use it to conceive the star. The operative assumption is not that the 'idea in the mind' intimately resembles the thing in the world but that the two things are different with relevant samenesses."[17] We may reject the Rorty/Taylor construal of Cartesian representation as inner mirroring of an outer reality, while maintaining that (at least some) representations are constructed. Taylor is correct to suggest, in a manner recalling the first paragraph of Vico's *De antiquissima Italorum sapientia*, that "thinking which is such a construction or gathering is rightly designated by '*cogitare*,' with its etymological links to notions like gathering and ordering."[18] Talk about theory-construction and the "creation of knowledge" is not to be taken for granted. It should, however, be detached from the conception of representing as mirroring or matching. As Yolton writes, "the seventeenth-century concept of representation and correspondence was not based upon the notion of glassy essence, mirrors and veils, or inspectable entities."[19]

None of this should be taken to deny that for Descartes a distinction remains between our representations and what is represented. Ian Hacking emphasizes that "people make representations," but urges a contrast between *homo faber* and *homo depictor*.[20] We conceive the star, but we do not make it. This view is eminently supportable. Descartes consistently professes that the world of nature is made by God, not the human mind.[21] Even here, however, the Cartesian commitment to construction may be deeper than that captured by the contrast between a representational knowledge that we make and a world of nature that we do not make. Some passages from *Le Monde, ou le Traité de la Lumière* suggest the remarkably small role played by the mind-independent world in the activity of the representational artist.

It conspicuously fails to provide a standard, a model to which he looks as he paints. The "fable of my *World*," as Descartes describes it to Mersenne[22], is not a copy of the existing world. It is "a wholly new one which I shall bring into being before your mind in imaginary spaces."[23] The *plenum* that constitutes its matter can be freely shaped: "we are taking the liberty of fashioning this matter as we fancy."[24] In describing *Le Monde* near the beginning of *Discours V*, Descartes compares himself to a painter who chooses to focus on representing one side of a solid body on a canvas and paint the other sides in relation to it. Like God, Descartes begins with light. He then adds strokes that depict the sun, celestial bodies, terrestrial bodies, and man in relation to light. It may seem that painting is nothing more than a colorful metaphor for what would more soberly be described as depiction of the real. Descartes adds, however, that he is not speaking of the real world, but rather "solely of what would happen in a new world," that is, a world of Cartesian making.[25]

What underwrites Cartesian making is not its ability to construct representations that mirror nature. The ultimate justification of Cartesian construction lies in its power to provide a vantage point from which "we could know the power and action of fire, water, air, the stars, the heavens and all the other bodies in our environment, as distinctly as we know the various crafts of our artisans."[26] Unlike the "speculative philosophy of the schools," the "practical philosophy" of Descartes (as he calls it himself) will furnish a maker's knowledge of nature. The aim is for the scientist to know nature with precisely the same clarity as the craftsman knows what he makes, in order that he might have the same degree of control over it. "We could use this knowledge—as the artisans use theirs—for all the purposes for which it is appropriate, and thus make ourselves, as it were, the lords and masters of nature."[27] The idea is not to mirror nature, but to master it.[28]

The Cartesian representation is a *factum*. Rousseau sees this when he asks the question "Did not Descartes construct the universe out of cubes and vortices?"[29] So does Pascal when he condemns the Cartesian desire to assemble the machine of the world from figure and motion.[30] Descartes has a general confidence that his representations will ultimately correspond (in some sense of that problematic term) to what is "out there." In this respect he may be taken to affirm the ideal of "accurate representation." It is doubtful, however, that "accuracy" is the primary Cartesian value. Descartes does not fundamentally understand the activity of representational artistry as one of matching, mirroring, or copying. One may even ascribe to Descartes a certain "pragmatism about representative devices," as Sepper does.[31] (Sepper makes the point about the early Descartes; the final section of this chapter will justify the claim as applied to the later Descartes.) But how are representations constructed? How are they to be distinguished from the "chimerical" ideas that we also make? What are the constraints on their making? Let us turn to these questions.

Representations as artifacts made from simple natures

The Cartesian text that offers the most detailed account of how representations are constructed is the *Regulae ad directionem ingenii*. *Rule VIII* broaches, and *Rule XII* elaborates, the doctrine that complex natures are put together by the intellect out of simple natures. Let us examine this doctrine in detail, before raising the distinct question about the origin of the simple natures themselves in the next section.

Rule VIII holds that we are to deal with *res ipsae*, "but only insofar as they are within the reach of the intellect."[32] There are two kinds of objects that are within the reach of the intellect: "absolutely simple natures" and "complex or composite natures."[33] Simple natures, as Marion observes, are neither natural or simple, as we will see for ourselves in the next section.[34] "As for composite natures, there are some which the intellect experiences as composite before it decides to determine anything about them: but there are others which are put together by the intellect itself."[35] This dichotomy is recast in *Rule XII* as a distinction between composites perceived or experienced by sense and composites that "we ourselves put together."[36] Composites experienced by sense are not constructed, which makes our knowledge of them uncertain, unless the intellect is able to assume control of the process by resolving them into intuited simple natures. The only composites that can truly be known are constructed by the intellect. Beyond intuited simple natures, "all the rest of what we know is put together out of these simple natures."[37] A composite that can be experienced or beheld, but not constructed out of simple elements, is *ipso facto* a composite that cannot be known. Its constitution can only be guessed at, or surmised about.

This linkage of constructibility and knowability is not confined to the early Descartes. In the Appendix to the *Fifth Objections and Replies*, Descartes considers the objection that his physics is imaginary and fictitious because it is derived from abstract mathematical extension, rather than from matter that is "real, solid, and not imaginary." Descartes answers that a physics confined to mere receptivity of nature obliges us "to accept as true only things which we do not conceive. We shall have to construct our doctrines out of these things, imitating others without knowing why, like monkeys, and uttering words whose sense we do not in any way understand."[38] The intelligibility of composite natures depends upon the capacity of mind to construct them out of simples.

Constructive composition, according to *Rule XII*, can occur through three ways: impulse, conjecture, and deduction. Neither impulse nor conjecture are radically deceptive, but they cannot be truth-bearing in the strict sense, since at best they furnish only probability. The mode of composition proper to the *mathesis* is deduction, "our sole means of composing things in a way that enables us to be certain of their truth."[39] Deduction is the operation of concatenating intuited simple natures into an ordered series. What certifies the solidity of the constructed chain is the capacity of the intellect to intuit the necessary connection of each item in the series. Descartes gives the example of knowing the nature of a magnet by composing it out of simple natures. As a preliminary, one gathers all available observations about magnetism. Then one attempts to deduce "what sort of mixture of simple natures is necessary for producing all the effects which the magnet is found to have."[40] Once the right mixture has been discovered by constructing the magnet out of material simple natures, using the common notional simple natures as links, one can legitimately claim to have grasped "the true nature of the magnet."[41] Such a grasp coincides with our ability to construct the magnet and its effects on the basis of simple natures.

How significant is the assimilation of deduction to construction? It might appear that construction is just a vivid metaphor for the operation of deduction, a mental process whose essence is entirely independent from the notion of construction. Descartes, however, judges himself able to provide a satisfactory explanation of deduction *only* when he depicts it as a type of construction. "What at the outset we were able to present only in a confused and rough-and-ready way,"[42] that is, the prior elucidations of *deductio* in *Rule III* and *Rule X*, receives its most distinct conceptualization at the heart of *Rule XII*, when it is explicated as a form of construction. If deduction is not fully intelligible apart from the image of construction, but explicable only in a rough way, one might infer the corollary that construction is the more fundamental idea, related to deduction as genus to species.

"The whole of human *scientia*," Descartes writes, "consists uniquely in our achieving a distinct perception of how all these simple natures contribute to composition of other things."[43] Rule 12 distinguishes four different kinds of simple natures: (a) "purely intellectual" simple natures, perceived by no corporeal image; (b) "purely material" simple natures, "which are recognized to be present only in bodies—as shape, extension and motion, etc."; (c) "common" simple natures, "ascribed indifferently, now to corporeal things, now to spirits—for instance, existence, unity, duration and the like, plus the "common notions" that "connect other simple natures together" and are known either by pure intellect or by the intellect as it intuits the images of material things; (d) privations and negations, for example, nothing, an instant, rest.[44] These are concepts which "will be helpful later on in enabling us to say that all the rest of what we know is put together out of these simple natures." That composite natures are constructed out of simple natures is clear enough. It also seems clear that, with the exception of purely intellectual simple natures, each kind of simple nature is utilized in the composition of complex bodies.[45] More could be said about which simple natures make up which composite bodies, and the rules that govern their connection. We shall elide these issues, however, and proceed to examine the depth of the Cartesian commitment to constructivism by posing the question: Are simple natures themselves constructed?

The constitution of simple natures

In one sense, simple natures are evidently *not* made. They are not constructed out of parts or elements. If they were, they would be composite rather than simple natures. Yet there may be an important sense in which simple natures, far from being merely beheld or gazed upon, are authentically *facta*, things made or constituted by the human mind.

Let us come at the question by turning to the first expansion of the *mathesis universalis* given from *Rule V* to *Rule VII*. Although the *mathesis* concerns both order and measure, the emphasis of these rules is on order. *Rule V* declares that "the whole method consists entirely in the ordering and arranging of the objects on which we must concentrate our mind's eye if we are to discover some truth."[46] After excoriating those who disregard the need for order, Descartes proceeds to identify *Rule VI* as "most useful" rule in the entire treatise, claiming that it contains the whole "secret" of his *ars*.[47] (The identification of the *mathesis universalis* as an *ars* is itself remarkable, suggesting a fusion of knowing and making.) The secret of the *ars* is to refuse "ontological" or "natural" classifications of things, which may allow intrinsic differences in being, in favor of their reduction to the rank of homogenous objects that can be placed in an ordered series. "All things can be arranged serially in various groups, not in so far as they can be referred to some ontological genus (such as the categories into which philosophers divide things), but in so far as some things can be known on the basis of others."[48] As Marion has argued, the *mathesis universalis* demands as its necessary complement a counter-Aristotelian ontology which denies that, at least from the standpoint of *scientia*, there are any irreducible differences in being.[49] It is this essential sameness that enables Descartes to postulate a *singular* "object of pure *mathesis*" in the *Meditations*.

Rule VI divides the objects of the method into "absolute" and "relative." An absolute object is "whatever has within it the pure and simple nature in question; that is, whatever is regarded (*id quod consideratur*) as being independent, a cause, simple, universal, single, equal, similar, straight, and other qualities of that sort. I call this the simplest and the easiest thing when we can make use of it in solving problems."[50] The *id quod consideratur* is crucial; simplicity is not an attribute that inheres in beings, or is predicated of them in a way that reflects their essence. Simplicity is construed from the standpoint of the *ars*; it may not possess, and in any case does not require, metaphysical anchorage *in rerum natura*. *Rule VI* specifically denies that we are "to inspect (*spectare*) the isolated nature of things." The goal is to construct a perspective that enables us "to compare them with each other so that some may be known on the basis of others."[51] Simplicity is not ontic, but whatever comes first in the construction of a problem.[52]

To say this another way: simplicity is a function of an order to be constructed. *Rule X* records Descartes' discovery that "the method usually consists simply in constantly following an order, whether it is actually present in the matter in question, *or is ingeniously read into it.*⁵³ Descartes gives the problem of reading an unfamiliar cipher that "lacks any apparent order."⁵⁴ The solution to any such problem is to construct an order, "so as to test every conjecture we can make about individual letters, words, or sentences, and to arrange the characters in such a way that by an enumeration we may discover what can be deduced from them."⁵⁵ Descartes never excludes the possibility that in any particular case, one may happen to stumble upon an order "already there," existing prior to construction. But such a "natural" order is neither a prerequisite for *scientia* nor related to it in any clear way. It will be unlikely to be found in more difficult problems, which Descartes says we must approach in the same constructive spirit, "just as if we were playing a game."⁵⁶ The first move of the game is to establish what is most simple or "absolute"—but relative to the problem under consideration. *Rule XII* links the "most useful way of conceiving everything within us that contributes to our knowledge of things" with "suppositions" which do not oblige his reader to believe that "things are as I suggest" (perhaps because they lack any obvious warrant in the world), but which nevertheless ought to be accepted because they "simply make everything much clearer."⁵⁷ Geometry makes certain assumptions about quantity "which in no way weaken the force of the demonstrations, even though in physics you often take a different view of the nature of quantity."⁵⁸ Simplicity, conceived as what comes first within a sequence, is determined or constructed according to the requirements of the problem at hand.

But what of the perception of simple natures by intuition? Is the intuition of simple natures compatible with their construction? It would seem that if simple natures are the object of our mental gaze, they cannot be constructed. Yet this antithesis is more apparent than real, because Cartesian *intuitio* does not correspond to anything like Aristotelian *nous*. Whatever intuition in Descartes may be, it is not the intellectual virtue of achieving insight into the nature of things. Descartes recognizes as much when, immediately after introducing intuition in *Rule III*, he declares that his use of the term is novel and differs profoundly from that of scholastic philosophy.⁵⁹ *Rule IX* compares intuition to vision, but the paradigmatic case of vision, according to Descartes, is precisely that of the craftsman, whose ability to see is judged by his success in making.⁶⁰ Simplicity is simplicity with respect to our (productive) intellect, not a property of things in themselves. The most essential feature of intuition, emphasized by the *Regulae*, is the self-grounding quality of its perceptions. Things intuited are known by themselves, rather than by a process of inference from other things, which is the hallmark of deduction. To intuit things is to know them "so clearly or distinctly that they cannot be divided by the mind into others which are more distinctly known."⁶¹ This is what entitles notions as diverse as existence, thinking, the fact that a triangle is bounded by three lines, and the limitation of a sphere by a single surface (to reproduce the list of *Rule III*) to be assimilated under the rubric of "simple natures."

If the Cartesian concept of intuition does not pose an obstacle to saying that simple natures are *facta*, it does not follow that each of the four kinds of simple natures is constructed, or constructed in the same way. Our reading has suggested that *in general terms* Descartes views simplicity as a construct, if one understands "construction" not as composition, but as postulation according to the needs of a problem. Pure and simple objects are not taken from being as perceived through the senses, but must be actively constituted by the mind—or *made* to conform to the demands of method. Far from "antecedently determining or regulating our knowledge," as Marion writes, "the 'natures' are simply the end products of our knowledge."[62]

Beyond the somewhat elusive sense of "making" as mental constitution, can anything more precise be said about the construction of simple natures? Answering this question would require a detailed examination of each of the four types of simple natures, not only as they receive initial articulation in the *Regulae*, but also as they appear in various guises in subsequent texts.[63] In lieu of such an examination, we may suggest that the purely intellectual simple natures (e.g., God, the *ego*, thinking) are not constructed, since they transcend the *mathesis universalis*. Material simple natures, however, *are* constructed by the *ego*, on Marion's reading, although their constructedness is not really apparent until the *Meditations*. Extension, to name one material simple nature, is not clearly perceived by sense. Its distinct perception presupposes the ego's ability to construct the concept by reducing it to a mode of thinking, that is, to a mode of itself. What is true of material simple natures also holds for common simple natures. Regarding duration and number, two of the common simple natures in the *Regulae*, Marion reads Descartes as holding that "the *ego* can construct these notions thanks to the variations in its own thinking."[64]

Full justification of Marion's attribution to the *ego* of the power to construct simple natures would require lengthy engagement with his work, as well as embroil us in a thicket of interpretive difficulties involving the entire range of Cartesian texts. These cannot be addressed here. But if something like Marion's interpretation can be sustained, then it seems that Descartes' constructivism runs considerably deeper than the view that composite bodies, to the extent that they are intelligible, are made from simples. It extends to the origination of the simple natures.

Construction in the determination of *quaestiones*

The first half of the *Regulae* offers a theory of order, according to which we understand composite natures by putting them together out of simple natures, which themselves are in part generated by the mind. We now turn to the second half of the *Regulae*, which moves from the consideration of *propositiones simplices* to the examination of *quaestiones* (or "problems"[65]) in which there is something to be sought. Rules XIII–XXI are concerned with what Descartes calls "perfectly understood *quaestiones*."[66] The thesis argued in what follows is that when Descartes speaks of a "perfectly understood problem," what he has in mind is a perfectly *constructed* problem. Demonstrating this will deepen our perception of the nexus between intelligibility and construction for Descartes.

Any *quaestio*, whether perfect and imperfect, must satisfy three conditions: (1) it must have something unknown, (2) the unknown must be "designated" in some way; it cannot be *purely* unknown; (3) the unknown must be designated by what is known; the known serves to point us in one way rather than another.[67] A perfectly understood *quaestio* will satisfy another condition: (4) it must be determined in every respect, so that nothing more is to be sought beyond what can be deduced *ex datis*.[68] The "data" of a problem, its "givens," does not mean "what is given from nature." It denotes what is contained in the problem itself. To consider the magnet's nature solely on the basis of given experiments performed by Gilbert is to pose a perfectly understood question. This example is revealing because it shows that the distinction between perfect and imperfectly understood *quaestiones* does *not* correspond to a distinction between non-empirical problems in mathematics and empirical problems in physics.[69] Problems involving an unknown and known arise paradigmatically in mathematics, which serves as a fertile source of illustrations of such questions, but facility in framing perfectly understood questions is the key to success in all disciplines that are part of the *mathesis universalis*. Rule XIII enjoins the practitioner of the method to "abstract a problem which is well understood from every irrelevant conception and reduce it to such a form that we are no longer aware of dealing with this or that subject-matter but only with certain magnitudes in general and the comparison between them."[70] The *mathesis* deliberately restricts the focus of *quaestiones* to magnitude, since its only legitimate *explananda* are points concerning order and measure, prescinding from any particular subject matter.

The components of a perfectly understood *quaestio* must be distinctly perceived. But can we distinctly perceive "magnitude in general"? Descartes' negative answer to this question underlies the imperative of *Rule XIV*: "The *quaestio* is to be re-expressed (*transferenda*) in terms of the real extension of bodies and should be pictured in our imagination entirely by means of bare figures. Thus it will be perceived much more distinctly by our intellect."[71] We approach truths about magnitude in general only by means of the *specific* magnitude of "the real extension of a body considered in abstraction from everything else about it save its having a shape."[72] All problems about secondary qualities perceived by sense must be recast as questions about figurate extension: "one thing can of course be said to be more or less white than another, one sound more or less sharp than another, and so on; but we cannot determine exactly whether the greater exceeds the lesser by a ratio of 2 to 1 or 3 to 1 unless we have recourse to a certain analogy with the extension of a body that has figure."[73]

Neither purely intelligible objects nor qualities perceived by sense can be handled by the *mathesis* until they are depicted in the imagination as bodies that have a figure. This is the burden of *Rule XIV*'s argument for the necessity of the aid of the imagination in framing *quaestiones*. Such a formulation, however, may be too weak, since it leaves open the possibility that a range of beings which cannot be depicted by the imagination may nonetheless exist. Descartes seems to reject this possibility when he holds that "we generally do not recognize philosophical entities of the sort that are not genuinely imaginable."[74] With the exception of the purely intellectual simple natures (this exception may provide the sense of the qualifying *generaliter*), objects that are not constructible, in the sense of being unimageable or undepictable, do not exist. To believe in "number as distinct from things numbered" is "sheer nonsense."[75] There is no "real distinction" between extension and things extended, number and things numbered, figure and things that have figure. Whether an extended thing is, and whether it can be understood, depend on whether or not it can be constructed in the imagination.

After connecting both intelligibility and being with imaginative construction, Descartes returns to the vital role of the imagination in constructing problems. In perfectly understood *quaestiones*, "our sole concern is to discover a certain extension on the basis of a comparison with some other extension which we already know."[76] In simple comparisons, the relation between the known and the unknown is manifest, since they "participate equally" in the nature of unity.[77] Other comparisons, however, require the determination of other relations or proportions that connect the unknown with the known. A *quaestio* is solved when one is able "to reduce these proportions to the point where an equality between what we are seeking and what we already know is clearly visible."[78] How can this be done? First, as we have seen, the problem must be transferred to the realm of figurate extension, the only species of magnitude that admits of certain comparison. Such transference requires the aid of imagination. Second, the intellect must make use of three marks of extension "which can help us in expounding differences in proportion."[79] These are dimension, unity, and figure.

"By *dimensio*," Descartes writes, "we mean simply a mode or aspect in respect of which some subject is considered to be measurable."[80] This includes not only length, breadth and width, but also weight, speed, and division into parts. Any object may have "countless different dimensions" that enable us to measure it. Whether any dimension is "real" or "merely intellectual" is irrelevant: the thing is measured in the same way whether its dimensions "have a real basis in the objects themselves or are arbitrary inventions of the mind."⁸¹ Another way to say this: measurement requires dimension; whenever necessary, dimensions may be created by the mind. Whether real or fictitious, all dimensions "function in the same way."⁸² Their reality is beside the point, something for the physicist to consider. From the point of view of the *mathesis universalis* (and hence of Cartesian physics, if not ordinary physics), the construction of dimensions in the imagination is both justified and necessary. The unit, similarly, may not be already present in the *quaestio*, in which case "either one of the magnitudes already given or *any other magnitude*" must be arbitrarily stipulated as "the common measure of all the others."⁸³ The objects of comparison must participate in unity, either directly or mediately. Participation cannot occur, however, until something is made to stand for the unit. The third mark of extension that facilitates comparison is *figura*. Corresponding to the distinction between discrete multitudes and continuous magnitudes are two kinds of figures that may be constructed in diagrams. *Rule XV* holds that "it is generally helpful if we draw these figures and display them before our external senses."⁸⁴ The depiction of extended bodies in the mind's eye and their graphic representation are complementary means of rendering "magnitude in general" accessible to distinct perception, which is the condition for finding the *ratio* between known and unknown. To arrange unknown extensions in relation to known extensions, without the imaginative construction of dimension, unit and figure, is an impossible task.

As useful as figures are, however, they have one serious disadvantage. Their construction is laborious, enervating the intellect and distracting it from its proper act of deducing one thing from another. The remedy for this problem is not to renounce graphic imaging in favor of pure conception, but to find a mode of construction that is less exhausting. Descartes theorizes precisely this in *Rule XVI*, which recommends the use of "very concise symbols," whose brevity permits the mind to "run through all of them with the swiftest sweep of thought and intuit as many as possible at the same time."⁸⁵ The incorporation of symbolization within the *ars* enables it to solve problems in the most effective way possible, and constitutes the most complete victory of writing over memory. It is in this Rule that Descartes lays the foundations of his "analytic geometry." The traditional habit of regarding the magnitude denoted by "square" as the area of a two-dimensional figure, and that denoted by "cube" as the volume of a three-dimensional solid, turns out to be of limited utility. "After the line and the square, nothing, it seemed, could be represented more clearly in my imagination than the cube and other figures modelled on these."⁸⁶ The route to a more distinct perception of magnitudes is to symbolize them with algebraic signs. This is to regard the root, square, cube, etc. as "nothing but magnitudes in continued proportion, which, it is always supposed, are preceded by the arbitrary unit."⁸⁷ These are not areas or volumes of figures, but simply the values captured in the series of proportionals $x/1 = x^2/x = x^3/x^2$.

What makes a *quaestio* perfectly understood? This is the question posed and answered by *Rules XIV–XVI*. The argument of these Rules is that if a *quaestio* is to be perfectly understood, its components must be re-expressed in terms of *extensio*. The work of re-expression requires the aid of imagination in picturing bare figures, its further deployment in rendering figures accessible to the external senses via the artifice of diagrams, and finally the representation of magnitudes not requiring immediate attention by symbols. The virtuosic performance of these operations enables the intellect to achieve its goal of "displaying the terms of the problem in such a pure and naked light that, while nothing useful will be omitted, nothing superfluous will be included."[88] A perfectly understood *quaestio* is one that is perfectly constructed. The agent of construction is not the pure intellect, but the intellect working in concert with the imagination, the indispensable auxiliary in making a *quaestio* transparent or, to use the Cartesian term, *nuda*.

Perfectly understood/constructed *quaestiones* pave the way for the operation that *Rule XVII* describes as the "intuiting, through a train of sound reasoning, the dependence of one term on another."[89] The objective of *Rules XVII–XXI* is to show that "no matter how many unknown magnitudes there are in a single proposition, they can all be arranged in a serial order."[90] *Rule XVII* confirms the role of construction in the method by explicitly describing the expedient of treating unknown terms in a serial order "as if they were known" as an *artificium*.[91] *Rule XVIII* reduces the operations required to deduce some magnitudes from others to addition, subtraction, multiplication, and division. To these operations correspond the procedures for finding some lines on the basis of other lines, procedures that supply all the necessary information for what the *Géométrie* will call the "construction des problèmes."

The division of the Cartesian inheritance

If our exposition is on the right track, the notions of making, construction, and creation play a vital role in Cartesian thought. It does not follow, however, that everything in our cognitive grasp is humanly made. The exemplary case of the non-coincidence of the true and the made for Descartes is God. Put as simply as possible: humans neither make God, nor their idea of God. They attend to it, they inspect it, they infer from it, but they do not make it. Only readings that accuse Descartes of radical dissimulation, treating *Meditatio III* as an elaborate smokescreen, would deny this.[92]

There is a sense, however, in which Descartes thinks that everything other than God is a *factum*. (In fact, even God may be a *factum*. As the *causa sui*, he is certainly a *causatum*.) The doctrine of continuous creation, whose scope Descartes considers to be universal, suggests that even what is of human making is also, in some sense, of divine making.[93] If continuous creation is taken seriously, then any neat division between human and divine making breaks down. Humans are at best co-creators. To the question: "What about things that are uncreated, but simply are the way they are because of their immutable essences?" Descartes answers that even truths which seem to be self-grounding (e.g., mathematical truths, the laws of logic) are true only by virtue of the divine choice to make them so. This is the notorious doctrine of the "eternal truths," which Descartes develops explicitly in the 1630 correspondence and alludes to in later writings.[94] A consequence of the eternal truths doctrine, conjoined with the affirmation of continuous creation, is that for Descartes there is no "secular" as such. To speak of the secular, in the modern sense of that term, is to imagine a space existing outside the divine *factum*. For Descartes there is no such territory. Contrary to Rorty's reading, Descartes would reject the "Naturally Given" as an incoherent concept.[95] All being is a *factum*, a product of human or divine will. There is no "intrinsic nature of things," on Descartes's view, apart from God.

This position, in a drastically modified version (the key modification will be a linkage of divine understanding and willing more thorough than that found in Descartes), is a central tenet of "radical orthodoxy." Descartes is fundamentally correct to deny the existence of a secular space that is somehow outside creation. How, then, can this denial be reconciled with Descartes' affirmation of the radical autonomy of human thinking, its essential independence from revelation and discourse about revelation? Within the Cartesian horizon, we suggest, there is *no* possible reconciliation. Our thesis may be put in a single sentence: Descartes paradoxically enshrines the secular while denying its possibility.

Let us begin to unpack this by agreeing with Pascal. Descartes needs God to set the world in motion with a flick of his finger, as Pascal said, but has no further use for him. Whatever the metaphysical work done by continuous creation, God plays no obvious role in the day-to-day practice of Cartesian science. His ends are irrelevant to an understanding of nature; his providence is of no help in understanding human action. It would be a *non sequitur*, however, to infer that God is thereby removed from the Cartesian system. A system that eliminates God, or wholly immanetizes him, is not a Cartesian system, but something else. Descartes is committed both to the view that a transcendent God created and continues to create all things, down to their very essences, and to the position that his wisdom in creating (to the degree that any involvement of divine wisdom in creation makes sense on Cartesian terms) is perpetually inaccessible to human beings. The createdness of things is a fact, but it offers no clue to the intelligibility of things. One may go further: the Cartesian understanding of reality as product of arbitrary divine fiat ensures its radical unintelligibililty.

Along with Leibniz, Peirce sees clearly that for Descartes the final answer to many questions of the form "Why is *x* the way it is?" can only be "Because God made it so." As Peirce suggests, Descartes renders "absolutely inexplicable" not only the mysteries of faith, but many other facts that pertain to created things.[96] In a reversal of the roles usually accorded to Cartesianism and pragmatism, Descartes might reply that ultimate explanations do not matter, as long as the knower can achieve the success appropriate to a practical philosophy bent on mastering nature. In this sense, Descartes would be the consummate pragmatist.

There is much evidence to support this view of Descartes. Although Descartes did care about attaining certainty, he did not view it as a lifetime quest. Once the principles of metaphysics are understood, he tells Elizabeth, "it would be very harmful to occupy one's intellect frequently in meditating upon them, since this would impede it from devoting itself to the functions of the imagination and the senses."[97] The *Meditations* has accomplished, once and for all, the work in metaphysics that needed to be done, "so everyone does not have to tackle the job for himself, or need to spend time and trouble meditating on these things."[98] One must simply remember the conclusions of that work, "and then employ the rest of one's study time to thoughts in which the intellect co-operates with the imagination and the senses."[99] Those who read the *Principia Philosophiae*, Descartes says, will find that "there is no need to look for any principles other than those I have provided."[100] The remaining work consists solely in application, in making use of the principles so that progress may be attained in physics and its three branches—mechanics, medicine, and morals.

The conventional stereotype of Descartes as a figure dominated by the "quest for certainty" is largely false.[101] Even when Descartes seems most consumed by the need for certainty, he never regards it as an end in itself, something desirable purely for its own sake. We see this in not only the final part of the *Discours*, which identifies the goal of philosophy as the mastery of nature, but also in its first part, where Descartes claims: "Above all I delighted in mathematics, because of the certainty and self-evidence of its reasons. But I did not yet notice its real use; and since I thought it was of service only in the mechanical arts, I was surprised that nothing more exalted had been built upon such firm and solid foundations."[102] As much as Descartes savors the certainty and self-evidence of mathematics, he chides himself for not seeing that it has a *use* beyond these attributes.

A contemporaneous letter also emphasizes the instrumental relation of truth to utility. The new mechanics is a part of the "true physics which, not being welcomed by supporters of the common sort of philosophy, took refuge with the mathematicians."[103] Why has mathematical mechanics "remained truer and less corrupt" than other philosophies? Precisely because it does *not* aim for a disinterested contemplation of truth. It "has useful and practical consequences, and so any mistakes in it result in financial loss."[104] The philosophy that deliberately seeks utility is the most likely to be true. Certainty is a good to be sought, but it is not the ultimate *telos* of inquiry. It is a proximate end that serves as a foundation on which more exalted things are constructed. Although Descartes views certainty as a desideratum, he profoundly instrumentalizes it. When Pascal writes "Descartes useless and uncertain," he indicates not only a sound grasp of the twin goals of Cartesian philosophy, but also the order of their importance.[105] The celebrated desire for certitude serves the ambition of constructing a practical philosophy whose outcome is the production of useful things, analogous to Bacon's *opera*.

The Cartesian defense against the charge common to Peirce and Leibniz—that his philosophy is deficient because it deprives us of the ability to know how things are—is that his approach is to be judged by its fruits. (The same pragmatic test also constitutes the best reason for rejecting Aristotle: "the best way of proving the falsity of Aristotle's principles is to point out that they have not enabled any progress to be made in all the many centuries in which they have been followed."[106]) This defense cannot succeed, however, because it requires us to say, counterfactually, that Cartesian science was a success. In this connection, we might not only attend to Leibniz's ground-breaking demonstrations of particular errors in Cartesian science, but also encourage a reconsideration of his argument that a primary source of these errors is the banishment of final causes and, more generally, all theological principles, from scientific knowing. That Leibniz was a better physicist than either Descartes or Locke is evident. What deserves more consideration is whether Leibniz's ability to identify Cartesian errors in natural philosophy and replace them with better theories is due, at least in part, to his deep sense that theological convictions about divine goodness and simplicity have an important role to play in guiding one's approach to nature. Leibniz may legitimately be read as offering a perspective that is both non-Cartesian and "radically orthodox." On his view, maintained against both Descartes and Locke, the createdness of things does not deprive them of their intrinsic intelligibility. A proper understanding of creation enhances our ability to understand reality.

We need not pretend that Leibniz offers the only possible option within modernity that goes beyond Descartes. Spinoza presents another mode in which nature is susceptible to being known by the human mind. Against Descartes, Spinoza denies that the world is the product of arbitrary divine will. His denial rests on the view that nature is not the product of any will at all. As a total system, nature cannot be said to be a *factum* caused by any creative agency outside itself. The *Deus sive natura* is an entirely impersonal order. One may say that Spinoza affirms the radical intelligibility of nature, but at the cost of denying createdness. How high is this cost? Is it worth paying? How one answers these questions determines, in large part, whether or not one is a Spinozist of some form or another.

This cost is unacceptably high. It ought not to be paid. Such is the view of any orthodox Judaism or Christianity, and *a fortiori* radical orthodoxy. Can this be argued persuasively? The accomplishment of at least two distinct tasks is required. The first is the articulation of an alternative model that preserves intelligibility by placing it in a *positive* relation to createdness. The second is a convincing rendition of the claim that the denial of createdness leads, both logically and historically, to nihilism. Our conclusion here is that Descartes affirms the convergence of the *verum* and the *factum* in multiple domains—in ways that are influential and important—but does so aporetically. On the one hand, he exudes confidence in the ability of the human mind to construct a method that, when rigorously applied, will issue in the mastery of nature. On the other hand, he is absolutely committed to the thesis that things are at bottom unintelligible. "That upon Cartesian principles the very realities of things can never be known in the least," Peirce writes, "most competent persons must long ago have been convinced," a truth of which Descartes himself may have been half-aware.[107] For another conception of human knowing as essentially directed toward the mastery of nature, a picture which similarly abandons the aspiration to know the "very realities of things" but more sharply foregrounds the role of the *factum*, let us turn to the thought of Thomas Hobbes.

5

THOMAS HOBBES

That Thomas Hobbes conceives a strong connection between knowing and making is evident. The *locus classicus* of the "Hobbesian *verum-factum*" is a passage from the Epistle Dedicatory of the *Six Lessons*:

> Of arts, some are demonstrable, others indemonstrable; and demonstrable are those the construction of the subject whereof is in the power of the artist himself, who, in his demonstration, does no more but deduce the consequences of his own operation. The reason whereof is this, that the science of every subject is derived from a precognition of the causes, generation, and construction of the same; and consequently where the causes are known, there is place for demonstration, but not where the causes are to seek for. Geometry therefore is demonstrable, for the lines and figures from which we reason are drawn and described by ourselves; and civil philosophy is demonstrable, because we make the commonwealth.[1]

We know the objects of geometry and civil philosophy, in the most rigorous sense of "to know," because we make them ourselves. The object of physics, by contrast, is either given by nature or made by God. Hence it evades our efforts to know it non-hypothetically. "But because of natural bodies we know not the construction, but seek it from the effects, there lies no demonstration of what the causes be we seek for, but only of what they may be."[2]

The main concern of this chapter is to come to grips with the Hobbesian conception of making. Does Hobbes think of making as essentially arbitrary, akin to voluntaristic free creation? Or does he view human construction as rigorously subject to constraints which are not of our making? Against those who have argued that Hobbes thinks of human making as arbitrary, we will attempt to show that Hobbes conceives making as technical craftsmanship. In both geometry and civil philosophy, we will show, Hobbesian construction requires the craftsman to possess clear definitions that express the generation of the thing made. Neither the *facta* made from definitions nor the definitions themselves are arbitrarily constructed. Our purpose is twofold. We want to read Hobbes in a manner that does justice to the power of his thought, against those who prematurely dismiss the Hobbesian conception of making on the ground that it amounts to little more than arbitrary stipulation. With a properly sympathetic reading of Hobbes in hand, we will be in a position to achieve our second aim, which is to mount a radical critique of the Hobbesian *factum*.

The making of geometrical definitions

Interpretations of Hobbes as a strong constructivist are not without precedent. Leo Strauss attributes to Hobbes the principle "we understand only what we make" and takes him to identify the "actualization of wisdom" with "free construction."[3] Knowledge, *scientia*, is demonstrative. Demonstration must begin with definitions, which, because they cannot themselves be demonstrated, are posited arbitrarily. "The world of our constructs," Strauss writes, "has an absolute beginning or is a creation in the strict sense."[4] A similar view of Hobbes may be found in Michael Oakeshott. Definitions express true propositions, but "a true proposition is not an assertion about the real world."[5] Definitions are the starting points for demonstrations that concern "the names of things, not the nature of things. With these philosophy must be satisfied, though they are but fictions. Indeed, philosophy must be defined as the establishment by reasoning of true fictions."[6] Definitions are creations of human will, neither possessing nor requiring anchorage in the real world.

If Hobbes actually regards definitions as fictions—free constructions, true by stipulation if true at all—we may expect him to hold this view with respect to the definitions employed in geometry. Implicit in many conventionalist accounts of Hobbes is the notion that he thinks of the geometer as the inventor of a purely formal system of definitions and inferences. The geometer has the freedom to make his own definitions, as long as he employs them consistently and without equivocation. The first reason for holding that such a view of Hobbes must be false is that Hobbes does not think the geometer makes his definitions at all. Far from being the autonomous creator of the elemental principles with which he operates, the geometer has no freedom whatever to make his definitions.[7] Against Wallis, who appears to grant the geometer this freedom, Hobbes writes: "It is not the work of the geometrician, as a geometrician, to define what is equality, or position, or any other word he useth, though it be the work of the same man, as a man. His geometrical part is, to draw from them as many true and useful theorems as he can" (*Six Lessons*, 222).[8]

Definitions *are* made, but not by the geometer. "The making of definitions, in whatsoever science they are to be used, is that which we call *philosophia prima*." This usage of "making" is not accidental. Summarizing the first three parts of *De corpore*—logic, *philosophia prima*, geometry—Hobbes writes:

"the truth of the first principles of our ratiocination, namely definitions, is made and constituted by ourselves, whilst we consent and agree about the appellations of things."[9] The referent of "ourselves" in this passage is the metaphysician (in Hobbes's sense). He alone has the right to make the definitions employed by the other sciences. The geometer may be the author of the particular lines and figures that "are drawn and described by ourselves," as when he uses ink, paper, ruler and compass in what Hobbes calls the "exposition of quantity."[10] But he does not say what a line is; he does not determine the definition of a line. To define a line is the prerogative of the metaphysician; accordingly, we find Hobbes defining a line in part 2 of *De corpore*, on *prima philosophia*, and not part 3, its geometrical part.

That the metaphysician *makes* a definition, in some sense, is unquestionable. The work is to establish the authentic Hobbesian sense of "to make." Does he mean that the metaphysician creates the definition arbitrarily, out of pure will? Or is his making of another kind, rigorously subject to extrinsic constraints? Hobbes denies that just any verbal construction qualifies as a definition. A well-made definition possesses no fewer than seven properties. Hobbes says that it must: (1) eliminate equivocation; (2) make a universal representation present to the mind; (3) exhibit a clear idea of the thing defined; (4) explicate a compounded name, and hence possess an intelligibility prior to and independent of that of the compound name; (5) be distinguished by subject matter, according to conventional usage; "a *parabola* and an *hyperbole* have one definition in geometry, and another in rhetoric"; (6) use more than a single word, since no word is sufficient for the resolving of one or more words; (7) avoid repeating the name to be defined.[11] These logical properties can serve as criteria for distinguishing between definitions that serve the goal of "accurate definition, for the avoiding of confusion and obscurity,"[12] and those that do not. Definitions are instituted, by human beings, but not arbitrarily. Hobbes says this himself: "definitions are instituted and serve for the understanding of the doctrine which is treated of."[13]

But what if there are rival and incompatible definitions that possess the seven properties enumerated by Hobbes? Are we not required to choose, arbitrarily, which definitions from this set will serve as the principles of demonstration? Even though the range of options is determined by logical constraints, does not the choice of definitions remain arbitrary? A positive answer to this question is premature, because Hobbes emphasizes the necessity for well-made definitions to fulfill another, not merely formal, requirement. This is the requirement that definitions be *generative*. Let us establish the presence of this view in *De corpore*, before examining the relevant passages in the *Six Lessons*. In the sixth chapter of *De corpore*, Hobbes declares that the "definitions of things, which may be understood to have some cause, must consist of such names as express the cause or manner of their generation, as when we define a circle to be a figure made by the circumduction of a straight line in a plane, &c."[14] Here the example is the generation of a circle. Hobbes thinks of the definition of line in exactly the same manner. *De corpore* 6.6 indicates the "generation" or "description" of a line: "a line is made by the motion of a point."[15] This already suggests the close relationship, if not identity, between a generation and a description. The formal definition of a line, its *quid sit*, comes in the appropriate place—in *prima philosophia*. "Though there be no body which has not some magnitude, yet if, when any body is moved, the magnitude of it be not at all considered, the way it makes is called a *line*, or one single dimension."[16] Definitions express, and must express, generation, the "way it makes."

Must the definition of a line express the way a line is actually made? Or does Hobbes only require hypothetical generation? Oakeshott gives a clear answer to this question: "from beginning to end there is no suggestion in Hobbes that philosophy is anything other than conditional knowledge, knowledge of hypothetical generations and conclusions."[17] Hobbes, however, is not quite so definite. Although examples such as the definition of a circle in the first chapter of *De corpore*[18] appear to support Oakeshott's account, the passages on definition and generation in the *Six Lessons* suggest that any definition which fails to express the *actual* way of making is a poorly made definition. Wallis objects to Hobbes's definition of a plane on the ground that it purports to describe the actual generation of a plane, when it should have confined itself to making a hypothetical claim. Hobbes summarizes the objection: "you require, first, that instead of *describe*, I should have said *can describe*."[19] Hobbes responds to the objection by claiming that, if Wallis is to be consistent, he should apply the same standard to Euclid: "Why do you not require of Euclid, in the definition of a cone, instead of *continetur, is contained*, he say *contineri potest, can be contained?*"[20] In fact, Hobbes counters, the modal operator is unnecessary; the distinction between hypothetical and actual generation is without point in geometry: "If I tell you how one plane is generated, cannot you apply the same generation to any other plane?"[21] Hobbes proceeds to reject Wallis's definition precisely because it is not generative. He is "deceived" in thinking that "the plane of a circle may be generated by the motion of the *radius*," because "the motion of a straight line resting, describeth with the other points several perimeters of circles, may as well describe a conic superficies, as a plane."[22] It is not enough for a definition to say how a figure *may* be generated. It must specify the actual generation of a figure. Hobbes defends Euclid's definitions to the degree that they capture authentic generation: he "saw that what proper passion soever should be derived from these his definitions, would be true of any other cylinder, sphere, or cone, though it were otherwise generated; and the description of the generation of any one being by the imagination applicable to all."[23] Hobbes acknowledges that we may be confronted with figures not of own making, but holds that ignorance of generation in this sense is irrelevant. The reason is that, in geometry, one can universally produce effects that are not merely similar to those that are given (such is the case in physics) but precisely identical.

The generativity requirement functions to exclude definitions that may pass purely formal tests. Distinguishing two types of "rules of demonstration," Hobbes writes:

> The rules of demonstration are but of two kinds: one, that the principles be true and evident definitions; the other, that the inferences be necessary. And of true and evident definitions, the best are those which declare the cause or generation of that subject, whereof the proper passions are to be demonstrated. For science is that knowledge which is derived from the comprehension of the cause.[24]

It is not enough for a definition to be "true and evident."[25] It must also, and more importantly, contain the generation of what it defines. "If the first principles, that is to say, the definitions contain not the generation of the subject, there can be nothing demonstrated as it ought to be."[26] That well-made definitions will satisfy this requirement is non-negotiable: Hobbes "thought it *necessary* in my definitions to express the motions by which lines, superficies, solids, and figures, were drawn and described."[27] Far from being arbitrary, the proper making of definitions is what distinguishes a good practitioner of a science from a charlatan. False inference from correct definitions is forgivable, an effect of "human frailty."[28] But he "that proceedeth from untrue, or not understood definitions, is ignorant of that he goes about."[29] This is the center of Hobbes's charge against Wallis: he makes poor definitions, principally because his definitions fail to conform to the generativity requirement.

Non-generative definitions, even if they happen to have all seven of the logical properties of definitions, are "false or unactive principles."[30] True and active principles, by contrast, are generative. "It is in sciences as in plants; growth and branching is but the generation of the root continued; nor is the invention of theorems anything else but the knowledge of the construction of the subject prosecuted."[31] Generative definitions are fecund in two overlapping but distinct senses: (1) they show how the subject is constructed—this is the "generation of the root"; (2) they enable the deduction of all the properties that belong to the subject—this is the "growth and branching." (We will see that *Leviathan* employs the definition of the commonwealth in both of these senses.) Hobbes does not think that *all* definitions will have this property. "And though definitions be the only principles of demonstration, yet it is not true that every definition is a principle."[32] Some may be self-consistent, and yet be utterly sterile. Hence "not every proposition that is evident is therefore a principle" of demonstration.[33]

Let us establish this in more detail by tracing one thread of the controversy with Wallis. That Hobbes does not think definitions are equally good, even if they are equally intelligible or free from contradiction, is evident near the beginning of the *First Lesson*. On the fifteenth Euclidean definition, Hobbes comments that it is true, but that its truth could not be known to someone who had never seen a circle generated "by the motion of a compass or other equivalent means."[34] We know the truth of a definition by concretely seeing that it is able to generate the reality it claims to define. Definitions whose truth cannot be so exhibited must be excluded from philosophy, "which seeketh the proper passions of all things in the generation of the things themselves."[35] Anything that is putatively described by a definition, but cannot be generated from that definition, is unintelligible. In the *Second Lesson*, Hobbes reiterates the point: "of true and evident definitions, the best are those which declare the cause or generation of that subject, whereof the proper passions are to be demonstrated."[36]

That definitions are something other than merely arbitrary stipulations is clear enough. Yet they *are* "made." We must seek to understand more clearly the procedure used to make definitions. The making of definitions corresponds to the invention of principles. The name for the technique used in the invention of principles is *analysis*. Analysis takes a composite given to sense and resolves it into its constituent parts. "I do not here mean parts of the thing itself," Hobbes says, "but parts of its nature."[37] For example, to understand "man," to define the term correctly, one must perform an analysis upon the composite that presents itself to sense, resolving it into "not head, shoulders, arms, etc., but figure, quantity, motion, sense, reason, and the like; which accidents being compounded or put together, constitute the whole nature of man, but not the man himself."[38] The product of analysis is the definition of man, its resolution into body, animated, and rational. Each of these terms in turn provide material upon which the technique may be applied to construct additional definitions, until one arrives at primitive terms which cannot be further analyzed. The terms correspond to "the causes of universal things, or of such accidents as are common to all bodies, that is, to all matter."[39] By "resolving continually," Hobbes says, one comes to "such things as are most universal."[40]

Definitions of complex things are made by applying the technique of analysis to material that is initially given by sense. But what of the "universal or simple things" which are not compounded out of anything more primitive? These things cannot be resolved; they cannot be known by analysis. How are they known? They are, Hobbes answers, "manifest of themselves, or (as they say commonly) known to nature; so they need no method at all."[41]

Some interpreters take this as the point of entry for a strong intuitionism into Hobbes's theory of definition. As we have seen, however, no definition can be justified *simply* because it is known through some faculty of intuition. It has to be generative of further consequences, which themselves serve as principles that can be used for the methodical generation of things. The reverse face of strong intuitionist interpretations is the view that the definitions of universal causes are arbitrarily made. Even though Hobbes sometimes writes as if he were an intuitionist, proponents of this view argue, he more typically sees that first principles are ultimately arbitrary, since they cannot be justified by anything prior to them. Their resistance to analysis deprives them of intelligibility. Although they are the "first principles by which we know the *dioti* of things,"[42] they do not have any intelligibility themselves. The extreme statement of this view may be found in Strauss: "Since we do not make the natural beings, they are, strictly speaking, unintelligible.... Man can guarantee the actualization of wisdom, not in spite of, but because of, the fact that the universe is unintelligible."[43]

The universal cause, the cause of the "universal things" that Hobbes names as body, matter, quantity, and extension, is motion. It is the absolute terminus of analysis, the only uncaused cause. "Motion cannot be understood to have any other cause besides motion."[44] Is the definition of motion arbitrarily stipulated, declared by an act of pure will? A positive answer to this question is defensible only if Hobbes thinks that the definitions of universal things are subject to no constraints whatever. Hobbes does not, however, think this. Universal causes "need no demonstration, though they need explication."[45] They require definitions which are "nothing but the explication of our simple conceptions."[46] Poor explications of simple conceptions will *ipso facto* be poor definitions. Not every attempt to explicate our simple conceptions succeeds. Attempted explications can go wrong by being self-contradictory or equivocal. Definitions of universal causes, far from being arbitrary, must faithfully explicate our natural discourse. Since they are "made by such circumlocution, as best explicateth the force of that name,"[47] they are not demonstrable, but it does not follow that they are unintelligible. We know that such names are "well enough defined, when, by speech as short as may be, we raise in the mind of the hearer perfect and clear ideas or conceptions of the things named."[48] Motion has been correctly defined when, upon hearing the definition, an idea of motion comes into our mind "clear enough."[49] Hobbes does not infer unintelligibility from indemonstrability, as Strauss thinks. The distinction that Hobbes recognizes between the demonstrable and the indemonstrable corresponds not to a gap between the intelligible and the unintelligible, but to a difference between *scientia* ("truth of consequences") and *cognitio* ("truth of fact").[50]

Neither our definitions of complex things nor our definitions of primitive, unanalyzable causes are arbitrary. Particular things whose generation is captured in definitions are also not made arbitrarily. There are not multiple, equally justifiable ways for a geometer to make a line. There is only one right "way of making," which will be captured in a non-arbitrary definition. (That Hobbes describes our use of the particular *term* "line" to stand for what we draw, when we draw a line, as "arbitrary" is not in question.) A line is made in accordance with the generative formula expressed by the correct definition of a line. Its properties can be demonstrated because they follow from the generation.

If this account of Hobbes is faithful to the texts, then it cannot be the case that he grounds the demonstrability of the geometrical art in the capacity of the geometer to create his lines and figures *ex nihilo*. No such capacity exists. A line cannot be created from nothing, because it requires a pre-existing receptacle ("space") in which to exist. It also requires motion. As is true of everything else in geometry, a line is nothing but a determination of "simple motion."[51] Motion itself exists prior to and independently of a line. George Steiner acutely observes, "technique channels; it does not initiate."[52] To draw a line is to channel motion, to determine it in a particular fashion. It is a feat of technique, not a creation *ex nihilo*. What is true of lines is true generally of things geometrical. They are constructed, and therefore have properties that may be demonstrated through the method Hobbes calls "synthesis."[53] Synthesis is a kind of making, the "composition" of elements into wholes. Any set of elements that a particular act of synthesis combines must exist prior to that synthesis. Hence synthesis, though constructive, is not creative in the primordial sense. It requires raw material to synthesize. The synthetic geometer is a technician who knows what he wants to construct or demonstrate. Because he has this knowledge prior to making, and would not be able to make unless he possessed this knowledge in advance, he is a craftsman rather than a creator.

To recapitulate: Conventionalist interpretations of Hobbes err in thinking that he conceives of definitions as essentially arbitrary; on the contrary, Hobbes considers them to be anchored in our conceptions or ideas of universal causes, which are rooted in the motion of corporeal bodies.[54] What is arbitrary is the decision as to which name ought to be paired with which conception. Only in this limited sense does Hobbes conceive of scientific definitions as arbitrary. Yet a genuine problem remains. How do we know when we our conceptions are "perfect and clear"? Must Hobbes not fall back upon a certain dogmatism, a decisionism that *we* must regard as arbitrary? These questions will resurface in the final section of this chapter. Let us now consider the status of the *factum* as it arises in the making of the commonwealth.

The commonwealth as feat of technical making

Like the lines and figures that are "drawn and described by ourselves," the commonwealth is a *factum*, something technically made by persons who possess the requisite skill. But, one may wonder, does Hobbes regard "making" as signifying univocally? Is the concept of making in civil philosophy the same as the concept of making in geometry? It is proper to read Hobbes as giving a positive answer to these questions, not only because he is generally committed to univocity in language, but also because the strong analogy that he envisages between civil philosophy and geometry demands a univocal sense of "to make." If what renders both civil philosophy and geometry demonstrable is the fact that we make their objects, and if civil philosophy is demonstrable in the same way and to the same degree as geometry, then "to make" ought to retain the same meaning across diverse contexts.

We may thus expect Hobbes to understand the commonwealth not as a creation, properly speaking, but as a feat of technical making. Pursuing the analogy to geometrical construction, one finds that Hobbes defines the object of civil philosophy in a manner that expresses its generation. Chapter 17 of *Leviathan* gives this definition of the commonwealth: "one person, of whose acts a great multitude, by mutual covenants one with another, have made themselves every one the author, to the end he may use the strength and means of them all, as he shall think expedient, for their peace and common defense."[55] This is a generative definition; it shows how the commonwealth comes to be. It is compact, but Hobbes can afford to be compact, since he has already taken great pains to define the terms used in the definition. (He will give a slightly expanded form of the definition in chapter 18.) The definition summarizes what has been said more loosely about the "cause and generation" of the commonwealth earlier in the chapter.

One may see that the construction of the Hobbesian commonwealth shares two salient features of technical making as described by R.G. Collingwood. First, commonwealths are always constructed with a preconceived end in mind. The maker knows what he wants to make before he makes it. He sets out to construct an artificial man modelled on the natural, "though of greater stature and strength than the natural, for whose protection and defense it was intended." An augmented version of natural man is the model upon which the commonwealth is made. He knows that he wants to construct an artificial body which possesses the specific property of promoting peace and the optimal pursuit of felicity. That the maker of the commonwealth finds no model in nature to imitate is less important than it may appear. The key point is that the political craftsman knows what he wants to make, with the requisite degree of precision, before he begins to makes it.

Second, the preconceived end is brought about through the transformation of a pre-existing material, which proceeds according to definite rules. The pre-existing material is the natural passions. The blueprint for transformation consists of the laws of nature, the rational theorems which, if agreed upon by individuals and then enforced by the sovereign, will transform natural man (the individual in the state of nature) into a social being (the "subject" of civil society). Like all technical makings, the construction of the commonwealth is a rule-governed activity. That Hobbes actually conceives of commonwealth-making in a strongly technical mode can be easily confirmed by passages throughout part 2 of *Leviathan*. For instance: "The skill of making and maintaining commonwealths consisteth in certain rules, as does arithmetic and geometry" (*Leviathan* 20.19). "When for the doing of anything there be infallible rules (as in engines and edifices, the rules of geometry), all the experience of the world cannot equal his counsel that has learnt or found out the rule" (*Leviathan* 25.13). "For to know who knows the rules almost of any art is a great degree of the knowledge of the same art, because no man can be assured of the truth of another's rules but he that is first taught to understand them" (*Leviathan* 30.25). Such rules have not been learned by pre-Hobbesian political architects, because teachers have not been sufficiently clear about them. "Knowledge of these rules is moral philosophy. But why have they not learned them, unless for this reason, that none hitherto have taught them in a clear and exact method?" (*De corpore* 8).

Geometry and civil philosophy both appear to be constructive activities in the same sense. They each possess a *factum* made according to certain rules, and whose generation can be expressed in a definition. The *Leviathan* itself is nothing but an attempt to supply the rules for making the commonwealth, and deducing the properties that can be deduced from its generative definition.

It is true, nevertheless, that Hobbes does not universally speak of the commonwealth as technically made rather than created. This may suggest that he recognizes, at least implicitly, that the technical analogy is subject to strain. In two passages he describes the construction of the body politic not as a technical making, but as a creation. The first is from the *Elements of Law*, where Hobbes identifies two ways of erecting a body politic. One is "by arbitrary institution of many men assembled together, which is like a creation out of nothing by human wit; the other by compulsion, which is as it were a generation thereof out of natural force" (*Elements*, p. 108). The second is from the Introduction of *Leviathan*. There Hobbes writes that "the *pacts* and *covenants* by which the parts of this body politic were at first made, set together, and united, resemble that *fiat*, or the *let us make man*, pronounced by God in the creation."

To say that the body politic is a like a creation *ex nihilo* appears to suggest a disanalogy to the geometrical *factum*. The geometer makes a line, but he does not create it *ex nihilo*, if he can be said to create it at all. For a line to be constructed, two prerequisites must be satisfied. There must be the following: (1) a pre-existing receptacle ("space") in which the line can exist; (2) motion, since the line is nothing other than a determination of "simple motion," and cannot exist without the prior reality of motion.

But do not the same conditions apply to the making of the commonwealth? Hobbes does not think that the commonwealth can literally be created out of nothing. It too requires material space and prior motion. Thus, in both of the passages quoted above, Hobbes does not say that the commonwealth actually *is* a creation from nothing. It only bears certain resemblances to a creation *ex nihilo*. Strauss is wrong to hold that for either geometry or civil philosophy the Hobbesian *factum* is a creation "in the strict sense." Hobbes undermines the analogy to creation *ex nihilo* almost as soon as he invokes it. He follows the above-quoted passage from the *Elements* with two decisive qualifications. The making of the body politic "proceedeth from the assembly and consent of a multitude" and it requires a prior understanding of what one is to make: "the knowledge of what covenants they must needs make, dependeth on the knowledge of the persons, and the knowledge of their end." Given these dependencies, the making of the body politic cannot be a case of creation *ex nihilo*. At best, it can only be *like* creation from nothing.

Is this likeness sufficient to demand a modification in our initial position? Ought we to say that the commonwealth, rather than only being a feat of technical making, is an authentic creation, even if not a creation of nothing? To create something, as Collingwood says, "means to make it non-technically, but yet consciously and voluntarily." Any act of creation, with the single exception of creation *ex nihilo*, assumes pre-existing conditions. To use Collingwood's example: when we create a nuisance—and we do speak of creating nuisances, rather that constructing them—it must be the case that there are persons capable of being annoyed. Moreover, "the person who creates the nuisance must already be acting in a manner which, if modified this way or that, would annoy them." The mere existence of prerequisites does not, by itself, show that constructing the body politic is an act of technical making rather than creation. It shows only that making the commonwealth cannot be an act of creation *ex nihilo*.

The Hobbesian texts seem to embody a certain tension between the notion of making as technical making and the notion of making as creation. Oakeshott's interpretation gives expression only to one side of the tension. "Civil association is artificial, the free creation of these absolute wills," he writes, "just as nature is the free creation of the absolute will of God." This is misleading. If humans are said to create the commonwealth at all, it cannot be "just as" God creates nature, since the "free creation of the absolute will of God" can only mean creation *ex nihilo*, whereas human creation cannot mean this. Moreover, the freedom of divine creation implies the utter lack of a predicament which impels Him to create. Humans, however, absolutely need the commonwealth if they are to escape their basic predicament, to use Oakeshott's own term. God does not need His creation in this sense, or in any other. That civil association is "artificial" is not in question, but Oakeshott overlooks the possibility that "artificial" can mean either "created" or "made by craft." If it does mean "created," it cannot bear precisely the same sense that it has in the sentence "God freely created the world."

We may give two reasons for concluding that, if the tension between artifice as creation and artifice as technical making in Hobbes is to be resolved at all, it is to be resolved in the direction of the latter. The first reason is that Hobbes invokes the analogy to divine creation only two times. He does not use, even once, the creation trope in the body of the *Leviathan*. It appears solely in the Introduction, and not at all in *De cive*. After the *Elements*, Hobbes rigorously avoids collating the distinction between the two kinds of commonwealth with that between creation *ex nihilo* and natural generation. The *De cive*, composed just two years after the *Elements*, speaks of the "two kinds of *civitates*, the one natural, such as is the paternal and despotical; the other institutive, which may also be called political" (*De Cive* 5.12). Creation does not appear as a category; the chapter is concerned with the "causes and generation" of the commonwealth. Similarly, the distinction between "the political commonwealth, or commonwealth by *institution*" and the "commonwealth by acquisition" in the *Leviathan* (17.15) is inscribed within the "causes, generation, and definition of a commonwealth." "Creation" is not used to illuminate either pole of the distinction, or the context in which the distinction appears.

The second reason for maintaining that Hobbesian artifice is ultimately technical making rather than creation is that construction of the commonwealth is always enabled by a prior knowledge of what one wants to make. Collingwood remarks that the hallmark of technical making, what most decisively distinguishes it from any act of creation, is that "the craftsman knows what he wants to make before he makes it." The authors of the Hobbesian commonwealth are not trying to express something that can be discovered only in the act of expressing it. They possess an antecedent knowledge of the essential characteristics of the *factum* before they begin to make it. The presence of this foreknowledge, along with the analogy to geometrical making, reinforces our initial position that the construction of the commonwealth is neither free creation (*pace* Strauss and Oakeshott) nor creation constrained by prerequisites. It is a feat of technique.

But why, then, did Hobbes have any truck at all with the parallel to creation? One may give a straightforward explanation. Hobbes's basic point is that man makes the commonwealth from a raw material which is identical to human nature itself. In this sense, there is a disanalogy with the craftsman who reaches for some matter outside himself. Man is both the artificer and the source of the raw material out of which the commonwealth is technically made. The function of the creation analogy is to provide a memorable image that expresses this point.

If the commonwealth were a creation, its matter would not be "given." It would actually be produced by its creator. But does Hobbes think that man literally, or even analogically, creates the human material out of which he constructs the body politic? Strauss consistently sees that his identification of Hobbesian making as "creation in the strict sense" requires a positive answer to this question. Accordingly, he attributes to Hobbes the view that "man is the animal which is the author or maker of itself" and takes him to reject any natural law tradition which still assumes "that there is a human nature which is given, not made."[56] As a reading of Hobbes, this is untenable. From beginning to end, "man" names a natural body. Human nature, a category of which Hobbes is quite fond, is not something we construct. This can be shown across the range of Hobbes's texts. The *Elements of Law* defines "man's nature" as "the sum of his natural faculties and powers, as the faculties of nutrition, motion, generation, sense, reason &c."[57] *De cive* finds that it consists of four faculties: "bodily strength, experience, reason, passion."[58] In *Leviathan*, human nature is known as the set of "consequences from the qualities of *men in special*," which are inferred from the "consequences from the qualities of *animals*."[59] These consequences are in turn inferred from the properties of terrestrial bodies, which are known from "bodies permanent," the knowledge of which is the branch of "natural philosophy" that Hobbes identifies as "physics."[60] As the *De corpore* has it, man is first of all a "work of nature" that is distinct from artificial bodies "made by the wills and agreement of men."[61] To be sure, he is not *just* a natural body. He is also a part of the body politic, as Hobbes says in the Epistle Dedicatory to *De homine*. This passage, however, does nothing to support the Strauss's notion that, according to Hobbes, man *never* discovers any part of his nature as given, but creates himself in the strict sense. (Strauss claims that Hobbes rejects the "traditional conception of natural law which was still adhered to by Grotius," which "had assumed that there is a human nature which is given, not made."[62]) It suggests, rather, that the natural body—human nature as given—will have to be shaped, molded, transformed until it becomes part of an artificial body politic. In this sense, one can and should speak of the commonwealth—the artificial man—as a *factum*. But the making is the transforming of a given, pre-existing material. It is not a creation. To say this concisely: Artificial man is not created, but made or generated from natural man.

None of the above precludes the view that the best knowledge of human nature, perhaps the only adequate knowledge, is attained by the process of making that Hobbes terms synthesis. Part 1 of *Leviathan* largely follows a synthetic procedure, attempting to arrive at a total knowledge of man by composing the elements of sense, imagination, natural discourse, speech, reason, and the passions into a whole, and using these definitions as principles from which to demonstrate particular properties of man. Any such synthesis, however, presupposes a whole that can be resolved into its primitive elements by analysis. The analysis of human nature into its elements is performed off stage, as it were. It is not present in *Leviathan*, to the degree that it follows the compositive method instead of the resolutive. But human nature itself is not an artifact of the synthetic method, even if its knowledge is best attained by the use of that method. In *De corpore*, Hobbes explicitly says that human nature can be known without any ratiocination. "The causes of the motions of the mind are known, not only by ratiocination, but also by the experience of every man that takes the pains to observe those motions within himself."[63]

Against "free constructionist" or "free creation" interpretations of Hobbes, we may observe that Hobbes plainly does not grant the human knower the freedom to conceive the simple constituents of reality as he or she likes. Persons who fail to understand that motion is the most simple reality, positing instead (for example) immaterial substance as primitive, are not free constructors of their own version of reality. They are, Hobbes thinks, either lazy thinkers or (worse yet) fools who have had "their natural discourse corrupted with former opinions received from their masters."[64] Those in whom natural discourse survives intact will understand that motion is the first cause. To explicate their natural discourse, they will have to define it. To define means to make what Hobbes calls an "accurate definition," not a definition that is true because we say it is.[65] The making of accurate definitions presupposes human access to natural or mental discourse, which is grounded in how things are outside the mind. Hobbes may not provide a satisfactory account of this correspondence. But he clearly believes that such correspondence exists, as when he instructs the reader of *De corpore* that "philosophy" is the "child of the world and your own mind." As natural discourse, it is "within yourself; perhaps not fashioned yet, but like the world its father, as it was in the beginning, a thing confused."[66] To fashion this reality is to un-confuse it, to explicate it through the making of definitions. At its most basic level, such making gives way to discovery: "Do, therefore, as the statuaries do, who, by hewing off that which is superfluous, do not make but find the image."[67]

And yet, Hobbes immediately proceeds to subvert any simple dichotomy between the made and the discovered by adding that the "order of contemplation" can be understood by analogy to the "order of creation." "Or imitate the creation: if you will be a philosopher in good earnest, let your reason move upon the deep of your own cogitations and experience; those things that lie in confusions, must be set asunder, distinguished, and every one stamped with its own name set in order; that is to say, your method must resemble the creation."[68] In his own way, Hobbes attests to the analogy that philosophical knowing bears to creation. One must insist, however, that "creation" in his particular sense of the term, when transferred to the domain of human method, presupposes something anterior to making. It is the ordering of a primal chaos, "those things that lie in confusions." As such, Hobbesian reason is not participation in divine creation. It is more akin to the making of the demiurge. All making for Hobbes turns out to be technical making, operation upon a pre-existing raw material, undertaken in order to realize an end conceived prior to making.

Science and power

Hobbes's general emphasis on the *factum*—as we have seen, he clearly regards definitions, lines, figures, and the body politic as constructs—amply justifies the attribution of some version of the *verum-factum* principle to him. It is possible, however, to overstate the thesis. Strauss finds Hobbes to hold that "we understand only what we make."[69] Does Hobbes really think that we understand *only* what we make? We have already seen why the answer to this question must be "no." Definitions are made, but to make them well requires clarity of conception. Clear conceptions are rooted in the reality of matter, which we do not make, *in any sense*. The commonwealth is a feat of technical making which, like all technical making, requires a pre-given raw material. We have access to human nature, Hobbes claims in the Introduction to *Leviathan*, not from self-making, but from self-reading. Self-reading does not furnish knowledge of what humans make. It provides insight into what they do not make, the "thoughts and passions" of all men which do not vary according to time or place.[70]

Ought it to bother either Hobbes or us that the made should repose on a foundation that is not made, but naturally given? Strauss suggests an affirmative answer to this question, because he finds Hobbes to affirm, whether implicitly or explicitly, that the sheerly given is unintelligible. What we do not construct ourselves, we cannot understand. This is true only if one takes "to understand" narrowly, as meaning "to demonstrate." In a wider sense of the term, Hobbes does think that we have noetic access to what we do not make—our simple conceptions and their corresponding realities. Such things may be indemonstrable, but Hobbes does not infer that they are unintelligible. Here the "intuitionist" interpretations of Hobbes provide a useful corrective. They remind us that Hobbes, at least on occasion, thinks of basic principles as "self-evident." Strauss's reading, nonetheless, is useful in that it forces us to ask: *How* are such principles intelligible? To the degree that Hobbes is an intuitionist, his view of the intelligibility of indemonstrables is vulnerable to the same criticism as any other appeal to self-evidence. What impress some observers as indubitable truths, apparent to all rational minds, strike others as nothing more than asserted dogmas, or postulates whose primary function is their argumentative utility.

One finds in Hobbes materials for another account of the intelligibility of indemonstrables. *Scientia propter potentiam*: "the end of knowledge is power."[71] All knowledge is for the sake of power. The ultimate warrant for rational assent to indemonstrable truths is not that we have some privileged intuition. It lies, rather, in our capacity to recognize that their postulation confers an increase in human power. (Hobbes justifies the acceptance of unproven postulates in geometry to the degree that they enable the "construction of problems."[72]) In common with Bacon and Descartes, but even more clearly, Hobbes describes the final cause of philosophy, its "end or scope," as *essentially* practical.

> [T]hat we may make use to our benefit of effects formerly seen; or that, by application of bodies to one another, we may produce the like effects of those we conceive in our mind, as far forth as matter, strength, and industry will permit, for the commodity of human life. For the inward glory and triumph of mind that a man may have for the mastering of some difficult and doubtful matter, or for the discovery of some hidden truth, is not worth so much pains as the study of Philosophy requires; nor need any man care much to teach another what he knows himself, if he think that will be the only benefit of his labour. The end of knowledge is power; and the use of theorems (which, among geometricians, serve for the finding out of properties) is for the construction of problems; and, lastly, the scope of all speculation is the performing of some action, or the thing to be done.[73]

The second part of *Leviathan* concludes on a similar note. The "theorems of moral doctrine" demonstrated by Hobbes are not valuable for their own sake. They exist so that some sovereign may "convert this truth of speculation into the utility of practice."[74] (31.41). If *scientia propter potentiam* is the slogan of Hobbes's philosophy, the question arises: "Power to do what?"

Hobbes does not evade this question. On the contrary, he forthrightly includes within the generative definition of the commonwealth a statement of its end. In chapter 18 of *Leviathan*, he writes:

> A *commonwealth* is said to be *instituted*, when a *multitude* of men do agree and *covenant, every one with every one*, that to whatsoever *man* or *assembly of men* shall be given by the major part the right to *present* the person of them ... every one, as well he that *voted for it* as he that voted *against it*, shall *authorize* all the actions and judgments of that man or assembly of men, in the same manner, as if they were his own, to the end, to live peaceably amongst themselves and be protected against other men.[75]

Here a problem arises, a difficulty serious enough for even as sympathetic an interpreter as David Gauthier to find Hobbes "guilty of a serious methodological oversight."[76] The oversight, we suggest, is not methodological in any narrow sense, but carries large implications for the claim of Hobbes's civil philosophy to be a science.

The difficulty may be stated simply. In demonstrable sciences such as geometry, the end is never included in the generative definition. Our ability to construct a circle and demonstrate its properties does not require us to know the final cause of a circle, or even to assume that such a concept makes sense. When Hobbes decides to include the final cause of the commonwealth in its definition, he breaks the parallel between geometry and civil philosophy at a crucial point. Gauthier comments that although the end, "the peace and defence of them all," is what "determines the intention of and provides the rationale for the acts by which the commonwealth is instituted, [it] cannot sensibly be treated as itself part of the generative cause."[77] If this is right—and surely it is—then Hobbes cannot justify his particular notion of the commonwealth's end by appealing to its necessary role in the generation of the commonwealth. In order for his definition to have sufficient content to serve as a principle for the demonstration of a host of properties that he thinks the commonwealth should possess, Hobbes must *inject* final causality into his definition.

Why is this problematic? Does Hobbes not have a right to put whatever he likes into his definitions, so that he may get whatever he needs out of them? One may grant Hobbes this right, but only at the cost of fatally compromising his claim to provide a "scientific" civil philosophy analogous to geometry. We may put the issue in the form of a dilemma. Hobbes can *either* assert dogmatically that his conception of the human end is correct, and build final causality into the generative definition of his commonwealth, *or* he can endeavor to adhere more rigorously to the geometrical model and abstain from including the end in the definition. The first horn is unpalatable, because Hobbes cannot openly admit to dogmatism. What distinguishes his approach, as he proclaims in the Epistle Dedicatory of the *Elements of Law*, is that his principles have nothing to do with the dogmatical learning that builds its principles in the air. Instead, it strives to emulate the mathematical reasoning that generates neither doubt nor controversy, but knowledge.[78] The second horn, however, is equally unpalatable. Hobbes *needs* a teleology to account for the generation of the commonwealth. It is not only that men would never make a commonwealth if they did not have some end in mind. More fundamentally, the properties of the Hobbesian commonwealth, the attributes that make up its very essence, cannot be fully enumerated or specified apart from the particular notion of the final end that Hobbes includes within its generative definition.

Our conclusion is that Hobbes's attempt to mark out a purely secular space on scientific principles fails. If Hobbes had limited himself to including only what is actually made—as opposed to the rationale that determines and inspires making—within his definition of the commonwealth, his new ideal would have been deficient in content, and therefore much less inspiring and persuasive than it was. Only a truncated version of the Hobbesian commonwealth would be demonstrable from a generative definition that omits final causality. Thus it is not surprising that Hobbes would come to declare that the final cause "hath place only in moral philosophy."[79] But what is the intelligibility of the final cause, if it lacks the intelligibility of a *factum*? Why would Hobbes think that all rational persons must accept his particular account of it? Neither intuition nor arbitrary stipulation are satisfying answers to this question, either exegetically or in themselves.

But the question persists. One of Hobbes's great merits is that he enables us to formulate the question, and to generalize it. How do we reconcile the *verum-factum* principle, which Hobbes articulates with a good deal of force and clarity, with the demand to preserve and elucidate the intelligibility of things not of our own making, for example, the human *telos*? As long as one is confined to a purely secular view, the question is intractable—or so the example of Hobbes suggests. One could attempt to abolish the question—either by singing hymns to "Nature" that would rob the *verum-factum* principle of its force, or by reducing all reality, so far as it is intelligible, to what is humanly made. Those who take the first path tend to downplay the significance of human artifice, assuming the only alternative to nihilism to consist in a root-and-branch dismissal of constructivism. Those who take the second path oscillate between self-deification (man as god of his own reality, liberated from all constraints) and self-abasement (whatever man constructs, he can deconstruct, with no sense of ultimate truth). An alternative to either of these options may be found in the theological and historical metaphysics of Giambattista Vico, to whom we now turn.

6

GIAMBATTISTA VICO

Making and truth

"For the Latins 'verum' and 'factum' are reciprocally related, or, as is said commonly in the Schools, convertible."[1] This first sentence of the opening chapter of *De antiquissima Italorum sapientia* is the *locus classicus* of Vico's "*verum-factum* principle," a principle that is more often quoted or mentioned than understood. What makes the principle difficult to interpret is not only that (as we have seen from our readings of Aquinas, Cusanus, Bacon, Descartes and Hobbes) the correlations between knowing and making vary significantly among diverse thinkers. It is also that Vico considers his *verum-factum* principle to be embedded in a broader metaphysics whose exposition occupies the fourth chapter of *De antiquissima*. This metaphysics, rather than the *verum-factum* principle in isolation, is what Vico takes to be the central theme (*proprium argumentum*) of the *De antiquissima*, as he says in the conclusion of that work, and reiterates first in response to its early critics, and later in his *Autobiography*. This would suggest that a grasp of Vico's metaphysics is a necessary condition for any satisfactory interpretation of the *verum-factum* principle. Yet one must admit that Vico's exposition of the central concept of that metaphysics—what he calls "metaphysical points"—is quite obscure. One may sympathize with the first critics of *De antiquissima*, who complain that Vico's use of the phrase "envelops the whole treatise in a darkness that is almost palpable."[2]

Our procedure in this section and the next will be to attend carefully to the initial articulation of the *verum-factum* principle in chapter one of the *De antiquissima*. Against the commentators who dismiss this text as too cryptic to merit interpretive attention, we will offer a clear, coherent reading of the *De antiquissima*'s first chapter. We will then be in a position to turn to the convoluted fourth chapter of the text, adjusting our interpretation of the *verum-factum* principle as necessary.

To quote the opening sentence in full: "Latinis 'verum' et 'factum' reciprocantur, seu, ut Scholarum vulgus loquitur, convertuntur; atque iisdem idem est 'intelligere,' ac 'perfecte legere' et 'aperte cognoscere.'"[3] In this sentence, Vico suggests some relation between *verum-factum* and the idea that "to understand" (*intelligere*) means "to read perfectly" or "to cognize openly, without distortion." One may hazard the following: if cognition attains a *verum*, and *factum* is interchangeable with *verum*, then cognition may also be described as attaining a *factum*. But a *factum* is attained only through some process of making. Therefore cognition may be understood as essentially a process of making. But making in what sense? The remainder of the first paragraph addresses this question. *Ratio* was held by the Latins to mean "a collection (*collectio*) of arithmetic elements."[4] *Legere*, "to read," is said of the person "who collects (*colligit*) the elements of writing, from which words are put together (*componuntur*)."[5] Cognition is making, in the precise sense of assembling or composing a set of elements into a whole. As the object of cognition, this whole may be described as a *verum*. Considered as the result of a constructive process, the whole obtained through the composition of elements is a *factum*. Thus the *verum* and the *factum* coincide.

Making is the collecting of elements into a whole. Reading, *legere*, is an exemplary case of element-collecting. To read perfectly, *legere perfecte*, is to *intelligere*. But what do either of these terms mean? Vico tells us: "intelligere sit colligere omnia elementa rei, ex quibus perfectissima exprimatur idea."[6] To understand, *intelligere*, is to collect *all* the elements—not just some of them. It is a complete collection, not an approximate gathering or partial assemblage. Because the collection of elements is absolutely perfect—a case of *perfecte legere*—it enables a correspondingly perfect expression of an "absolutely perfect idea" (*perfectissima idea*). Understanding is a flawless collection of real elements into a whole that either leads to or is identical with the expression of something perfect. *Intelligere*, in this sense, is possible only for God: "in God is the first truth, because God is the first maker."[7] The *primum verum* is the *perfectissima idea*, expressed from the *colligere omnia elementa rei*. From the nature of perfection, Vico is able to deduce two attributes of the first truth. First, the *primum verum* is *infinitum*, without limit. Because God is the maker of all things, there is nothing outside of God that would impose a limit on the first truth. (If there were, it would not be the most perfect idea.) Second, the *primum verum* is *exactissimum*, absolutely precise, because there is nothing outside the first truth that would cause it to require qualification. The perfection of God's *primum verum* entails its ability to perfectly "represent to himself the elements of things, both outer and inner (*cum extima, tum intima*), since he contains them."[8]

Are humans capable of knowing a truth that is unlimited and absolutely precise, arrived at by a perfect gathering of all the elements of things? Vico answers "no": the human being is a *particeps* in reason, not reason itself. It follows, then, that *intelligere* is a divine activity, not a human one. But if divine knowing is a process that can be described by recourse to activities with which humans are familiar (making, reading, collecting), there must be some analogy between God's perfect *intelligere* and our imperfect *legere*. Thus the formula "to know is to compose the elements of things" (*scire autem sit rerum elementa componere*) applies to both divine and human mind, but one must add that "*cogitatio* is proper to the human mind, but *intelligentia* is proper to the divine."[9] *Cogitatio* is an imperfect composition of elements, a flawed imitation of divine *intelligentia*. *Cogitatio* is the product of *cogitare*, a word that Vico has already equated with the vernacular *andar raccolgiendo*. (In chapter 4, Vico will say "può andarle raccogliendo, ma non gìa raccoglierle tutte"—"one can keep on picking things up, but never get them all together."[10]) The *verum* known by *cogitare* is not the *primum verum*, because it is neither unlimited nor absolutely precise.

But why not? What is the ground of the distinction between *cogitare* and *intelligere*? What makes the human mind unable to perfectly compose the elements of things? Once again, Vico invokes the reading paradigm: "God reads all the elements of things, both outer and inner (*cum extima, tum intima*) because he contains them and disposes them."[11] The human mind, however, is *terminata*—limited and bounded, and therefore "outside of all things that are not itself."[12] Because of its distance from *res*, it has access to only their *extrema*, their outer edges, and consequently "never collects them all" (*nunquam omnia colligat*).[13] Yet because it can at least grasp the *extrema*, it is able to engage in a certain imitation of God, composing into wholes what it manages to glean of the *elementa rerum*. "Thus the human mind can indeed think about things (*cogitare*), but it cannot understand (*intelligere*); whence it is a participation in reason, but not its master."[14] *Cogitare* is thus a making, but a making that assembles its *factum* from shadows of realities. Vico illustrates with a "likeness" (*similitudo*): "divine truth is a solid image of things, like a *plasma*, whereas human truth is a monogram or plane image, like a picture."[15] The likeness both distinguishes human truth from divine truth and preserves what they have in common, i.e. that both are wholes made from elements. "As divine truth is what God, when he knows it (*cognoscit*), disposes and generates, so human truth is what man, when he knows it (*novit*), in like manner (*item*) composes or makes."[16] Vico does not want to conflate God's *disponere/gignere* with man's *componere/facere*. But he does want to connect the two, by portraying the latter as an imitation of the former.

To hold that the *verum* is a *factum*, a whole achieved through the synthesis of elements, leads Vico to a definition of *scientia*. *Scientia* is "cognition of the genus, or mode, by which a thing comes to be." To have *scientia* of *x*, does one actually have to originate *x*, or must one merely be capable of such origination? Vico seems to affirm the first option: "when the mind has cognition of the mode, it makes the thing, since it composes its elements."[17] One might protest that we often have cognition of how a thing comes to be, without ever having made it. We know, for example, how the universe came to be, viz. through the Big Bang. Vico's response would be that this is precisely the sort of the thing about which we do not—and cannot—have *scientia*. However plausible our hypotheses, whatever the force of our conjectures, they will always fall short of pure *scientia*, since we did not compose the elements that make up the universe. Thus Vico reasserts the ontological difference: God makes a solid image "because he comprehends everything"; man makes a plane image "because he comprehends the outer edges (*extima*)."[18]

There can be little doubt that Vico means to emphasize the gap between human and divine making. Although its status as a *rationis particeps* distinguishes it from brute animals, the mind that makes human truth is strictly limited, external to things not itself, capable of possessing only the outer edges of the *elementa*. Whether it can have true *scientia* of anything appears doubtful. These characteristics of the human mind are, Vico conjectures, known to the Latins. But Vico proceeds to say that the things discussed so far in the first chapter of *De antiquissima* need to be "woven together" (*componantur*) with the teachings of "our religion."[19] What have the "ancient philosophers of Italy" missed? This question is crucial for interpreting Vico. One might suppose that Vico does not take the ancient pagan understanding of the principle *verum esse ipsum factum* to lack anything of significance. On this account, the final paragraph of *De antiquissima* 1.1 would appear as only so much pious window dressing, perhaps written to ward off the Inquisition. Any such account is persuasive only if the paragraph fails to add anything substantial to Vico's explication of the difference between divine and human truth. Does the paragraph fail in this manner? The only way to answer this crucial question is to examine the paragraph with care, in order to assess whether it is the key to the entire account or an irrelevant coda.

Vico links the pagan *verum-factum* with the belief that the world is eternal. Because of this belief, Vico claims, the pagan philosophers "worshipped a god who always operated *ad extra*, which our theology denies."[20] One may think of the Platonic demiurge, who makes the world by working at an eternally existent material which lies outside of himself, and does so by looking to forms which likewise have an eternal existence independent of him. Clearly Vico wishes to deny the cogency of such a description of God. What allows Vico to locate a form of *intelligere* that differs radically from human *cogitare* is precisely the idea of a God who has an internal (and therefore perfect) possession of the *elementa rerum*. Because such elements are underived, they cannot themselves be made by composition—they are not *facta* in this sense. But neither can they exist outside the mind of the creator; if they did, the *primum verum* would not exist *in Deo*.

Vico does not write the final paragraph of *De antiquissima* 1.1 because he wishes to affect a pious attitude. He does so because he thinks that if God is to be coherently described as possessing the *elementa rerum* internally, he must generate them from his own substance. Internal possession of the elements necessitates a distinction between two kinds of divine truth: *verum creatum convertatur cum facto, verum increatum cum genito*.[21] To the extent that pagan accounts place the elements outside the divine mind, they are unable to apprehend the ground for holding that God grasps the elements perfectly and humans only their *extrema*. Scripture, by contrast, understands this rationale profoundly. "With truly divine elegance, it calls the wisdom of God, which contains in itself the ideas of all things and thus the elements of all ideas, *Verbum*."[22] Vico is thus able to account for both God's internal comprehension of the elements and the particular disposition of those elements which constitute "this universe of things" (*hanc rerum universitatem*).[23] Some distinction between these is required in order to preserve a sense of the difference between the *Verbum* and creation. Yet Vico does not wish to sunder the two. Both the *factum* and the *genitum* are related to divine activity (*disponit et gignit*), and both have their being through "the comprehension of the elements of all things" (*comprehensio elementorum omnium*).[24]

Far from being an arbitrary or merely prudential appendix, the final paragraph of *De antiquissima*'s first chapter provides the key for understanding the distinction between *cogitare* and *intelligere*. It does so by replacing the half-coherent idea of a demiurgic God with the notion of a total divine *comprehensio*, the acknowledgment of which possibility is the only way between dogmatism and scepticism—or so Vico will argue at the end of the chapter. In the *Prima Risposta*, Vico associates the failure to think this notion with "innumerable errors" committed by those "who have the opinion that God operates like a craftsman (*fabro*) and that created things are the causes of other things, instead of being parts of the modes which the eternal mind of God comprehends"[25] Assimilations of *verum-factum* to secular efforts to replace God by *homo faber* are entirely misleading. *Verum-factum*, as Vico understands it, is inscribed within a theological metaphysics.

Abstraction as creation

Vico has described human truth as a *factum* that is arrived at through a synthesis of elements that are only partly grasped, because they exist outside the mind which grasps them. If the human mind is essentially outside the *elementa rerum*, how does it manage to grasp even their outside edges? Vico proceeds to answer this question: "God knows everything, because he contains within himself the elements from which all things are composed; man seeks to know these elements by a process of dividing (*dividendo*)."[26]

What is the relation of "dividing" to making? Is *dividendo* creative or destructive? Vico's answer is "both." *De antiquissima* 1.2 begins with an homage to the fecundity of dissection. The "anatomy of nature's works" gives birth to the range of human *scientiae*. It does so by inventing their objects. One can divide man into body and spirit. From body, human science has "picked out (*excerpsit*) or, as men say, abstracted figure and motion, and from these, as well as from all other things, it has extracted (*extulit*) being and unity."[27] The objects obtained through abstraction give rise to the human *scientiae*: metaphysics (whose proper object is *ens*), arithmetic (*unum*), geometry (*figura*), mechanics (*motus* from the edge), *physics* (motion from the center), medicine (*corpus*), logic (*ratio*), and ethics (*voluntas*).

The fecundity of dissection comes at a cost. Man creates the human *scientiae* by fragmenting, and therefore destroying, the whole. Vico licenses *abstractio* as a synonym for *dividendo*, but nearly always follows his use of the term with an "as they say" clause (*ut dicunt* or *quam dicunt*). He does this, first, because he does not want his usage of the scholastic term to lend an unwarranted prestige to any process that sunders the whole, and second, because he thinks that *dividendo* is the basic notion in terms of which *abstractio* should be understood, and not vice versa. The entities created by abstraction—being, unity, figure, motion, shape, intellect, will—are "one thing in God, in whom they are one, and another thing in man, in whom they are divided."[28] Ripped from the whole in which they have life, humanly obtained elements are *disiecta membra*. "In God they live, in man they perish."[29] Our efforts to understand nature by cutting it up supplies us with theories rather than works: "in nobis sunt ratiocina, in Deo sunt opera."[30] All that man acquires through dividing the whole, is like man himself, *nihil prae Deo*; all finite and created beings are nothing but *disposita entis infiniti ac aeterni*.[31] Etymology confirms the connection between division and diminution: Vico asserts that *minuere* means both "to lessen" and "to separate."[32]

The limitations of abstraction ensure that we have access only to the *extrema* of the *elementa rerum*. In what is likely to be an allusion to Lucretius, Vico declares that when man starts to investigate the nature of things (*naturam rerum vestigabundus*), he finds that "he does not have within himself the elements from which composite things exist."[33] This lack (*brevitas*) is not a morally neutral feature of the human condition, but a "vice of the mind" (*mentis vicium*).[34] It is an effect of fallenness, a decline from a primordial state in which mind and nature were integrated. (Vico uses *nefas* to characterize physicists who think they can provide real definitions of things.) Man responds to this condition by turning the *mentis vicium* to good use, by performing an operation that relies solely upon the mind and bypasses, as it were, the material world. "By abstraction, as they say, he fabricates (*configit*) two things for himself: the point that can be drawn and the unit that can be multiplied."[35] The association of *abstractio* and *confingere* suggests that abstraction is creative. The suggestion is confirmed most clearly in the *Prima Risposta*, where Vico writes that mathematics "procedono a similglianza della scienza di Dio, perché si han creato in un certo modo gli elementi con definir certi nomi."[36] This passage establishes beyond any reasonable doubt that abstraction is a kind of making—a creation of the elements. But this type of making must be distinguished from *De antiquissima* 1.1's sense of *facere* as compositive. Unlike compositive making, abstraction either presupposes no prior elements, or presupposes them in a way that does not involve their composition (the verbs *componere* or *colligere* do not appear in this section). Thus Vico writes: "man defines the names themselves, and on the model of God with no underlying thing he creates (*creat*) the point, line and surface as if from nothing, as if they were things."[37] Possessing these elements internally, man is able "to establish (*condidit*) for himself a certain world of forms and numbers, which he embraces entirely within himself: and by producing, shortening, or composing lines, by adding, subtracting, or reckoning numbers, he effects infinite works because he knows infinite truths within himself."[38]

Mathematics is the privileged discourse in which it is most true that "scientia humana divinae sit imitatrix."[39] But the geometer's creation is only analogous to divine making. Vico does not think that the mathematician succeeds in creating things. Even at its most creative, abstraction yields only names. These names are *ficta*: "the point, when you draw it, is not a point: the one, when you multiply it, is no longer fully one."[40] The procedural parallel, however, seems intact: "man, containing within himself an imaginary world of lines and numbers, operates in it with his abstractions, just as God does in the universe with reality."[41] But this parallel turns out to be analogical as well. Creation of mathematical elements is creation *in un certo modo*. It is not literally *ex nihilo*, but "as if (*tamquam*) from nothing."[42]

Abstraction is the mind's way of coping with its estrangement from things. Because he cannot possess "the *elementa rerum* by which things themselves exist with certainty,"[43] he resorts to the fabrication (*confingere*) of *elementa verborum*, elements which, despite their unreality, are able to "stimulate ideas with no controversy."[44] Abstractions may be false in themselves, and yet humanly useful. Vico draws parallels between mathematics and mechanics, and chemistry and pharmaceutics. Both mathematics and chemistry arise from the vice of the mind; both display the tendency "to seek a truth that is denied to man by nature."[45] Yet both give rise to useful arts, that is, pharmaceutics and mechanics. But the utility of these arts does nothing to justify the pretensions of human science. "It pretends to know things it does not contain, and because it does not contain the truths it seeks, it is unable to put them into operation."[46] Heuristic success is never a reason to confuse our shadowy abstractions with real things. Although abstractions give us the power to manipulate things, they do not help us to know them, since they tell us nothing about the genus or mode by which natural things come to be. The exception is mathematics, which does not concern natural things at all. The objects of mathematics are not things, but *nomina* regarded "as if they were things" (*res veluti*).[47] Because the point and the unit simply *are* abstractions, a retracing of the abstractive process will perfectly disclose the genus or mode by which they come to be.

To summarize our exposition so far: the first two sections of *De antiquissima* 1 contain two distinct concepts of making: (1) *facere*, understood as an activity of gathering or composing elements into a whole; (2) *dividendo/abstractio*—

the process of obtaining the elements, whether from nature or from the mind itself. There are two major points of obscurity so far. First, why does Vico use "abstraction" to describe *both* the dissection of elements from a given whole and the creative process by which the mind makes the point and the unit? Second, why does Vico consistently say that the creation of the mathematician is creation "*as if* from nothing, or creation "in a certain way?" Why does Vico ascribe something less than full creative power to the geometer?

These questions must wait until we examine Vico's discussion of the relation between mathematical and metaphysical points. In the remainder of *De antiquissima* 1.2, Vico uses his account of the origin of the sciences and their elements to arrange them in a hierarchy displaying their degrees of certainty. The hierarchy is as follows: mathematics (the science of the point and the one), mechanics (motion from the edge), physics (motion from the center), medicine (body), logic (reason), ethics (the soul). Mathematics stands at the top of the hierarchy. It is the *scientia* in which truth is most fully made by its human practitioner. Because the mind creates its elements itself, it comprehends them internally, and therefore has full control over their origination and composition. Mechanics and physics, by contrast, are less certain than mathematics. "We are not able to prove from causes in physics, because the elements of natural things are outside us."[48] We do not make the natural elements of motion. Nonetheless, *verum-factum* is applicable. Although the physicist cannot pretend to give real definitions of things, he can use the elements created by mathematics to construct useful hypotheses. These hypotheses are useful precisely to the extent that they permit experiments "in which we make something similar to nature."[49]

Vico considers the adoption of artificial dissection and construction enormously useful in the *scientiae* of the upper part of the hierarchy. Although the anatomy of nature as practiced by modern physics, mechanics and chemistry can never provide access to the *elementa rei*, it does facilitate the production of useful goods. In these sciences, *verum* and *factum* give rise to *bonum*. This is not the case, however, for the *scientiae* that occupy the lower part of the hierarchy. Here dissective procedures are useless and uncertain. In *De ratione* VI, Vico holds that the elements which medicine seeks to know, the causes of disease, are deeply hidden, and recommends ancient preservation over modern cure.[50] To this analysis, the *De antiquissima* adds that efforts to possess the relevant elements are doomed to failure because the parts of a corpse are no longer organs in a living system. Consequently their actual uses in an animate body, Vico says, cannot be explored. Medicine does not teach the genera or modes by which its subject matter comes to be; it is thus what Vico will call a "conjectural" art.[51]

The *scientiae* below medicine on the hierarchy are also conjectural. Logic, in the broad sense that Vico uses the term, seeks to know the operations of the mind. Dissective procedures do not provide *scientia* about the mind, because "the mind does not make itself as it gets to know itself, and since it does not make itself, it does not know the genus or mode by which it knows itself."[52] Thus "our clear and distinct idea of the mind cannot be the criterion of the mind itself (let alone of other truths)."[53] Vico develops this contention in *De antiquissima* 1.3. Like Pascal, he thinks that Descartes does not really understand the power of scepticism. "Although the sceptic is aware (*conscius*) that he thinks, he does not know the causes of his *cogitatio*, that is, by what means his *cogitatio* comes to be."[54] Because he lacks this causal knowledge, he has only "awareness" (*conscientia*) of thinking. The attempt to derive real knowledge of one's being, *scientia entis*, from *conscientia cogitandi* is hopeless, because *scientia* requires a knowledge of causes, which for Vico is the equivalent to the ability to produce the thing from causes: *probare a caussis esse ipsum efficere*."[55] Since we cannot produce our own being, we lack access to the genus or mode by which we were made. Thus the *cogito* is not so much false as idle; it merely provides us with the awareness that we exist, which we already had prior to Cartesian meditation, and which the true sceptic has no particular need to contest. Because we cannot know the mind by creating its elements through abstraction, our knowledge about the mind is mostly uncertain. (The interminable character of the disputes among contemporary "philosophers of mind" suggests how little has changed in this respect.[56])

Below medicine and logic comes moral philosophy, the *scientia* in which abstraction proves most useless. The fruit of abstraction in ethics is the proliferation of manuals containing rules about what to do and what not to do. In *De ratione X*, Vico rejects this sort of "artificial" approach to ethics: "in those subjects in which *prudentia* is supreme, a great number of *artes* is no more helpful than their absence."[57] Why *artes* are not helpful in moral philosophy may be discerned from examining its elements. These are the end (*finis*, which Vico identifies as the principal cause in ethics), the will directed toward the end (*voluntas*), desire for the end (*libido quae est infinita*), and the "motions of spirits, which are most hidden" (*motus animorum, qui penitissimi sunt*"), caused by infinite desire. The *telos* is God, the *primum verum* who cannot be grasped by human abstraction. In ethics, abstractions are not only inadequate to the good that we want to know—this is also true for mechanics, physics, and chemistry—but do remarkably little to help us draw us nearer to that *telos*, and even push us farther away from it. To have *scientia* of a thing is to compose it from its elements, to know the genus or mode by which it comes to be. This is equivalent to making the thing itself from its causes ("to prove something from causes is the same as to make it"[58]). To have *scientia* of God would entail our ability to prove God from allegedly prior elements, which is to say, to make God by composing him out of these elements. Those who attempt to provide *a priori* proofs of God are thus "guilty of impious curiosity"; they "make themselves the God of God and deny the God whom they seek."[59]

Verum-factum functions as a principle by which Vico is able to rank human *scientiae* according to their degrees of certainty. Against the impression that Vico is simply exalting mathematics, it may be observed that he considers the degree of certainty with which one knows the elements of a science to be inversely proportional to the reality of those elements. If there were a science in which the mind could *both* possess its elements within itself by internal generation, *and* be correct in regarding these elements as real things (unlike mathematics, which delusively treats its *ficta* "as if they were *res*"), this would be a higher science—indeed, a *scienza nuova*.

Making within metaphysics

Although its elements are already in place, Vico has not meditated the *Scienza nuova* in 1710. He does, however, have the idea of a master architectonic discourse, a science of the whole. This science is necessarily superior to any of the sciences on the hierarchy; it is what enables Vico to construct the hierarchy. In the *De antiquissima*, Vico calls this science "metaphysics." Metaphysics is the *omnis veri fons, et unde in alias scientias omnes derivatur*, chapter 4 of *De antiquissima* declares.[60] The *Prima Risposta* reaffirms this view: metaphysics "è la scienza che ripartisce alle altre i loro propri soggetti, e, poiché non può darle il suo, dà loro certe immagini del suo. Onde la geometria ne prende il punto, e 'l disegna; l'arithmetica l'uno, e 'l moltiplica; la meccanica il conato, e l'attaca a' corpi."[61]

This passage contains an initial clue to addressing both of the perplexities mentioned in the previous section. Mathematics may be described as abstractive because, like physics, it draws (*prendere*) its elements from another source, although without the mediation of matter. It may also be said to create its elements. But this creation cannot be purely autonomous, if mathematics takes its subject matter from metaphysics. Thus Vico ascribes to the mathematician the power to create his elements only "in a certain way," or "as if from nothing." Even the creation of the *punctum* and the *unum*—the closest approximation of human making to divine creation—presupposes something beyond itself. The geometrical point is a *fictum*, because the point that can drawn is a self-negating contradiction. Yet it is not *only* a fiction. It is also a "certain image" of the subject matter proper to metaphysics.

On the basis of this passage alone, one may recognize the inadequacy of any purely nominalist interpretation of Vico's conception of making in mathematics. But to see how—or whether—Vico is able to coherently claim *both* that the geometrically constructed point is a fictive name, *and* that it is an image of reality, possessing a degree of ontological weight beyond its status as a nominal definition—one must examine the very difficult fourth chapter of the *De antiquissima* in some detail.

Vico begins by attributing to the Latins the view that metaphysics is the one true *scientia* because it treats of *virtutes* that are eternal, immutable, indivisible, and infinite. Physics deals with body and motion; metaphysics examines that which makes body and motion possible. The conditions of body and motion are the *virtus extensionis* and *conatus, qui virtus movendi est*. These *virtutes* of extension and motion are the *materia propria* of metaphysics. Thus Vico claims, invoking the authority of Doria, that "in physics there are acts (*actus*), in metaphysics there are *virtutes*."[62] These *virtutes*, Vico claims, have been most convincingly treated by the Stoics through the "hypothesis of the metaphysical point."[63]

No one doubts, Vico says, that geometry and arithmetic either possess truth or its near likeness. In order to maintain *both* the commonly accepted opinion that mathematics seeks and to some extent attains truth and the "enlightened" view that the elements of geometry and arithmetic are in themselves *ficta*, Vico asserts that mathematics must derive its truth from another source. This is metaphysics, the *omnis veri fons*. But through what path (*via*) does geometry derive truth or its likeness from metaphysics? There is no other *via* but "through the malign gateway of the point" (*per malignum aditum puncti*).[64] What makes the gateway malign is evident: when the geometer defines *punctum* as "that of which there is no part," he is giving a *definitio nominis*, "because there is no thing that is extended, which has no parts, and yet you draw it in the mind or with a pencil."[65] The arithmetician likewise supplies a definition of a name, because the *unum multiplicabile* cannot be a true *unum*.

The "Zenonians," however, provide an alternative definition of a point. They consider the point to be a "definition of a thing, insofar as the point is an image (*instar*) of what the human mind is able to think (*cogitare*) concerning the *virtus* of indivisible extension and motion."[66] The practice of the geometer who constructs a world of lines and surfaces from the *punctum* supplies a model of how the physical world is generated from and dependent upon metaphysical points—points which "virtually" contain the physical world, and yet cannot be reduced to material extension, or described in physical terms. Analysis of the purest case of human creation thus provides a degree of insight into the divine creation of things, without furnishing *scientia*. But there is no justification for holding that human making based on geometrical points is capable of providing even this limited insight into the mode of divine making, *unless* the geometrical point has some positive connection to the metaphysical point. However malign and fictitious the *aditum puncti* is, it must *also* be thought to contain a semblance of truth. Thus in the *Seconda Risposta*, Vico claims that "il punto geometrico sia una simiglianza del metafisco, cioè della sostanza."[67] Against those who think that humanly constructed points or numbers are literally constituents of the physical world, Vico understands them as nominal definitions.[68] But this is not his final word. He agrees with the "Zenonians" who consider *puncta rerum principia esse*.[69] Mathematical images of the metaphysical point are potent indicators of the punctiliar constitution of the world.

Why does Vico refuse to say that geometrical entities simply *are* the constituents of physical bodies, as Descartes seems to imply when he writes that "my physics is nothing but geometry."[70] To identify geometrical points with metaphysical points would *either* entail that the elements of nature are created by human beings, and consequently that nature itself is made by the human mind, *or* it would imply that the geometrical point is not a human construction. Both positions are equally unacceptable for Vico: any notion that men originate physical nature would strike him as self-evidently absurd; any denial that geometrical points are humanly created would entirely undermine his account of the certainty of geometry. Thus geometrical points cannot be seen as literally making up the world of nature, even if they provide an image of how nature is created. But why should one grant that geometrical points possess any such capacity to image the metaphysical *principia* of physical things? Vico's answer would be that if no such capacity is allowed, then there is no basis for thinking that geometry attains either truth or the *species veri*. Mathematics would be an entirely arbitrary exercise in manipulating counters. In keeping with his aim to mediate between dogmatism and skepticism, Vico wants neither to deny that mathematics attains truth, nor to affirm that mathematics exhausts truth. Thus he writes that the Pythagoreans and their Platonic followers did not hold that "nature is actually constituted by numbers," but rather "sought to exhibit (*explicare*) the world outside themselves through the world which they contained within themselves."[71] Such *explicare* belongs to *cogitare* rather than *intelligere*; it proceeds from images of the metaphysical points, not the real elements of things. But since *cogitare* involves something of the elements—a *legere* of their outer edges—the mathematical points used to explicate the outside world must be a likeness of truth.

What guarantees our knowledge that geometrical points are in fact images of metaphysical originals? Vico refuses, on principle, to provide any ironclad epistemological warrant. To make the attempt would be to lapse into dogmatism. His reply, rather, is that if the geometer turns philosopher—as he must if he is to defend his enterprise from the charge that it is merely a nominal game whose elements are self-negating fictions—he will be brought to acknowledge the rational possibility that he creates the elements of his science, without making them arbitrarily. The truth of this perspective cannot be apodictically demonstrated, but it can be confirmed by its ability to adjudicate between Aristotelian and Cartesian approaches to nature, and by its power to harmonize the view that we grasp mathematical truths with certainty because we make them with the opinion that mathematics is truth-seeking. Near the end of *De antiquissima* 4.2, Vico writes: "Geometry receives its truth from metaphysics, and returns what it has received to this very metaphysics: that is, it expresses human *scientia* on the model of divine *scientia*, and in turn confirms divine *scientia* from human *scientia*."[72] The practice of geometry itself confirms and gestures towards the existence of metaphysical points, which serve as the basis for the "Zenonian" construal of the geometrical point as more than a mere *fictum*.

This perspective enables Vico to mediate between those who would regard human making as null, and those who regard it as absolute. (These are really two sides of the same coin.) Vico clearly conceives the ontological dependence of what is humanly made upon that which is not humanly made. In the *Vita*, Vico speaks of eternal truths that exist in the mind, and yet which are not "from us" (*da noi*).[73] As Lachterman suggests, a mathematical creation can be more than a nominal fiction "if *and only if* its construction is shaped in accordance with a non-mathematical and non-human original."[74] This captures the "Platonism" of Vico. And yet, it is not the case that Vico grants the geometer the ability to direct his gaze toward a metaphysical archetype prior to his creation of the point. Milbank clearly understands that "it is not true for Vico there is an intimation of the divine transcendent unity *before* our human making. On the contrary, it is only *in* this making that we receive an intimation of transcendence."[75] There are truths which the mind does not construct, but there is no *mode of access* to these truths that bypasses human making. Lachterman himself suggests as much when he equates the creative motions of mathematical mind with "gestures of recollective imitation," gestures which are "governed by the metaphysical originals they mimic and are the sources of our acquaintance with those same originals."[76] Making is the *source* of our acquaintance with eternal truths that are not of our making. There is no human access to metaphysical archetypes prior to construction.

How can human making, especially if it is as limited and contingent as Vico suggests, provide a glimpse of the eternal? Although mathematics provides us with an example of how human making can be a participation of divine making—with respect to both its procedure ("*creato in un certo modo*") and its substance ("*il punto geometrico sia una simiglianza del metafisico*"), it remains the case that no finite human endeavor is sufficient to attain the infinite. It can, however, participate in the infinite. Synthetic geometry provides a paradigm of such participation. Vico affirms this not only in the *De antiquissima*, but well after the composition of the first two version of the *Scienza nuova*. In 1737, he writes to Msgr. Gaeta: "l'uomo è Dio nel Mondo delle grandezze astratte, e Dio è Geometra nel Mondo delle concrete, che è tanto dire quanto nel Mondo della natura e de' corpi."[77]

Making as imaginative mythopoesis

The status of geometry in Vico's thought, early and late, will surprise those whose knowledge of the Italian thinker is derived from commentaries that expound him as the champion of a humanism which privileges the imagination over reason. Such interpretations take their point of departure from the fact that Vico places *fantasia* at the center of the first major concept of "making" in the *Scienza nuova*. This we may label "mythopoesis." Vico ascribes the activity of imaginative myth-making to the first humans of the gentile nations, whom he calls the "theological poets." These makers are both the "first sages" of the gentile world and "stupid, insensate, and horrible beasts"[78] Precisely because these men are so crude, they are dominated by *fantasia*. The operation of *fantasia* in these cyclopean figures gives rise to the first comprehensive world-view, "poetic metaphysics." Because it depends upon *fantasia*, the metaphysics of the theological poets is not "rational or abstract like that of learned men now, but felt and imagined as that of these first men must have been, who, without power of ratiocination, were all robust sense and most vigorous imagination."[79] The poetic metaphysics is a *metafisica fantastica*, created by the theological poets who are "unable to make use of the understanding (*intendimento*)."[80]

How does *fantasia*, the organ of poetic metaphysics, work? Vico is sceptical about the possibility of laying down invariant rules according to which the imagination operates. The "obstinate study of art" does not tell one how to become a poet.[81] But he does not think that *fantasia* is simply unanalyzable. At least four sources provide important clues about its operation in poetic man. First, we know something about *fantasia* by reflecting on the "modifications of mind," in particular the property of human nature insofar as it is like that of animals: "the senses are the sole way in which it knows things."[82] Second, texts from the tradition, such as those of Lactantius and Tacitus, attest to the role of *fantasia* in the imaginative creation of gods. Third, there is evidence from contemporary societies that still exist in a primitive state. In a manner that recalls Hobbes's attempt to confirm empirically what he knows best by inference from the passions, Vico cites the American Indians. Such "rude and very simple nations help us to a much better understanding of the founders of the gentile world with whom we are now concerned."[83] Fourth, and perhaps most importantly, children provide an observable analogue of the act that Vico considers as absolutely basic to the primitive poetic mind. This is the act of giving "sense and passion to insensate things."[84] Here Vico sends us back to the axiom in the Elements which claims "it is characteristic of children to take inanimate things in their hands and talk to them in play as if they were living persons."[85] That Vico privileges this fourth source of evidence about the operation of *fantasia* in poetic man is suggested by its prominence among the Elements, and throughout the entire *Scienza nuova*.[86] In sections 32–6 of the Elements, Vico holds that the first men were ignorant of natural causes. Such ignorance issues in a "*volgar metafisica*" characterized by superstition and wonder.[87] The best analogue we have for the operation of *fantasia* that grows out of ignorance, superstition, and wonder is the activity of children. Watching children in the act of endowing inanimate things with life suggests the manner in which the theological poets gave the objects of their wonder the "being of substance from their own ideas."[88] Our own children, if we understand them properly, provide a link to the poets of the *mondo fanciullo*.

Like young children, the theological poets possess a certain innocence, a naiveté that renders their myth-making truthful. But Vico does not himself believe in the gods created by the theological poets. His own perspective is not, and cannot be, that of poetic man. Vico is quite clear that poetic man *imagines* the gods (§446 speaks of "men who imagined the gods") in a way that is ignorant and superstitious.

> The first nature, by a powerful deceit (*inganno*) of imagination, which is most robust in the weakest at reasoning, was a poetic or creative nature which we may be allowed to call divine, as it ascribed to physical things the being of substances animated by gods, assigning the gods to them according to its idea of each. This nature was that of the theological poets, who were the earliest wise men in all the gentile nations, when all the gentile nations were founded on the belief which each of them had in certain gods of its own. Furthermore it was a nature all fierce and cruel; but, through that same error (*errore*) of their imagination, men had a terrible fear of the gods whom they themselves had feigned (*finti*).[89]

In this short passage, Vico emphasizes the falsity of what the imagination creates. He speaks of the "inganno di *fantasia*" and the "errore di *fantasia*." He is quite clear that the gods created by the theological poets are fictions of the imagination. There is no hermeneutic problem on this point: Vico speaks openly about "la falsa divinitá di Giove."[90] But Vico also thinks that what is false in itself is capable of pointing to what is true. As we have seen, Vico has affirmed the capacity of ontological fictions to model truth, which portrays the geometer's creation of a world of points, lines, and surfaces from mathematical points that are *ficta* as a model of the divine creation of the world through metaphysical points that are *res*. In this respect, the fictions created by the theological poets take on a certain dignity. "Through the thick clouds of those first tempests, intermittently lit by those flashes, they made out this great truth: that divine providence watches over the welfare of all mankind."[91] They also understand something of divine omnipotence. Analysis of Jove as a "credible impossibility"—"it is impossible that bodies should be minds, yet it was believed that the thundering sky was Jove"—leads us to notice "a hidden sense that the nations have of the omnipotence of God."[92] Through its creation of poetic characters, *fantasia* providentially guides the first humans to truth, although the first humans do not consciously intend any such thing, not least because they lack the concept of truth, being driven only by their desire for utility and necessity. Vico does not romanticize the first humans: he insists that "le nazioni erano stordite e stupide."[93] That they could perceive a theological truth, however dimly and crudely, testifies to the power of divine providence.

Vico clearly thinks that gentile superstition is false, the product of nations that are confused and stupid. Yet he does not think that it is sheer nonsense, or unintelligible garbage: the fables are true in their form, but false in their matter. Once deciphered, the fables are reliable documents of how the primitive mind operates. By humanizing their creators, they lead providentially to the development of civilization. But this happens quite against the intentions of the theological poets, who were not intending to found a civilization, but merely to pursue their own utility. The conclusion of the section on Poetic Morals summarizes Vico's overall perspective.

> We may conclude from all this how empty has been the conceit of the learned concerning the innocence of the golden age observed in the first gentile nations. In fact, it was a fanaticism of superstition which kept the first men of the gentiles, savage, proud, and most cruel as they were, in some sort of restraint by main terror of a divinity they had imagined. Reflecting on this superstition, Plutarch poses the problem whether it was a lesser evil thus impiously to venerate the gods than not to believe in them at all. But he is not just in weighing this cruel superstition against atheism, for from the former arose the most enlightened nations while no nation in the world was ever founded on atheism.[94]

The myths of the theological poets, despite their falsehood—Vico accepts the Aristotelian description of poetic characters as "lies beyond equal"[95]— deserve our rational appreciation, since they are instruments used by divine providence in the slow education of the race. They cannot, however, be endorsed as true by anyone who understands their fictive character as clearly as Vico does.

Primitive mythopoesis issues in falsehood. It is driven by the imagination, not the understanding. Yet, even if we ought not to accept the content of the ancient myths, should we not attempt to learn from the creativity of the poetic mind, and strive to emulate it? Do not the theological poets practice a mode of making that is genuinely creative, and thus provide an alternative to the stale and derivative cognition of the modern age? Those who pose such questions often understand the brilliance of the *New Science* as deriving from Vico's ability to recover the creative power he sees in the primitive poetic mind. This power, *fantasia*, is the key to going beyond the arid abstractions of modern rationalism. If this is true, then Vico does not simply take imaginative *mythopoesis* as his subject-matter, but himself regards *fantasia* as the force that drives his own procedure in the *New Science*. It is difficult to reconcile this understanding of Vico, however, with what he actually says about the imagination. Reflecting in his *Autobiography* on what he calls the calls the "negative manner of demonstrating" (*maniera negativa di dimostrare*), Vico concludes that "though it is intriguing to the *fantasia*, it is repugnant to the understanding, since by it the human mind is not enlarged." The program of this work was to bring to light the "improbabilities, absurdities and impossibilities which his predecessors had rather imagined (*immaginato*) than reasoned out (*raggionato*)."[96] Whatever we might say about Vico's science of imagination, it does not seem that Vico is especially kind to *fantasia*.[97]

The argument that Vico's intention is to emulate on the philosophical plane the creativity found paradigmatically in the theological poets requires the assumption that Vico in fact regards the theological poets as essentially creative. There is some textual evidence for this view. In the first paragraph of opening section of Book 4, Vico describes the first nature as a "nature poetic or creative (*natura poetica o sia creatrice*)."[98] The adjective *creatrice* recalls the verb that Vico uses in the Poetic Metaphysics: the "first men of the gentile nations, the children of nascent mankind, created things according to their own ideas" (*dalla lor idea criavan essi le cose*).[99] It seems evident that Vico's theological poets are genuinely creative.

Despite this, we should be suspicious. Mythopoesis, the making of the first gentiles, man is "creative"—but in what sense? To what degree? There are serious textual reasons to suspect that Vico did not intend to ascribe any but the lowest degree of creativity to the theological poets. One may begin with the observation that Vico takes the creativity of poetic man to fall infinitely short of divine creativity. Immediately after he claims that the first men created things according to their own ideas, Vico notices an *infinita differenza* between their creation and God's creation For God, creation is a product of the *purissimo intendimento*. For poetic man, creation occurs through *fantasia*, which Vico emphasizes is entirely corporeal (*corpolentissima*) and operates under conditions of radical ignorance. Vico proceeds to describe the "creation" of theological poets as an exercise in fabrication, repeatedly employing the past perfect of *fingere*, which might be translated as "to fabricate" or (following the example of *Leviathan*, chapter 12) "to feign." (This is obscured by the Bergin and Fisch translation, which variously renders *finsero* by "pictured" or "created.") The giants "feigned (*finsero*) the sky to themselves as a great animated body, which in that aspect they called Jove."[100] They "feigned (*finsero*) the first divine fable, the greatest of those they had ever feigned (*finsero*)."[101] For poetic man, creation is fabrication, an "act of epistemic self-deception," as Lachterman puts it.[102]

Is the description of *fantasia* in poetic man as fabrication compatible with a conception of primitive imagination as authentically creative? One might acknowledge that in comparison to the limiting case of divine creation, *all* human making falls short of true creativity, but nonetheless insist that the creativity of poetic man remains the closest human approach to the divine. But further examination suggests that mythopoesis is creative only in a weak sense. The theological poets make fables about the gods by projecting the familiar upon the unfamiliar. Their construction of the fables presupposes at least two things: (1) an already existent self; (2) some material outside the self, namely the "vast bodies" of sky, sea and earth upon which the attributes of sense and passion are (falsely) imposed.[103] Rather than make something out of nothing, poetic man produces certain imitations of himself, through a process that can be understood clearly and distinctly by tropological analysis. This form of making may be described as "divine" or "creative," since it brings into primitive consciousness some notion of the divine which was not there before. But in itself, it is essentially mimetic, a corporeal self-projection.[104]

This reduction of poetic man's creativity to imitation may strike some as deeply alien to the spirit of Vico. But the source for understanding the creation of the theological poets as crudely mimetic is Vico himself. In Axiom 52, Vico declares that "children excel in imitating (*nell'imitare*), and hence we observe that they generally amuse themselves by simulating (*assembrare*) whatever they are capable of apprehending."[105] From this axiom, he concludes that *il mondo fanciullo*—the world in its childhood—was composed of "poetic nations, poetry being nothing other than imitation (*non essendo altro la poesia che imitazione*).[106] The mythopoesis characteristic of primitive man and his analogue in the contemporary child turns out be essentially mimetic. We may thus conclude, at least provisionally, that *fantasia* falls short of radically creative power.

To say that Vico's own procedure is driven by *fantasia* would serve not to affirm, but actually *weaken*, the view that the new science is creative. Yet Vico does conceive his *Scienza nuova* as exemplifying the conversion of the true and the made. The new scientist is both knower and maker, constructor and contemplator. To understand the sense in which the procedure of the new scientist is creative, we must turn to Vico's second major concept of making.

Making as the creation of elements

The *New Science* is not the work of *fantasia* but of *intendimento*. Its procedure should be compared not to the fantastic mythopoesis of the theological poets, but to the creative operation of the synthetic geometer. The geometer who creates the elements of his science "as it were from nothing"—as Vico says in the *De antiquissima*—may be regarded as *more creative* than the theological poets. Although Vico certainly thinks that geometrical making falls short of pure creation, he nowhere suggests that it can be analyzed in mimetic terms.

How does the making of the new scientist compare with respect to synthetic geometry? In the section on Method, Vico writes:

> Thus this Science proceeds exactly as geometry, which, when it constructs or contemplates the world of size from its elements, makes that world for itself, but with a reality greater by just so much as the orders (*ordini*) concerning human makings or doings

(*faccende degli uomini*) are more real than points, lines, surfaces and figures.[107]

The new scientist is a kind of geometer of the civil world, composing its elements into wholes, and thereby knowing effects together with their causes. Somewhat like Hobbes, Vico holds that we can demonstrate truths about the civil world because we make it. He takes the link between intelligibility and construction as a fundamental truth: "in the night of thick darkness enveloping the earliest antiquity, so remote from ourselves, there shines the eternal and never failing light of a truth beyond all question: that the world of civil society has certainly been made by men, and that its principles are therefore to be found within the modifications of our human mind."[108] As we have seen, Hobbes also holds that physics is hypothetical: because God made the world of nature, only he can know its true causes. Vico agrees with Hobbes, finding it a source of wonder that "philosophers should have bent all their energies to the study of the world of nature, which, since God made it, He alone knows."[109] Vico contrasts the world of nature with "the world of nations, or civil world, which, since men had made it, men could come to know."[110]

Because we are able to demonstrate the effects of the *mondo civile* from their causes, we are able to possess *scientia* of the civil world. Vico regards the demonstration of effects from causes as a kind of making. But it is important to distinguish this sense of making from "free construction." The interpretive difficulty may be stated as follows: How can Vico express the doctrine that the new scientist creates the civil world, down to its very elements, without reducing creation to arbitrary postulation? If we are to maintain the procedural analogy with geometry that Vico explicitly claims in §349 ("questa Scienza procede appunto come la geometria"), we must insist that the new scientist somehow creates the elements of the civil world. Lachterman, despite the general excellence of his studies of Vico on geometry, is not quite right to speak of the elements as "already existent."[111] But we must also explain the sense in which the created elements of the civil world depend upon, and are derived from, the "modifications of our own human mind." To explain this sense will illuminate the first concept of making proper to the new scientist—the creation of the elements of the *mondo civile* from the modifications of mind.

The modifications of mind are clearly not products of human making. In the *Autobiography*, Vico holds that "in our mind there are certain eternal truths which we cannot mistake or deny," and therefore are not "from us."[112] The modifications of mind are essential truths about the mind that are *not* products of our own making. Vico seems to lack any epistemological anxiety about our capacity to know what the modifications of mind are. He leaves open the possibility of introspection; if one is sufficiently industrious, one can "attend to oneself."[113] But Vico is not Descartes; he does not privilege introspection. He conceives the modifications of mind not as privately contemplated theorems, but as publically accessible truths, knowable most readily through the mediation of tradition.

The modifications of mind that will enable us to understand poetic man cannot be the exclusive property of esoteric wisdom. They must be accessible, in some fashion, through the tradition, especially that part of the tradition which contains *sapienza volgare*. The primary authority on *sapienza volgare* for Vico is Tacitus. Like Vico himself at the beginning of the *Scienza nuova*'s section on Method, Tacitus in the *Autobiography* is portrayed as "descending" (*discendere*) into the characteristics of the mind as it is, the "counsels of utility." As an observer of human nature, Vico thinks that Tacitus has no serious equal. "With an incomparable metaphysical mind Tacitus contemplates man as he is."[114] In the *Autobiography*, Vico considers his discovery of Tacitus to be precisely the point at which he is able to conceive a "sketch" (*abozzo*) of the ideal eternal history.[115] The same relationship is present in the *Scienza nuova*, which presents the modifications of mind as the ground of the ideal eternal history. In the *Autobiography*, Vico associates his reading of Tacitus with his own ability to grasp "certain eternal properties of civil things (*certe eterne propietà delle cose civili*)."[116] The correspondence of these *propietà* with the *modificazioni* of the *Scienza nuova* may be seen by attending to Vico's use of Tacitus in the Elements. In the first part of this section, Vico says that *magnifiche oppenioni* about antiquity may be exposed as such "through the property of the human mind (*per tal propietà della mente umana*) adverted to by Tacitus in the *Life of Agricola* with this motto: "*omne ignotus pro magnifico est.*"[117] Some paragraphs later Tacitus is again credited with adverting to a "true property of human nature" (*vera propietà di natura umana*), namely that "minds once cowed are prone to superstition."[118] In the poetic metaphysics, Tacitus gives "noble expression" to an "eternal property" (*eternal propietà*) of the nature of human things, viz. that frightened man "no sooner imagine than they believe" (*fingunt simul creduntque*).[119] It is the "property of human mind adverted to by Tacitus" that enables Vico to conclude that what primitive men identify as "Jove" is really whatever they are seeing, imagining, or doing themselves.[120]

These examples are useful not only because they suggest the importance of Tacitus—we must dissent from Momigliano's judgment that Vico made little use of Tacitus[121]—but also because they indicate the direction of Vico's argument. The new scientist does not arbitrarily construct the elements of the civil world. He derives or constitutes them from the modifications of his own human mind. These are the eternal properties of mind which the new scientist makes neither by abstraction nor by composition. The creation of the elements of the civil world from the modifications is a "making," but one that depends on what we do not make. Because of this dependence, the civil world is not the product of free construction. It does not occur in a desacralized sphere, a sealed-off territory ruled by human beings with no divine influence. Vico understands all human making to occur under the "seeing eye of God with the aspect of his providence."[122] Providence not only sees, but also governs the world of nations, leading its makers to produce effects that are often different from and contrary to their intentions. Human creativity is real, but not absolute: it is situated within a providential context. Man is not the absolute creator, but the co-creator of the *mondo civile*. (We may see this even more clearly in the *Scienza nuova prima*, which describes providence as the "architect of the world of nations," and the human mind as its "craftsman" (*fabbro*).[123] Voegelin notices this text and comments that for Vico, "the process of the human mind in history is part of the process of divine creation."[124]

But how do humans create, or co-create, the elements of the *mondo civile*? To answer this question, one might desire greater clarity on precisely what Vico regards as the proper elements of the civil world. Near the end of his explanation of the *dipintura*, Vico recapitulates a comprehensive set of "all the prime elements of this world of nations."[125] Elsewhere in the text, he reduces the number to four, speaking of "the immense number of civil effects, which may all be traced back to these four causes, which, as will be observed throughout this work, are four elements, as it were, of the civil universe: that is, religion, marriage, asylum, and the first agrarian law."[126] If we identify the elements of the civil world with its principles, we may reduce them to three—religion, marriage, and burial. Whatever the precise identity of the elements of the *mondo civile*, it is evident that "religion" counts as a primary element. To make more concrete our contention that the elements of the civil world are genuine creations, we will attempt a brief elucidation of the sense in which the new scientist creates religion by deriving it from the modifications of mind.

To create religion as an element of the new science by deriving it from the modifications of mind is problematic for at least three reasons. First, the new science presumes that we possess a true understanding of what the modifications of mind are. It requires that we have access not merely to our own contingent notions about the mind, but to the eternal truths that belong to the human mind as such. Second, if the new science creates the elements of the *mondo civile* by deriving them from the modifications of mind, what makes Vico's particular derivation of the elements from the modifications necessary? Is an alternative derivation of "religion" possible? If so, what becomes of Vico's claim to provide a science that conforms to the Aristotelian requirement that *scientia debet esse de universalibus at aeternis*?[127] Third, if the scientific creation of elements is to prove illuminating for the apprehension of actual human origins, there must be some correspondence between "religion" as an artifact of the science and what is actually known about the particular "Joves" attested by the surviving texts.

Vico is vividly aware of each of these problems. They underlie his attempt to conceive a science that combines "philosophy" and "philology." The derivation of religion from the modifications will be "philosophical," since only philosophy is capable of understanding a concept as abstract as the "modifications of mind." (The poets down to the time of Homer, Vico says, are utterly unable to grasp the concept of the human mind.[128]) Yet it must also be philological—we cannot deduce the essential attributes of religion in a void, as if we had never learned anything about the concept through reading about it, or from the testimony of others. Philological evidence provides an indispensable but limited constraint on what the philosopher can derive from the modifications. The constraint is indispensable. Without it, philosophy will not recreate the elements of the civil world, but generate its own private fantasies that bear no relation to the historical experience of the race. This is why Vico insists that the *senso comune* must function as a criterion, a standard against which philosophical thinking about human origins can and must be tested. The grounds of truth from which the authentic elements of the civil world may be reconstructed are necessarily public. Yet the constraint is limited. Vico does not think that we have a repository of solid, unambiguous textual evidence ("facts") against which we can measure the accuracy of theoretical reconstruction. The textual evidence itself has been distorted and corrupted through the ages. What counts as solid philological evidence must itself be judged by some theory capable of distinguishing what belongs to the authentic *vera narratio* of the first humans—the fables that are *vere e severe istorie de' costumi*—and what ought to be consigned to the *museo dell'impostura*.[129] Vico's science must be guided by the textual remains, without being determined by them, since a central part of its task is to piece together the fragments of antiquity that have come down to us. ("The great fragments of antiquity, hitherto useless to science because they lay begrimed, broken, and scattered, shed great light when cleaned, pieced together, and restored."[130])

The rational reconstruction of the new scientist will not enable the new scientist to discover every contingent feature of every particular religion. But discovering the effects known by "certain history"—that is, the discovery of historical particulars—is not the chief aim of the *Scienza nuova*. Philosophy examines philology because it wants to discover the necessary and universal principles that underlie the contingent and particular. These are "the inseparable properties (*le propietà inseparabili*)" of things, which are "produced (*produtte*) from the modifications or guise with which the things are born."[131] The first essential property of mind from which Vico derives religion is fear (*timore*). To derive religion as a consequence of fear, Vico must first establish that fear is an essential property of the primitive mind. He does this by reflecting (with the assistance of Livy) on the general case in which a nation has become savage: "whenever a people has grown savage in arms so that human laws have no longer any place among it, the only powerful means of reducing it is religion."[132] Because the primitive mind is essentially savage, the only force that can bring it to any respect for order is religion, understood precisely as fear. It is only through the "terror" (*spavento*) of an imagined divinity that the fierce and violent *bestioni* are led to put themselves in order.[133] Vico reaffirms this in the Method: the "savagery and unbridled bestial freedom" of the giants can be tamed only by "the frightful thought of some divinity, the fear of whom is the only powerful means of reducing to duty a liberty gone wild."[134]

Fear, by itself, is not enough to account for the production of the gods. If it were, then Vico could simply accept the traditional saying that "fear first created gods in the world" (*primos in orbe deos fecit timor*).[135] Such fear, however, does not arise out of knowledge or the will to power. It is connected to the ignorance of the savage mind. Thus Vico concludes that "false religions were born not of imposture but of credulity."[136] Ignorance is thus the second essential modification of mind from which, together with fear, the new scientist must derive religion. The savage mind has only a "confused idea of divinity"[137]—an idea that, as we have seen, is a magnified projection of its own nature. That the first idea of the divine is self-magnification is not a contingent fact—it does not just *happen* to be the case that all gentile nations have a corporeal immanent idea of divinity—but a necessary consequence of ignorance. "The human mind, because of its indefinite nature, wherever it is lost in ignorance makes itself the rule of the universe in respect of everything it does not know."[138] Thus in the primitive case, "Jove" follows necessarily from the conjunction of fear and ignorance. Jove's necessity is confirmed by the fact that all gentile nations, acting independently and without knowledge of one another, produce a god that has the same essential characteristics of Jove. We may see this by juxtaposing Vico's dictum "Jove hurls his bolts and fells the giants, and every gentile nation had its Jove" with the axiom that "uniform ideas, born among peoples unknown to each other, must have a common ground of truth."[139]

As modifications of our own human minds, fear and ignorance seem jointly sufficient to account for the production of Jove. But if Vico exhibited all religion as a simple deduction from the nature of fearful and ignorant man, his position would be reducible to that of later naturalists, such as Condillac (as Milbank observes).[140] Moreover, Vico's descriptions of the way in which primitive man perceives the gods would make little sense. In the Poetic Logic, Vico writes that "the heavens were observed as the aspect of Jove by all the gentile nations the world over, to receive therefrom their laws in the auspices which they considered to be his divine admonishments or commands (*divini avvisi o comandi*)"[141] The giants do not simply fear the thundering sky because it threatens to destroy them. They also perceive it as a being who expresses moral disapproval. In order to perceive it in this way, they must have—in some form—the idea of *shame*. When Vico says that the nations were born in the "persuasion" of divine providence,[142] he presumes that something exists in the giants with which Providence, understood as an orator, is able to make contact. The giants could not be "persuaded" unless they had some capacity to feel shame. Hence, along with fear and ignorance, we must regard shame as the third essential modification from which the new scientist is able to derive "religion" as an element of the *mondo civile*. Though one can derive shame as a seed of religion from the *Scienza nuova*, a more direct confirmation of this reading is supplied by the *De constantia philologiae* of 1721, in which Vico locates *pudor* as a *principium humanitatis*.[143] The *bestioni* are not entirely non-human; traces of their original human nature remain, despite the magnitude of their fall from an original state of integrity. (It is relevant that Vico implies that they once had families, which were later "broken up" by the descent into promiscuity.[144])

To summarize—the new scientist proceeds on the model of the synthetic geometer, because he creates his own elements. This is not "pure" creation—just as the geometer ultimately abstracts his elements from metaphysical points, the new scientist draws his elements from the modifications of mind. But the mathematical analogy has its limits. Unlike both the geometer who "feigns" his point that is not a point, and the theological poet who imagines and feigns the gods, the new scientist does not feign his elements. He makes the *mondo civile* for himself, "but with a reality greater by just so much as the orders concerning human makings or doings (*faccende degli uomini*) are more real than points, lines, surfaces and figures."[145] If Vico considered that the elements of the *mondo civile* were merely feigned or arbitrarily posited, the new science itself would be hypothetical. But Vico understands his science as being anchored in reality. Its necessity is not simply that of conditional necessity. He expressly describes it as a metaphysics, that is, a discourse which is more than hypothetical. In Platonic terms, it belongs not to the third but to the final stage of the Divided Line.

The first type of making proper to the new scientist is the creation of the elements of the *mondo civile* from the modifications of mind. That the elements are created, yet ontologically dependent on that which is not humanly made, conforms precisely to the relation set forth in the *Idea of the Work* between "the world of human minds, which is the metaphysical world" and "the world of human spirits, which is the civil world or world of nations."[146]

Making as composition from elements

The second type of making that is practiced by the new scientist is the composition of the totality of the *mondo civile* from its primary elements. To show in detail how Vico reconstructs the world of nations from its origins would be to interpret the whole of the *Scienza nuova*. Once again, we must examine a single example of Vico's procedure. In the section entitled Poetic Politics, Vico endeavors to show that the state of nature has a character quite different from that described by thinkers like Grotius and Hobbes. For

Hobbes, the state of nature is a theoretical artifact, a construction whose nature is known by inference from the passions. Vico faults Hobbes neither for presuming the state of nature, nor for reducing the state of nature to a theoretical construction. In Axiom 31, Vico expresses a qualified but genuine approval of Hobbes's project, understood as the enrichment of Greek philosophy, by adding to it what it had lacked, the study of man in the whole society of the human race.[147] His criticism is that Hobbes misconstructs the state of nature. By neglecting the primacy of religion, he does not proceed from the authentic elements of the civil world.

The "state of nature" is "the state of the families, out of which, by general agreement of political theorists, the peoples and cities later arose."[148] Marriage, the second basic element of the civil world, produces the family through yielding children that are acknowledged by man and wife as their own. Without marriage, there are no families, but only copulations between partners who neither recognize one another nor their children. It is only with marriage—"a chaste carnal union consummated under the fear of some divinity," sealed by the sexual act performed in hiding and therefore with *pudore*[149]—that men couple with "certain women" who bear "certain children."[150] Religion and marriage, then, are the elements out of which Vico constructs the family, understood as a unit that includes husbands, wives and children.

But this construction of the family is not yet complete. Not every giant is able to become a father and thereby constitute a family with certain women and certain children. Only a small group of the *bestioni*, those capable of "checking their bestial habit of wandering wild through the great forest of the earth," are able to perform such a feat.[151] This requires both the moral strength of *conatus* and the physical act of taming the forests and cultivating the fields. Thus "from the nefarious state of the outlaw world some few of the sturdiest first withdrew and established families, with whom and by whom they brought the fields under cultivation."[152] If only a few of the giants were able to become fathers, the remaining giants were left to run wild and fight amongst themselves. But such a state could not last forever. Impelled to seek their own preservation, the more perceptive of these giants would have brought themselves under the yoke of the fathers. These are the giants whom Vico calls the *secondi*, the second comers who approach the families created by the fathers "through the necessity of saving their lives."[153] Thus they "gave an origin to 'society' as it is properly said, through the communication principally of utility, and in consequence, base and servile."[154]

Vico is thus able to perform a complete construction of the family by combining the first two elements of the science—religion and marriage—in accordance with two eternal truths about human nature—first, the necessity of strength to overcome passions, second, the natural desire of humans to seek their own preservation. The complete construction of the family thus contains four components: fathers, wives, natural children, and the refugees who "were called *famoli*, from whom principally the families (*famiglie*) were named."[155] Though Vico takes his own account of the family to be superior to that of the princes of the natural law, who either neglect the family altogether or construe it anachronistically, he does not entirely disown their accounts. Rather, he considers them as containing partial truths that must be woven together to form a coherent whole. The perceptive refugees who seek protection are "the simpletons of Grotius" and "the abandoned men of Pufendorf." Those from whom they seek protection correspond to "the violent men of Hobbes."[156] Vico evidently wants to preserve the "realism" of the early modern princes of natural law, while rejecting their tendency, in accordance with the conceit of scholars, to impose advanced rationality onto the primitive mind. Thus he is able both to construct his own account from the elements of his science, and to rule out alternative accounts which imagine the first men using conceptually advanced language—one must always remember that the "cyclopses" are still mute—to deliberate about the advantages of peace and the means that most efficiently lead to peace.

The absurdity of other accounts, juxtaposed with the consistency of Vico's own, supplies the latter with a kind of "negative confirmation." To the extent that it respects the crude nature of the primitive mind, its plausibility far exceeds that of the competing theories. Philology provides a more positive sort of confirmation. It enables Vico to "ascertain" what is known from philosophy. In addition to the (perhaps somewhat dubious) etymology of *famiglie* from *famoli*, the surviving textual remains point to the inclusion of refugees within the original families. "In all ancient nations," Vico declares in the Axioms, "we find everywhere clients and clienteles, which are best understood as vassals and fiefs."[157]

Why does this matter? If our access to the nature of the family state proceeds by making, why not hold that one theoretical construction is as good as another? A sense of how Vico would answer this question may be had from the following passage:

> Philologists and philosophers have commonly supposed that families in the so-called state of nature included children only; whereas in fact they included *famoli* also, and that was the original reason for their being called families. On this maimed economy (*manca iconomica*) a false politics (*falsa politica*) has been erected.[158]

Vico evidently thinks that a sound construction of the state of nature—that is, a composition that proceeds from the authentic elements of the *mondo civile* and is governed by the relevant modifications of mind, has political consequences of the first importance. It is difficult, as recent commentators have begun to see, to follow Croce's estimate of Vico's thought as "essentially apolitical."

The construction of the new scientist, as we have seen, is not arbitrary making. It is governed by the modifications of mind, the eternal truths about human nature with which it must cohere, and by the *senso comune*, which Vico conceives as a criterion, respect for which will ensure that the scientific construction of the world of nations will remain continuous with beliefs actually held by those nations, rather than being a private fantasy of the advanced philosopher. Because the creation of the new scientist is subject to philosophical and philological constraints, it cannot accurately be described as free construction. But neither does it seem to be "rule-governed" in any clear sense. Although method is useful for disposing of the fruits of human creativity, it is not a substitute for creativity.

The new science cannot be reduced to a rule-governed method. But to infer that it is therefore a work of *fantasia* would be not only a gross *non sequitur*, but also violate the texts. Vico describes his work as *una severa analisi de' pensieri umani*.[159] Advising prospective readers of the *Scienza nuova* in 1730, Vico describes the work as composed according to a geometrical method, "entirely metaphysical and abstract in conception."[160] To understand it, it is necessary to "divest yourself of everything corporeal and of everything to which this gives rise in pure mind, and therefore, for a while, to put the imagination to sleep and lull the memory."[161] Vico does not seem to think that imaginative empathy is the key to understanding the original form of the civil world.[162] Although he describes his journey into the mind of primitive humanity as a process of "descending" (*discendere*) from refined to savage nature, he nowhere describes the descent as accomplished by the imagination.[163] The descent is achieved through the painstaking labors of the scholar. "To discover the way in which this first human thinking arose in the gentile world, we encountered exasperating difficulties which have cost us the research of a good twenty years."[164] This research produces understanding of the authentic constitution of primitive reality, but not the capacity to imagine it. Vico holds that it is "naturally denied to us to enter into the *vasta immaginativa* of those first men, whose minds were not in the least abstract, refined, or spiritualized, because they were entirely immersed in the senses, buffeted by the passions, buried in the body."[165] Understanding the operation of poetic *fantasia* is extremely difficult, but imagining it is literally impossible. Our civilized natures ensure that "we cannot at all imagine and can understand only by great toil the poetic nature of these first men," Vico says in the *Idea of the Work*.[166] He repeats this theme—"difficult to understand, impossible to imagine"—three times within the body of the *Scienza nuova*.[167] In his final citation of the theme, he describes it as an "important observation" (*importante osservazione*).[168]

Vico consistently privileges the understanding over the imagination, which he considers to play an auxiliary and subordinate role. What most visibly separates his notion of reason from "rationalistic" conceptions is his emphasis upon the creative power of *ingenium* (*l'ingegno*). This is not to be confused with *fantasia*—Vico clearly distinguishes it from *ingenium*, despite the conflation of the concepts that one finds in any number of commentators. For example the *Autobiography*'s digression on learning speaks of memory, imagination, and *ingenium* as distinct powers to be trained by distinct studies, viz. poetry, history and synthetic geometry.[169] Within the *Scienza nuova*, one may cite Vico's statement that Homer never mentions anything painted because "painting abstracts the surfaces absolutely, and this is a labor calling for the greatest *ingegno*."[170] Homeric man thus possesses *fantasia* to an extraordinary degree, as do all men who are weak in reason,[171] but he does not excel in the highest form of *ingegno*. That *ingegno* is more creative than *fantasia* may be seen in the ninth philosophical proof of the true Homer, where Vico ascribes the conflation of *fantasia* and *ingenium* to the returned barbarian times. There he holds that the two, although both aspects of memory, must be distinguished. Imagination is memory when it "alters or counterfeits things" (*l'altera e contrafà*).[172] (Bergin and Fisch's rendering of *contrafà* as "imitates" is misleading—it dulls the sharp edge of Vico's critique of *fantasia*.) *Ingegno* is memory when it "gives things a new turn or puts them into proper arrangement and relationship" (*le contorna e pone in acconcezza ed assettamento*).[173] *Ingegno* is closer to *scienza* than *fantasia*, because its exercise is closer to divine making. Vico never compares the use of *fantasia* to divine operation, but he does not hesitate to liken human and divine *ingegno*. In the *Prima Risposta* to critics of the *De antiquissima*, he writes: "l'ingegno umano delle arti è, come la natura nell'universo è l'ingegno di Dio."[174]

What is *ingegno*, if not another name for *fantasia*? In the *De antiquissima*, Vico defines *ingenium* as the power "by which man is capable of contemplating and constructing (*facendi*) likenesses."[175] As Lachterman observes, Vico brings *ingenium* in close relation to *scientia*, as when he declares that "*scientia* itself is nothing but making things correspond to themselves in beautiful proportion, which only those who excel in *ingenium* can do."[176] *Ingenium* is "the power to connect disparate and diverse things."[177] The whole of the *New Science* may understood as a massive exercise of *ingenium* that enables Vico to know the nature of the *mondo civile*. Vico engages in historical construction on the grandest possible scale, as he narrates the ideal eternal history.

Is this type of reconstructive narration advisable? Nietzsche hopes for "a time when one will wisely refrain from all constructions of the world process or of the history of mankind."[178] Nietzsche's complaint in *The Use and Abuse of History for Life* is about those who fail to recognize sources of life and energy that lie outside the historical. Can Vico be accused of this failure? When the reader contemplates the causes and effects of the civil world, he will "experience in his mortal body a divine pleasure as he contemplates in the divine ideas this world of nations in all the extent of its places, times, and varieties."[179] This is not possible, however, for any reader. It can happen only for the exceptional reader who is willing to purify or spiritualize his mind, to put his imagination to sleep for a while. The reader must take seriously Vico's rendition in the oration *De mente heroica* of the Platonic concept of wisdom—*purgatrix, sanatrix, consummatrix* of the interior man.[180] Only a mind so purged can share in the creation proper to the "divinity of an infinite free mind."[181] Such a mind will taste—and not just speculate about—the divine pleasure in which "to know and to make (*il conoscer e 'l fare*) are the same thing."[182]

This divine pleasure is accessible to those who, in contradistinction to either the Stoics and the Epicureans, have the "clean and pure heart" that Vico ascribes to metaphysics.[183] To have a clean and pure heart requires humility, a radical loss of self: "in metaphysics the one who profits is the one who suffers the loss of himself in the meditation of this science," Vico tells the critics of his metaphysics."[184] At the highest point of self-loss, we discover not that we exist, or that we exist as a thinking thing, but that God thinks in us. "Deus in me cogitat; in Deo igitur meam ipsius mentem cognosco."[185]

Citing the work of Gentile, Christian Moevs writes: "the *Scienza nuova* is ultimately not about the things it seems to be about. It is a mapping, a coming to self-knowledge, of the human spirit."[186] The point of the "New Science, or metaphysics"[187] is to know oneself. Not, of course, as an isolated, autonomous being—considered this way, we are "nothing before God," as the *De antiquissima* says. But self-nullity is not Vico's final word. To know oneself as a being that is finite and created is to know oneself as a "disposition of infinite and eternal being."[188] In the *De mente heroica*, Vico reminds those who despair that the origins of their mind are divine, and that they must not wait for learning to drop into their bosoms from heaven while they slumber. The remedy is for the mind to become creative—"stir yourselves up with a effective desire (*efficaci desidero*) for wisdom," Vico exhorts his auditors. "Stir your minds up, enkindle the divinity that fills you."[189] By enkindling this divinity, we not only experience a divine pleasure caused by God thinking in us, but come to know ourselves as that in which divinity dwells. When we recreate the *mondo civile* with purified mind by remaking the *corso che fanno le nazioni*,[190] we come to experience a divine pleasure that testifies to the divine within us.

The divine lives in us—but it is not imprisoned in us. Vico thinks that we are finite dispositions of the infinite—*nosse, velle, posse finitum, quod tendit ad infinitum*.[191] The finite cannot contain the infinite. The active reader with pure and clean heart participates in the construction of the *mondo civile*. In so doing, he is able not only to know himself, but what is beyond himself. Those who can "unite themselves to the infinite wisdom of God"—the only real goal of the learned, as the penultimate sentence of the *Scienza nuova* suggests[192]—will learn something about God. The philosophers have attempted to contemplate God by seeking to understand the divine will as it operates in the world of rocks, stones, and stars. If Vico is right, a better route to such a union—a way that is more creative and more pleasurable—is to be had by retracing the providential design of God within the world of nations. Thus, above the order of natural things, metaphysics contemplates God in an act of ecstasy.[193]

EPILOGUE

The six authors we have considered are committed to some version of the principle *verum et factum convertuntur*. We have distinguished between theological and secularizing applications of the principle. Although we began our exposition with Aquinas, one might hazard a guess that the true origin of the 'theological' version of the principle is to be found in John 3:21, where Christ tells Nicodemus: "ὁ δὲ ποιῶν τὲν ἀλήθειαν ἔρχεται πρὸς τὸ φῶς." The Vulgate renders the Greek precisely: "*qui autem facit veritatem, venit ad lucem.*" Vernacular translations, from Tyndale and Luther through the King James Version to contemporary editions, have avoided precision in favor of "he who does what is true" or something similar. But, as James O'Donnell observes in his magisterial edition of St. Augustine's *Confessions*, "what 'doing the truth' might mean is anybody's guess, and the phrase is probably preferred out of fear of the implication in 'making truth' that the truth does not exist until it is made."[1] This fear may be unmasked as a product of the modern assumption that no real alternative to the secular *verum-factum* exists. For both Radical Orthodoxy and the tradition, this fear is unjustified. It is coherent to follow the words of Christ and think of human beings as making the truth, in a sense which affirms that human making is more creative than the imitation of nature, yet is not cut off from the divine *Logos*, because its creativity is fundamentally a finite participation in the infinite *Verbum*.

This, we have argued, is the perspective common to Aquinas, Cusanus, and Vico, with deep roots in Augustine. One may locate the Augustinian *verum-factum* with precision in Book 10 of the *Confessions*. In this book, Augustine wants to supply the fruit of his confessions by telling the reader not what he has been, but what he is. For God to disclose the essence of man would be simple, Augustine says: "you know all of him, for you made him" (*scis eius omnia, quia fecisti eum*).[2] For humans, the situation is different. Self-knowledge is difficult because we did not make ourselves. Yet it is not impossible. Though we do not originate ourselves, we can remake ourselves through narrative, isolating defining moments, describing relevant episodes, composing the existential and the intellectual into a work that is integral but incomplete.³ Augustine makes the truth about himself, but he does not make it up. The *Confessions* are able to narrate the role of providence in Augustine's life because they are multiple acts of self-fashioning, weaving the broken fragments of his life into a providential unity, manifesting his works that are wrought in God.

But what enables Augustine to have any assurance that his narrative is an authentic self-construction, rather than a merely contingent act that serves to promote his own interests against others? What must be the case if human construction is to participate in truth, and not just an exercise in the augmentation of power and utility? Augustine's answer to this question is also contained in Book 10 of the *Confessions*. If Augustine is to understand himself, he must do so by productively arranging what lies scattered and confused in his memory. If he is to seek happiness, he must already know what happiness is—otherwise he would be unable to recognize it when he found it. This requires that happiness be somehow present in the memory. But if happiness is nothing other than union with God, it follows that God must also exist in the memory, although (as Augustine notes) he cannot be confined to memory. Human effort does not cause God to exist in the memory, but God has left a trace of Himself in creaturely memory. There is no desire for happiness without a memory of happiness, no memory of happiness without a prior taste of happiness, and no prior taste of happiness without grace. Neither true knowledge nor right action, the modes of the human ascent, are possible without a memory illumined by grace.

Augustine, in short, never thinks of human *ratio* as anything other than participation in the *ratio divina*. The *libri Platonicorum* teach him that reason is not a material thing but a spiritual substance that derives its authority from its participation in the *Logos*, although they fail to teach him that this *Logos* was made flesh, and thus prove incapable of inspiring charity. In correspondence with Leo Strauss, Eric Voegelin acutely raises the question "whether a *ratio* that, unlike the classical and Christian, does not derive its authority from its share in divine being is still in any sense a *ratio*."[4] Our argument has been that the secularizing architects of modernity—Bacon, Descartes, and Hobbes—engage in the willful detachment of human *ratio* from divine *ratio*, and thus paradoxically inaugurate postmodern irrationalism and nihilism.[5] They do so through preserving—and indeed emphasizing—the constructive character of reason, while severing construction with its connection to recollection and illumination.

Such an assertion may seem odd, given the heavy investment of secular Enlightenment in the rhetoric of illumination. Consider the example of Bacon once again. That Bacon preserves the rhetoric of illumination is clear enough. But where does the light of Baconian science come from? It is not entirely impossible to read Bacon as a kind of divine illuminationist. One can appeal to the aphorism where Bacon declares *principium autem sumendum a Deo*: "now the beginning is to be taken from God," who is the *author boni*, *et pater luminum.*⁶ But the actual function of this passage is to give religious sanction to a project that seeks to drive a wedge between faith and reason, giving to faith "only what belongs to faith." The real source of illumination appears to be the *lumen naturae*, which cannot be conclusively identified with either experience or the understanding, both of which themselves stand in need of illumination. It is true that Bacon urges the necessity of purgation, but he does not think that cleansing the mind of its idols is sufficient to overcome the feebleness of the mind and the subtlety of nature. According to Coleridge, Bacon "tells us that the mind of man is an edifice not built with human hands, which need only be purged of its idols and idolatrous services to become the temple of the true and living Light."⁷ Coleridge's misreading of Bacon is ingenious and perhaps exemplary for a radically orthodox appropriation of modern thought (something similar would apply to Vico's use of Bacon), but it is not Bacon himself. It is Bacon placed within a Platonic framework.

But why might Bacon require positioning within such a framework? His declared intention is to effect a harmony between the nature of mind and the nature of things, to prepare the bridal chamber of the mind and the universe.⁸ No such harmony can be discovered or constructed, however, unless we already have some anticipation of what this harmony would look like. In Platonic terms, we must already have an acquaintance with its *eidos*, if we are to engage in a quest which can terminate in the recognition of this harmony. In detaching reason from faith, by insisting on the totally autonomous and non-overlapping character of what he calls the "two differing illuminations,"⁹ Bacon deprives us of the resources whereby we might possess some confidence in attaining or approximating this harmony. Bacon loves to quote Solomon: "the glory of God is to conceal a thing; but the glory of the king is to find it out."¹⁰ But he fails to add that the divine–human game of hide and seek cannot be meaningfully played unless we already have an anticipation of what God has concealed, an anticipation that comes through grace by (as Augustine would have it) the action of the eternal teacher in all acts of knowing.

In separating himself from the Platonic–Augustinian tradition, Bacon must devise another way to judge the success of human reason. He does so by measuring knowledge not according to its potency to facilitate recollection or participation, but through its ability to "establish and extend the power and dominion of the human race itself over the whole universe."¹¹ The project of nourishing the *libido dominandi* enables man to emulate divine creation in his own autonomous sphere, and to become God. *Hominem homini Deum esse*, the penultimate aphorism of *Novum Organum* Book I concludes. Man is a God to man.¹² The seeds of Nietzsche are already in Bacon, as the homage to Bacon in *Ecce Homo* itself suggests: "we are very far from knowing enough about Lord Bacon, the first realist in every great sense of that word, to know everything he did, wanted, and experienced in himself."¹³

Bacon and Nietzsche share an optimistic exaltation of human creativity, conceived in secular fashion. With Bacon, creation and reason seem to go together. For Nietzsche, it may appear that man cannot be particularly rational, but (pending the overcoming of nihilism) is able to be creative. But at least one reader has suggested the questionable character of Nietzsche's donation of creative power to man. Stanley Rosen argues that it is "superficially correct, but at a deeper level profoundly wrong, to say that man creates value. No human being creates anything, despite Nietzsche's exoteric rhetoric: the world is a work of art giving birth to itself. It is 'the will to power—and nothing beyond that!'"[14] Behind Nietzsche is not only the Spinozist *amor fati*, as Rosen correctly suggests, but also the Lucretian *natura creatrix*, in which humans are utterly powerless. As Vico saw clearly, "fate" and "chance" appear to be diametric opposites, but in fact are only different strategies for the radical denial of Providence.

Post-Nietzschean strategies consist largely of accommodations to nihilism, or the invention of narcotics designed to counter its effects. Against this, Radical Orthodoxy seeks to recover a tradition according to which human reason is indeed constructive and creative—not despite its sharing in divine *ratio*, but precisely *because* it is a participation in the divine. If we deny the participation of the human in the divine, and the hidden but real presence of the divine in the human, it is difficult to see how the mind can be either rational or creative, unless one restricts these terms to denote knowledge and manipulation of a fixed, spatialized secular order in which it is increasingly difficult to find meaning.[15]

Vattimo perceptively remarks that God is dead, and man is not doing so well either. If we restrict ourselves to the secular concept of knowing-as-making, such an outcome appears inevitable. Man becomes the prosthetic God that Freud lamented. Our hope is that a retrieval of the theological conception of creative knowledge can play some role in reclaiming the dignity of making, which secular modernity superficially affirms but ultimately denies. *Qui autem facit veritatem, venit ad lucem, ut manifestentur eius opera, quia in Deo sunt opera.*

NOTES

PROLOGUE

1. Hacking, *The Social Construction of What?* p. 1.
2. Hacking, *The Social Construction of What?* p. 41.
3. Hacking, *The Social Construction of What?* p. 47.
4. Hacking, *The Social Construction of What?* p. 49.
5. F.H. Jacobi, quoted in David Lachterman, *The Ethics of Geometry: A Genealogy of Modernity*, p. 9.
6. Stanley Rosen, *The Question of Being: A Reversal of Heidegger*, pp. xx, 285. And cf. xix, where Rosen writes that it "remains permanently unclear why Heidegger's resolution of the problem of nihilism is not itself nihilism on the grand scale."
7. Lachterman, *The Ethics of Geometry*, p. 6.
8. Lachterman, *The Ethics of Geometry*, p. vii.
9. Lachterman, *The Ethics of Geometry*, p. 4.
10. Lachterman, *The Ethics of Geometry*, p. 1.
11. Lachterman, *The Ethics of Geometry*, p. ix.
12. Lachterman, *The Ethics of Geometry*, p. 6.

1 THOMAS AQUINAS

1. R.G. Collingwood, *The Principles of Art*, pp. 15–17. The reader will note that we have collapsed Collingwood's (2) and (3) into our (2).
2. Collingwood, *The Principles of Art*, p. 16.
3. Collingwood, *The Principles of Art*, p. 16.
4. Collingwood, *The Principles of Art*, p. 16.
5. On this point, see L.P. Hemming, "*Quod Impossibile Est! Aquinas and Radical Orthodoxy*," in *Radical Orthodoxy?—A Catholic Enquiry*, p. 89.
6. St. Thomas, *Summa theologiae*, 1.14.8.corp.
7. St. Thomas, *Summa theologiae*, 1.14.11.corp.
8. St. Thomas, *Summa theologiae*, 1.14.11.corp.
9. St. Thomas, *Summa theologiae*, 1.14.11.corp.
10. St. Thomas, *Summa theologiae*, 1.45.1.corp.
11. Collingwood, *The Principles of Art*, p. 16.
12. St. Thomas, *Summa theologiae*, 1.45.2.corp.
13. St. Thomas, *Summa theologiae*, 1.45.2.corp.
14. St. Thomas, *Summa theologiae*, 1.14.8.ad 3m.
15. St. Thomas, *Summa theologiae*, 1.14.8.corp.
16. St. Thomas, *Summa theologiae*, 1.15.3.corp.
17. St. Thomas, *Summa theologiae*, 1.15.3.corp.

18 St. Thomas, *Summa theologiae*, 1.14.16.ad 2m.
19 St. Thomas, *Summa theologiae*, 1.14.16.corp.
20 See Jacques Maritain, *Creative Intuition in Art and Poetry*, pp. 83–4, and p. 101 for the clearest distinction between the poet and the craftsman.
21 Maritain, *Creative Intuition in Art and Poetry*, p. 81.
22 See St. Thomas, *Summa theologiae*, 1.41.2.corp.
23 See St. Thomas, *Summa theologiae*, 1.41.3.corp. for the rejection of "genitus de nihilo."
24 St. Thomas, *Summa theologiae*, 1.32.1.ad 3m.
25 St. Thomas, *Summa theologiae*, 1.32.1.ad 3m.
26 St. Thomas, *Summa theologiae*, 1.32.1.ad 3m.
27 St. Thomas, *Summa theologiae*, 1.32.1.ad 3m.
28 Compare St. Thomas, *Summa theologiae*, 1.27.1.corp. and *Summa theologiae*, 1.44.2.ad 1m.
29 St. Thomas, *Summa theologiae*, 1.27.1.corp.
30 St. Thomas, *Summa theologiae*, 1.45.6.corp.
31 St. Thomas, *Summa theologiae*, 1.45.5.corp. Cf. *Summa theologiae*, 1.31.3.ad 3m, "solus Deus creat."
32 Maritain, *Creative Intuition in Art and Poetry*, p. 100.
33 Maritain, *Creative Intuition in Art and Poetry*, p. 100. Although Maritain's habit of speaking of the exemplar in the human mind as the "creative idea" (which is possessed by a "creative Self") may not be strictly faithful to the texts, he is on solid ground when he contends that the Thomist exemplar, in both the divine and human case, is not "an ideal model sitting for the artist in his own brain, the work supposedly being a *copy* or portrait of it. This would make of art a cemetery of imitations." As Maritain says, "the work is an original, not a copy" (*Creative Intuition*, p. 100).
34 Collingwood, *The Principles of Art*, p. 133.
35 St. Thomas, *Summa theologiae*, 1.44.3.corp.
36 Although Aquinas does not think that God's speaking and his making are separate, he does think they must be distinguished, unless His *genitum* is to be confused with a *factum*. "Speaking" and "creating" are not at all synonymous for Aquinas.
37 Maritain, *Art and Scholasticism and the Frontiers of Poetry*, p. 60.
38 Thomas Aquinas, *In 1 Sent.*, d. 32, q. I, 3, 2, quoted in Maritain, *Art and Scholasticism and the Frontiers of Poetry*, p. 60.
39 Josef Pieper, *The Silence of St. Thomas*, p. 48.
40 St. Thomas, *Summa theologiae*, 1.22.3.corp.
41 See St. Thomas, *Summa theologiae*, 1.14.16.ad 1m., 1.15.3.corp.
42 Maritain, *Art and Scholasticism and the Frontiers of Poetry*, p. 60.
43 St. Thomas, *Summa theologiae*, 1–2.94.4.corp.
44 St. Thomas, *Summa theologiae*, 1–2.94.5.corp.
45 St. Thomas, *Summa theologiae*, 1–2.95.2.corp.
46 Maritain, *Art and Scholasticism and the Frontiers of Poetry*, p. 195. Cf. Maritain, *Creative Intuition and Poetry*, pp. 75–108.
47 This strikes us as a departure from the Aristotelian paradigm of *techne*, which takes precise foreknowledge to be a condition of making. But it may be possible to find traces of another conception of *techne* in Aristotle. In his thoughtful treatment of Aristotelian *phronesis* and *techne*, Joseph Dunne suggests that in passages where Aristotle emphasizes the analogy of *techne* to nature and downplays the role of conscious deliberation, he approaches a concept of *techne* "in which *noesis* and *poiesis* are not separable, linear sequences, such that one retraces in reverse order the steps marked out by the other, but are, rather,

NOTES

interwoven in one process which is at the same time intelligent *and* productive." See Dunne, *Back to the Rough Ground*, p. 334.

48 Maritain, *Art and Scholasticism and the Frontiers of Poetry*, p. 60.
49 Mark Jordan, "Creation and Intelligibility in Aquinas: A Reading of the *Contra Gentiles*" (unpublished Ph.D. thesis, 1977), p. 103.
50 Jordan, "Creation and Intelligibility in Aquinas: A Reading of the *Contra Gentiles*," p. 103.
51 Cajetan, *Scripta Philosophica. De nominum analogia. De Conceptu Entis*, n. 3, quoted in Ralph McInerny, *Aquinas and Analogy*, p. 5.
52 Cajetan, commentary on Aquinas, Summa theologiae 1.16.6, quoted in McInerny, *Aquinas and Analogy*, p. 15.
53 Cajetan, *De nominum analogia*, n. 11, quoted in McInerny, *Aquinas and Analogy*, p. 20.
54 Cajetan, *De nominum analogia*, n. 11, quoted in McInerny, *Aquinas and Analogy*, p. 20.
55 See James Anderson, *The Bond of Being*, pp. 132–40.
56 See Anderson, *The Bond of Being*, p. 292.
57 Anderson, *The Bond of Being*, p. 312.
58 See McInerny, *Aquinas and Analogy*, pp. 3–29.
59 See David Burrell, *Analogy and Philosophical Language*, pp. 14–15.
60 E.L. Mascall, *Existence and Analogy*, p. 106.
61 Mascall, *Existence and Analogy*, p. 110.
62 Milbank even goes so far as to detect an "alliance of the post-critical perspective with proper proportionality." See John Milbank, *The Word Made Strange*, p. 9.
63 This has been argued by many. See, for example, Anderson, *The Bond of Being*, p. 238 and J-L. Marion, *On Descartes' Metaphysical Prism*, p. 225.
64 Barth, *Church Dogmatics* I (preface), quoted in Fergus Kerr, *After Aquinas: Versions of Thomism*, p. 35. Kerr's discussion of the entire problem merits consultation.
65 Mascall, *Existence and Analogy*, pp. 99–100.
66 Anderson, *The Bond of Being*, p. 112.
67 St. Thomas, *Summa theologiae*, 1.44.1.corp.
68 See Rudi te Velde, *Participation and Substantiality in Thomas Aquinas*. See also Kerr, *After Aquinas*, pp. 42–51.
69 Anne Davenport, *Measure of a Different Greatness*, p. 291.
70 Davenport, *Measure of a Different Greatness*, p. 285 (author's emphasis).
71 Davenport, *Measure of a Different Greatness*, p. 296.
72 Davenport, *Measure of a Different Greatness*, p. 193. It should be noted that Davenport approves of the tendencies in Olivi and Scotus that lead to Descartes and the modern scientific project. Accordingly, her work cannot be dismissed by those who want to domesticate Scotus, or to distance his thought from the intellectual origins of modernity, as a quest for villains.
73 St. Thomas, *Summa theologiae*, 1.45.8.ad 4m.
74 St. Thomas, *Summa theologiae* 1.117.1.corp. Cf. Maritain's helpful clarification of the meaning of this maxim in *Art and Scholasticism*, p. 202.

2 NICOLAUS CUSANUS

1 Dorothy Sayers, *The Mind of the Maker*, p. 22.
2 The explicit linkage of *imago dei* with human creativity first occurs in the Renaissance, with writers like Petrarch. See Charles Trinkaus, *In Our Image and Likeness: Humanity and Divinity in Italian Humanist Thought* and, more recently, the subtle readings of Giuseppe Mazzotta, *Cosmopoiesis: The Renaissance Experiment*.

3 Gadamer was among the first to suggest that Cusanus's "real importance" lies in his having "turned the distinction between the divine and the human mind into something positive" (*Truth and Method*, p. 434).
4 Karsten Harries, *Infinity and Perspective*, p. 191.
5 *Idiota de Mente*, p. 41. At times I have further literalized the already very literal renderings of Miller's edition. Also worth consulting is M.L. Führer, *The Layman on Wisdom and the Mind*.
6 The term "coniectura" is central for Cusanus, as the very title of his *De coniecturis* of 1440 would suggest. Vico will later couch his *Liber Metaphysicus* in "conjectural" terms, although existing translations tend to suppress his frequent use of the verb *coniecere* in that work.
7 *Idiota de Mente*, p. 43. Cf. St. Thomas, *De veritate*, question 10, article 1 (body).
8 *Idiota de Mente*, p. 43.
9 *Idiota de Mente*, p. 43.
10 *Idiota de Mente*, p. 45.
11 *Idiota de Mente*, p. 45.
12 *Idiota de Mente*, p. 45.
13 *Idiota de Mente*, p. 45.
14 *Idiota de Mente*, p. 45.
15 *Idiota de Mente*, p. 45.
16 *Idiota de Mente*, p. 45.
17 *Idiota de Mente*, p. 45.
18 *Idiota de Mente*, p. 45.
19 *Idiota de Mente*, p. 45.
20 *Idiota de Mente*, p. 45.
21 *Idiota de Mente*, p. 47.
22 *Idiota de Mente*, p. 47.
23 *Idiota de Mente*, p. 47.
24 *Idiota de Mente*, p. 47.
25 *Idiota de Mente*, p. 47.
26 *Idiota de Mente*, p. 47.
27 *Idiota de Mente*, p. 47.
28 *Idiota de Mente*, p. 47.
29 *Idiota de Mente*, p. 47.
30 *Idiota de Mente*, p. 47. This lack of straightforward identification suggests that things are more complicated than recognized by those (e.g., Kristeller) content to describe Cusanus as a "15th-century Platonist." Gadamer more adequately notices that Cusanus's use of the *Verbum* in *De docta ignorantia* leads him to a conception where "the word is for him no less than the mind itself, not a diminished or weakened manifestation of it. Knowing this constitutes the superiority of the Christian philosopher over the Platonist" (*Truth and Method*, p. 435).
31 *Idiota de Mente*, p. 47
32 *Idiota de Mente*, p. 47.
33 *Idiota de Mente*, p. 49.
34 See *Idiota de Sapientia*, trans. M.L. Führer in *The Layman on Wisdom and the Mind*, p. 25.
35 *Idiota de Mente*, p. 49.
36 *Idiota de Mente*, p. 49.
37 *Idiota de Mente*, p. 49.
38 *Idiota de Mente*, p. 49.
39 *Idiota de Mente*, p. 51.
40 *Idiota de Mente*, p. 51.

NOTES

41 *Idiota de Mente*, p. 51.
42 *Idiota de Mente*, p. 51. See *Idiota*, p. 86 for a similar formulation. In his mastery of copious discourse, the layman has appropriated the function of the orator as well as the philosopher.
43 *Idiota de Mente*, p. 51.
44 See *Idiota de Mente*, p. 53.
45 *Idiota de Mente*, p. 51. Here I follow Miller in rendering *virtus* by "power."
46 *Idiota de Mente*, p. 51.
47 *Idiota de Mente*, p. 53.
48 *Idiota de Mente*, p. 53.
49 *Idiota de Mente*, p. 63.
50 *Idiota de Mente*, p. 55.
51 *Idiota de Mente*, p. 55.
52 *Idiota de Mente*, p. 57.
53 *Idiota de Mente*, p. 57.
54 *Idiota de Mente*, p. 57.
55 *Idiota de Mente*, p. 61.
56 *Idiota de Mente*, p. 63.
57 I am indebted to Jason Taylor for discussions of this passage and his assistance in formulating this point.
58 *Idiota de Mente*, p. 63–5.
59 *Idiota de Mente*, p. 65.
60 *Idiota de Mente*, p. 65.
61 *Idiota de Mente*, p. 65.
62 *Idiota de Mente*, p. 65.
63 *Idiota de Mente*, p. 65.
64 *Idiota de Mente*, p. 65.
65 *Idiota de Mente*, p. 65.
66 *Idiota de Mente*, p. 67.
67 *Idiota de Mente*, p. 67.
68 *Idiota de Mente*, p. 67. Some association between rustic simplicity and power of apprehension may also be found in Aquinas. See John Milbank and Catherine Pickstock, *Truth in Aquinas*, p. 14.
69 *Idiota de Mente*, p. 67.
70 *Idiota de Mente*, p. 67.
71 *Idiota de Mente*, p. 71.
72 *Idiota de Mente*, p. 71.
73 *Idiota de Mente*, p. 71.
74 *Idiota de Mente*, p. 71.
75 *Idiota de Mente*, p. 71.
76 *De coniecturis* 2.14 (Hoffmann, Wilpert, Bormann p. 170), "homo enim deus est, sed non absolute, quoniam homo; humanus est igitur deus." Watts comments on this passage in her introduction to *De ludo globi*, p. 19. Beck cites it in *Early German Philosophy*, p. 70, though he misstates both the book and chapter in which the passage appears. (Isaiah Berlin quotes Beck and further disseminates his mistake in *Vico and Herder*, p. 142.) Cf. the opening of *De Beryllo*, cited by Harries in *Infinity and Perspective*, p. 187.
77 *Idiota de Mente*, p. 71.
78 *Idiota de Mente*, p. 71.
79 *Idiota de Mente*, p. 73.
80 *Idiota de Mente*, p. 73.
81 *Idiota de Mente*, p. 73.
82 *Idiota de Mente*, p. 73.

83 See *Idiota de Mente*, p. 51.
84 *Idiota de Mente*, p. 51.
85 *Idiota de Mente*, p. 75.
86 *Idiota de Mente*, p. 75.
87 Ernst Cassirer, *The Individual and the Cosmos*, p. 44. Milbank notes Cassirer's (mis)reading in *The Religious Dimension in the Thought of Giambattista Vico 1668–1744*, vol. 1, p. 31. Watts calls it "fascinating but dated"; see her introduction to *De ludo globi*, p. 13.
88 *Idiota de Mente*, p. 75–7.
89 *Idiota de Mente*, p. 75.
90 *Idiota de Mente*, p. 75. In the *Idiota de sapientia*, the layman argues that we must have some knowledge of eternal wisdom, because we desire it, and "nothing utterly unknown is desired." See Führer, *The Layman on Wisdom and the Mind*, p. 27.
91 *Idiota de Mente*, p. 77.
92 *Idiota de Mente*, p. 77.
93 *Idiota de Mente*, p. 77.
94 *Idiota de Mente*, p. 77.
95 *Idiota de Mente*, p. 77.
96 *Idiota de Mente*, p. 77.
97 *Idiota de Mente*, p. 77.
98 *Idiota de Mente*, p. 79.
99 *Idiota de Mente*, p. 79.
100 *Idiota de Mente*, p. 79. Cf. the second chapter of Vico's *De antiquissima Italorum sapientia*, which makes precisely this identification on etymological grounds.
101 *Idiota de Mente*, p. 79.
102 *Idiota de Mente*, p. 81.
103 *Idiota de Mente*, p. 81.
104 *Idiota de Mente*, p. 83.
105 *Idiota de Mente*, p. 87.
106 *Idiota de Mente*, p. 87.
107 *Idiota de Mente*, p. 87.
108 *Idiota de Mente*, p. 87.
109 *De coniecturis* 2.14 (Hoffmann, Wilpert, Bormann p. 170). Watts comments on this passage in her introduction to *De ludo globi*, p. 20.
110 See Führer, *The Layman on Wisdom and the Mind*, p. 21.
111 *Idiota de Mente*, p. 93.
112 *Idiota de Mente*, p. 93.
113 This point has been recently noticed by Karsten Harries, who observes that Cusanus "invites consideration as a precursor of Vico." Harries also links Cusanus and Descartes: for both thinkers, as for Vico, "there is a sense in which we understand things precisely to the extent that we can make them." See Harries, *Infinity and Perspective*, pp. 193, 199.

3 FRANCIS BACON

1 *NO* 1.129. Eva Brann calls attention to Bacon's designation of overseers of the "scientific research complex" in *New Atlantis* as "the College of the Six Days' Work." See "The Roots of Modernity," *St. John's Review*, Spring 1984, p. 68.
2 *Distributio Operis*, p. 26.
3 Preface to *Novum Organum*, p. 39.
4 Peirce, "An Essay toward Improving Our Reasoning in Security and in Uberty," p. 464n.

NOTES

5   Cf. the *Distributio Operis*, p. 26, where Bacon speaks of the need to find "a kind of experiment far more subtle and simple than those that present themselves."
6   Preface to *Novum Organum*, p. 38.
7   *Distributio Operis*, p. 26. Cf. *NO* 1.98 for another use of "vexations of nature."
8   *NO* 1.117.
9   Preface to *Novum Organum*, p. 38.
10 *NO* 1.13, 1.29; *Distributio Operis*, p. 20.
11 For example, *NO* 1.14, 1.127.
12 *Distributio Operis*, p. 20.
13 *NO* 1.33.
14 Malherbe, "Bacon's Method of Science," p. 76.
15 *Distributio Operis*, p. 21; *NO* 1.127.
16 Malherbe, "Bacon's Method of Science," pp. 97–8.
17 Peter Urbach curiously writes that "Bacon's comparison of scientific method with the drawing of a circle by means of a compass was certainly an unfortunate one" (*Francis Bacon's Philosophy of Science*, p. 192). On the contrary, the metaphor is illuminating because it suggests at once that Bacon's instrument is a man-made device and that one of its functions is to indicate, to point in a direction. I owe the latter point to Malherbe, "Bacon's Method of Science," p. 86.
18 *Secare naturam* and kindred expressions are used frequently in *Novum Organum*. See, for instance, *Distributio Operis*, p. 21 and *NO* 1.51, 1.59, 1.66, 1.124, 2.16, 2.43, 2.52.
19 Pérez-Ramos assumes that Bacon is criticizing Aristotelian induction here (*Francis Bacon's Idea of Science*, p. 201). It is, however, not clear that Bacon has Aristotle in mind when he condemns the method of "simple enumeration." Neither *NO* 1.62 nor *NO* 1.105 give much support to the view that Aristotle is the target. Bacon does link Aristotle with the syllogism, of course, but the syllogism is quite different from ordinary induction, as *NO* 1.17 makes clear. Simple enumeration is more characteristic of the empiric than the rationalist or sophistical philosopher, and Bacon clearly places Aristotle among the latter group (see *NO* 1.71). Urbach plausibly suggests that "ordinary induction" refers to a procedure described and codified in logic textbooks of his day, for example, Thomas Wilson's *The rule of Reason, conteinyng the art of Logique, set forth in Englishe* (1551). See Urbach's edition of *Novum Organum* (Chicago, 1994), p. 47n.10.
20 *Distributio Operis*, p. 21.
21 *NO* 1.124.
22 *NO* 1.51.
23 *NO* 1.124. Cf. *NO* 1.23.
24 *NO* 1.129.
25 A generally perceptive essay by Richard Kennington describes Bacon's target as "Greek contemplative philosophy." This description obscures the point that contemplation in itself is not, for Bacon, the besetting sin of Greek thought. See Kennington, "The Reform of Nature," p. 44 in John C. McCarthy (ed.), *Modern Enlightenment and the Rule of Reason* (Washington, D.C., 1998). In the *Advancement*, Bacon chides the philosopher who "while he gazed upwards to the stars fell into the water." But the moral is not that one should eschew contemplation, but that one should contemplate in the right way, beginning with the small and ascending to the greater. "For if he had looked down he might have seen the stars in the water, but looking aloft he could not see the water in the stars. So it cometh often to pass, that mean and small things discover great, better than great can discover the small" (p. 71).
26 *Distributio Operis*, p. 25.

27 Rossi notes the importance of this passage. See "Ants, Spiders, Epistemologists," p. 250.
28 *NO* 1.70. See also *Distributio Operis*, p. 25.
29 Eva Brann notes the human–divine analogy in Bacon and implies a connection between the "luciferic" experiments of Baconian natural philosophy and the "satanic" pride, manifested in the desire to be a creator rather than a creature, which she takes to lie at the roots of modernity. See Eva Brann, "The Roots of Modernity," *St. John's Review*, Spring 1984, p. 68. Brann's characterization of modern thinkers as imitators of God who "want to be next to him and like him" seems to fit Bacon in some respects. But it should be noted that while Brann charges Bacon with a desire for *scientia boni et mali*, Bacon himself explicitly distinguishes the "ambitious and headstrong greed for moral knowledge—of telling good from evil" which caused the Fall from the quest for "pure and spotless natural knowledge, by which Adam gave names to all things according to their kind" (Preface to *Instauratio Magna*, p. 15). Since the latter was not the origin and occasion of the Fall, it may be pursued without fear of pridefully usurping the divine prerogative. Bacon does not crave *scientia boni et mali* (he is content to leave this to non-Baconian inquiry) but a return to the prelapsarian state. This may indeed be pride of a sort, but Bacon at least would deny that it is satanic.
30 *NO* 1.70. See also *Distributio Operis*, p. 25 and *NO* 1.121.
31 *NO* 1.129.
32 Preface to *Instauratio Magna*, p. 15.
33 Preface to *Instauratio Magna*, pp.14–15 and *NO* 1.89.
34 *Distributio Operis*, p. 19.
35 *Distributio Operis*, p. 23.
36 Preface to *Novum Organum*, p. 38.
37 Preface to *Instauratio Magna*, p. 12.
38 *Distributio Operis*, p. 22.
39 *NO* 2.3. Charles Whitney makes the point well in his analysis of the pursuit of novelty in Bacon's science. "Human culture thus becomes a superinduction upon nature; our purpose on earth becomes to bring the novel into being by such superinduction." See Whitney, *Francis Bacon and Modernity* (New Haven and London, 1986), p. 110.
40 *NO* 2.9.
41 Bacon himself does not speak of entrails. I am echoing the image used by Collingwood in *The New Leviathan*, p. 248.
42 This connection is explored more fully by Rossi in "Ants, Spiders, Epistemologists," p. 252.
43 See *NO* 1.125 for this suggestion.
44 *NO* 1.63. Cf. *NO* 1.44, where Bacon regards "all the philosophies that have been received or invented as so many stage plays creating fictitious and imaginary worlds," and *NO* 1.54, where Bacon says that Aristotle enslaved his natural philosophy to his logic.
45 *NO* 2.6 speaks of "the stupid and downright useless web of so-called learning." Such vitriolic passages in Bacon co-exist uneasily, to say the least, with the irenic posture assumed in the Preface of the *Novum Organum*.
46 Compare *NO* 1.121, where Bacon says that scholastic subtleties were "spent on words, or at least on common notions (which is much the same thing), not on things or Nature."
47 *NO* 1.120.
48 *NO* 1.11.
49 *NO* 1.40.

50 *NO* 1.106.
51 *NO* 1.24.
52 Also at *NO* 1.100. Kant uses this image repeatedly in the Preface to the second edition of the *Critique of Pure Reason*. The motto chosen by Kant for this edition strongly suggests a Baconian derivation.
53 *NO* 1.82.
54 For the suggestion the positivist reading of Bacon is itself a bad construction, "invented by the strong and agitated wit of the epistemologists," see Rossi, "Ants, Spiders, Epistemologists," p. 259. This misreading may originate in the nineteenth century, as Pérez-Ramos suggests ("Bacon's Legacy," pp. 324–7). One should note, however, that even some "epistemological" nineteenth-century thinkers knew that anti-theoretical readings of Bacon were gross distortions. For instance, John Stuart Mill writes in his *Autobiography*: "the accusations against the Benthamic theory of *being* a theory, of proceeding *a priori*, by way of general reasoning, instead of Baconian experiment, shewed complete ignorance of Bacon's principles, and of the necessary conditions of experimental investigation." See Mill, *Autobiography*, ed. J. Stillinger (Boston, 1969), p. 95.
55 On Bacon's use of garden imagery, see Michèle Le Doeuff, "Man and Nature in the Gardens of Science," in William A. Sessions (ed.), *Francis Bacon's Legacy of Texts*, pp. 119–38, particularly pp. 126–34.
56 *NO* 1.102. *NO* 2.10 uses nearly identical language, without the army metaphor.
57 Rossi rightly comments that "the *digestion* of experience is a very important notion in Bacon's philosophy." See "Ants, Spiders, Epistemologists," p. 255.
58 *NO* 1.102. For connections between Bacon's tables and the *inventio* of commonplaces in the rhetorical tradition, see Paolo Rossi, *Francis Bacon: From Magic to Science*, tr. Sacha Rabinovitch (Chicago, 1968), pp. 201–19.
59 *NO* 1.102. See also *NO* 1.125, where Bacon speaks of the ancients who "prepared vast numbers of examples and particulars, and digested them by subject and specific topic in notebooks."
60 *NO* 2.10.
61 *NO* 1.118.
62 *NO* 1.101.
63 *NO* 1.125.
64 *NO* 1.121.
65 The language used even by commentators who do not approach Bacon with the topic of "making" in mind often presupposes the link between tabulation and construction. For example, see Mary Hesse, "Francis Bacon's Philosophy of Science," in Brian Vickers (ed.), *Essential Articles for the Study of Francis Bacon* (Hamden, Ct., 1968), pp. 114–39, which speaks of "natures out of which the inductive tables are to be constructed" (p. 137n).
66 And yet perhaps we should not despise it. Peirce speaks of "the instructive example that *liber secundus* puts before us of how the crudest observations, skillfully used, may anticipate by two centuries the conclusions of minuter science." See Peirce, "An Essay toward Improving Our Reasoning in Security and in Uberty," p. 465n.
67 The phrase is also used at *NO* 1.81.
68 *NO* 2.10.
69 *NO* 1.124.
70 *NO* 1.98.
71 *NO* 1.100.
72 Brian Vickers, "Francis Bacon and the Progress of Knowledge," p. 499.
73 *NO* 1.126.

74 Collingwood, *The New Leviathan*, p. 254. In his *Autobiography* (Oxford, 1939) Collingwood draws upon *Novum Organum* in articulating his "logic of question and answer" (cf. pp. 30–7).
75 Rossi rightly faults commentators who do not compare their interpretations of Bacon with "comments, articles, or books published outside the parochial community of English-speaking epistemologists," but it should be noted that Collingwood constitutes an English-speaking exception to the tendencies associated with the community that Rossi scorns.
76 *NO* 1.104.
77 *NO* 1.104.
78 *NO* 1.104.
79 *NO* 1.106. For other uses of pointing metaphors, see *NO* 1.8, 1.24, 1.82, 1.103.
80 See *NO* 1.125. Bacon is aware that one can fiddle with the axiom until it does not formally conflict with the new particulars and rejects this solution at *NO* 1.25 and 1.46.
81 The common interest in falsification does not demand that one go as far as Urbach does and interpret Bacon as a kind of Popperian. But as Rossi puts it, "some coincidences between passages from Bacon and Popper (published in parallel) [in Urbach's work] are impressive." See Rossi, "Ants, Spiders, Epistemologists," p. 258.
82 As Hesse recalls, in the *Advancement of Learning* Bacon actually quotes Plato when he formulates this problem. See "Francis Bacon's Philosophy of Science," p. 122.
83 *NO* 1.66.
84 *NO* 1.66.
85 *NO* 1.116.
86 *The Advancement of Learning*, p. 91.
87 *The Advancement of Learning*, p. 91. Connections between Bacon and Plato have been noticed by a select group of thinkers going back to Vico and Coleridge. A provocative examination of Coleridge's attempt to link Bacon with Plato may be had in Michael Raiger, "Coleridge's Metaphysics and the Method of Deconstruction from Bacon to Heidegger," *The Coleridge Bulletin* 14 (1999), pp. 16–25.
88 *The Advancement of Learning*, p. 94.
89 *NO* 1.15.
90 *NO* 1.60.
91 *NO* 1.15.
92 *NO* 1.15.
93 Pérez-Ramos, "Bacon's Forms and the Maker's Knowledge Tradition," in *The Cambridge Companion to Bacon*, p. 99.
94 To which branch of knowledge does inquiry into final causes belong to? Bacon's thinking on this question may develop. The view of the *Advancement* seems to be that while speculation on final causes is impertinent in physics, it is legitimate in "metaphysique" (cf. p. 91). *Novum Organum* repeats the polemic against final causes in physics, but seems to imply that it has no place in metaphysics either, since true metaphysics is occupied with the knowledge of forms, a category that he takes pains to distinguish from final causes. Final causes now have nothing to do with metaphysics, but are relegated to sciences "concerned with human actions" (*NO* 2.2). These are the sciences that Bacon separates from natural philosophy, the "sciences that are based on supposition and opinion," which properly use anticipations and dialectic, since their object "is to command assent, not master the thing itself" (*NO* 1.29). If this description of the mature Bacon is correct, then Sachiko Kusukawa's view that Bacon assigns both formal

NOTES

and final causes to metaphysics demands serious qualification. See Kusukawa, "Bacon's Classification of Knowledge", p. 57 in *The Cambridge Companion to Bacon*, pp. 47–74

95 *NO* 2.2.
96 *NO* 2.2.
97 *NO* 2.2. Hesse, "Francis Bacon's Philosophy of Science," is helpful on the issue of what Bacon understood by a "law of nature." As she says, the word "law" in this context "does not . . . connote a 'correlation' of phenomena, for, as we have seen, mere correlations do not express forms; it has rather the older association with order imposed by the civil power: 'the first congregations of matter; which like a general assembly of estates, doth give law to all bodies'" (p. 129).
98 *NO* 2.4.
99 *NO* 2.4.
100 Pérez-Ramos, "Bacon's Forms and the Maker's Knowledge Tradition," p. 111. Pérez-Ramos is aware of the equation of forms with elementary components of nature. What he fails to recognize is that Bacon's identification of forms with simple, material natures necessarily excludes them from being rules, even if knowledge of forms is generated only through the observance of rules. To say that the rules *are* the forms, to reduce the simple natures to a practical heuristic, seems to involve an elementary category mistake that Bacon does not make. There is no "verbal" part of the Baconian Form, as Pérez-Ramos suggests at p. 109; the verbal component is located in *axioms* which attempt to express or indicate the form.
101 *NO* 2.5.
102 The close analogy, but *not* identity, between "cause" in contemplation and "rule" in operation is consistently implied throughout *Novum Organum*, beginning with *NO* 1.3: "We can only command Nature by obeying her, and what in contemplation represents the cause, in operation stands as the rule."
103 *NO* 2.3.
104 *NO* 2.5.
105 *NO* 2.5.
106 *NO* 2.5. Bacon does not take this to imply a teleology of nature. Cf. *NO* 1.66, which rejects the analogy between the operation of nature and the operation of a craftsman working to achieve an end.
107 *NO* 2.5.
108 This may be seen clearly in both *NO* 2.1 and *NO* 2.2.
109 *NO* 2.6.
110 *NO* 2.7. Bacon illustrates the necessity of moving from operation to discovery by suggesting that "we must pass, it is clear, from Vulcan to Minerva." (Compare to *The Advancement of Learning*, p. 64.) The illustration provides further evidence that Bacon does not mean to assert the identity of the two activities. If he did, the metaphor would lose its sense entirely.
111 *NO* 2.8. The exact nature of Bacon's relation to atomism is controversial. This passage and *NO* 1.66 seem to clearly disavow atomism, but an approving reference is given at *NO* 1.51. An exhaustive treatment of the issue may be found in Graham Rees, "Atomism and 'Subtlety' in Francis Bacon's Philosophy," *Annals of Science* 37 (1980), pp. 549–71.
112 *NO* 2.8.
113 For instance, Anthony Quinton remarks that "it has long been a familiar, and well-founded, criticism of Bacon's philosophy of science that it does not adequately recognise the role of science in mathematics . . . he does not recognise the *indispensable* place of mathematics in science" (Quinton, *Francis Bacon* [Oxford, 1980], p. 47, quoted in Urbach, *Francis Bacon's Philosophy of*

NOTES

Science, p. 134). And Pérez-Ramos writes that "Bacon did not espouse or openly recommend mathematically oriented patterns of reasoning and spurned the use of mathematics in physics" ("Bacon's Legacy," p. 314 in *The Cambridge Companion to Bacon*, pp. 311–34). To speak of the "use" of mathematics is precisely correct: Bacon does not think that physics is mathematics, but he certainly allows that it makes instrumental use of mathematics.

114 *NO* 2.8.
115 *NO* 2.8.
116 *NO* 2.9.
117 *NO* 2.9.
118 *NO* 1.23.
119 *NO* 1.124.
120 Bacon, *The Advancement of Learning*, p. 204.
121 Bacon, *The Advancement of Learning*, p. 7.
122 Bacon, *The Advancement of Learning*, pp. 7–8.
123 Bacon, *The Advancement of Learning*, p. 165.
124 See Thomas Aquinas, *Summa theologiae* 1–2.62.4.
125 Bacon, *The Advancement of Learning*, p. 147. See also Preface to *Instauratio Magna*, p. 15.
126 Bacon, *The Advancement of Learning*, p. 166.
127 Bacon, *The Advancement of Learning*, p. 164.
128 Bacon, *The Advancement of Learning*, p. 26.
129 Bacon, *The Advancement of Learning*, pp. 26–7.
130 Bacon, *The Advancement of Learning*, p. 27.
131 Bacon, *The Advancement of Learning*, p. 25.
132 Bacon, *The Advancement of Learning*, p. 146.
133 Bacon, *The Advancement of Learning*, p. 165.
134 Bacon, *The Advancement of Learning*, p. 146.
135 Preface to *Instauratio Magna*, p. 15.
136 Quoted in Taylor, *Sources of the Self*, p. 405.
137 Bacon, *The Advancement of Learning*, p. 83.
138 Bacon, *The Advancement of Learning*, p. 83.
139 Bacon, *The Advancement of Learning*, p. 195.
140 Bacon, *The Advancement of Learning*, p. 57.
141 Bacon, *The Advancement of Learning*, pp. 199–200. Compare *NO* 1.65.
142 Bacon, *The Advancement of Learning*, pp. 200.
143 See Augustine, *Confessions* VI.5.
144 Bacon, *The Advancement of Learning*, p. 201.
145 Bacon, *The Advancement of Learning*, p. 200. Compare *NO* 1.65.
146 William Ames, *Technometria* §44 (trans. Lee W. Gibbs, p. 100).
147 Ames, *Technometria* §48 (Gibbs, p. 101).
148 Ames, *Technometria* §48 (Gibbs, p. 101).
149 Ames, *Technometria* §111 (Gibbs, p. 112).
150 Ames, *Technometria* §46 (Gibbs, p. 100).
151 For these labels, see Bacon, *The Advancement of Learning*, p. 9.
152 At *NO* 1.79, Bacon writes that natural philosophy "ought to be regarded as the great mother of the sciences."
153 *NO* 1.65. See also Preface to *Instauratio Magna*, pp. 14–15
154 Whitney, *Francis Bacon and Modernity*, p. 29.

4 RENÉ DESCARTES

1 See David Lachterman, *The Ethics of Geometry* (New York and London: Routledge, 1989), pp. 126–40.

NOTES

2 Lachterman, *The Ethics of Geometry*, pp. 141–87.
3 See the Letter to Mersenne, 27 February 1637 (AT I, 349; CSMK 53): "I have also inserted a certain amount of metaphysics, physics and medicine in the opening *Discourse* in order to show that my method extends to topics of all kinds." See also the letter to an unknown correspondent written near the end of May 1637: "in order to show that the method can be applied to everything, I have included some brief remarks on metaphysics, physics and medicine in the opening discourse" (AT I, 370; CSMK 58).
4 *Rule VIII* (AT X, 397; CSM I, 31).
5 *Rule VIII* (AT X, 397; CSM I, 31).
6 *Rule VIII* (AT X, 397; CSM I, 31).
7 *Fifth Set of Replies* (AT VII, 368; CSM II, 253). I have modified the CSM translation.
8 Even Lachterman, the reader most eager to provide a comprehensively constructivist reading of Descartes, acknowledges that other, non-constructivist things "may appear appropriate to say about the role of Cartesian *intuitions* or clear and distinct ideas grasped reflectively or introspectively by the *ego cogitans*." See *The Ethics of Geometry*, p. 148.
9 *Meditatio III* (AT VII, 38; CSM II, 26). I have modified the CSM translation.
10 *Fifth Set of Replies* (AT VII, 362; CSM II, 250), translation modified. This passage economically suggests the flaw in Anthony Kenny's attempt to interpret Descartes as holding that all ideas are both innate ("*qua* capacity") and adventitious ("*qua* episode accompanied by extra-mental judgment"). Descartes plainly views ideas *a nobis factas* as neither innate (though their components may be innate ideas or reducible to innate ideas) nor adventitious. See Kenny, "Descartes on Ideas," p. 233 in *Descartes: A Collection of Critical Essays*, ed. Willis Doney (Notre Dame: University of Notre Dame Press, 1968).
11 *Meditatio III* (AT VII, 37; CSM II, 26).
12 *Meditatio III* (AT VII, 37; CSM II, 26).
13 *Meditatio III* (AT VII, 39; CSM II, 27).
14 Rorty, *Philosophy and the Mirror of Nature* (Princeton: Princeton University Press, 1979), p. 126. See also pp. 3, 10–12, 40–69, 113, 126, 160, 163–4.
15 Charles Taylor, *Philosophical Arguments* (Cambridge, Mass.: Harvard University Press, 1995), p. 3.
16 John Yolton, "Mirrors and Veils, Thoughts and Things: The Epistemological Problematic," p. 64 in *Reading Rorty*, ed. Alan Malachowski (Oxford: Blackwell, 1990). Rorty makes the claim quoted by Yolton in *Philosophy and the Mirror of Nature*, p. 45.
17 Dennis Sepper, *Descartes's Imagination* (Berkeley: University of California Press, 1996), p. 52.
18 Charles Taylor, *Sources of the Self* (Cambridge, Mass.: Harvard University Press, 1989), p. 145.
19 Yolton, "Mirrors and Veils, Thoughts and Things: The Epistemological Problematic," p. 64.
20 Ian Hacking, *Representing and Intervening* (Cambridge: Cambridge University Press, 1983), p. 132.
21 This implies for Descartes, as Marjorie Grene points out, that "any account we invent will be, however true, literally a fiction compared to the absolutely true account which we accept, even though we cannot strictly understand it, on God's own word." See Grene, *Descartes* (Indianapolis and Cambridge, Mass.: Hackett Publishing, 1998), p. 78.
22 Letter to Mersenne, 25 November 1630 (AT I, 179; CSMK 28).
23 *Le Monde*, chapter 6 (AT XI, 31; CSM I, 90).

24 *Le Monde*, chapter 6 (AT XI, 33; CSM I, 90).
25 *Discours V* (AT VI, 42; CSM I, 132).
26 *Discours VI* (AT VI, 62; CSM I, 142).
27 *Discours VI* (AT VI, 62; CSM I, 142–3).
28 "But doesn't Descartes still think that we have to mirror nature? Isn't mastery dependent on mirroring?" Perhaps, but (as Yolton argues) it is questionable that the Cartesian conception of representation has much to do with "mirroring" in any important sense. Moreover, even if one does think of Cartesian representation as mirroring, Rorty's contrast between "knowledge as a mirror" and "knowledge as a tool" still fails to distinguish Descartes from ostensibly more pragmatic conceptions of knowing. A mirror can be a tool!
29 Jean-Jacques Rousseau, *Discourse on the Sciences and the Arts*, p. 11 in *The Basic Political Writings*, trans. Donald Cress (Indianapolis and Cambridge, Mass.: Hackett Publishing, 1987).
30 Pascal, *Pensées* §84, trans. A.J. Krailsheimer (London: Penguin Books, 1966), p. 52.
31 Sepper, *Descartes's Imagination*, p. 109.
32 *Rule VIII* (AT X, 399; CSM I, 32).
33 *Rule VIII* (AT X, 399; CSM I, 32).
34 See Marion, *Cartesian Questions: Method and Metaphysics* (Chicago and London: The University of Chicago Press, 1999), p. 47.
35 *Rule VIII* (AT X, 399; CSM I, 32).
36 *Rule XII* (AT X, 422; CSM I, 46).
37 *Rule XII* (AT X, 420; CSM I, 45). In the same Rule, Descartes declares: "it is not possible for us ever to understand anything beyond those simple natures and a certain mixture or compounding of one with another" (AT X, 422; CSM I, 46).
38 *Appendix to Fifth Objections and Replies* (AT IX-A, 212; CSM II, 275).
39 *Rule XII* (AT X, 424; CSM I, 48).
40 *Rule XII* (AT X, 427; CSM I, 49).
41 *Rule XII* (AT X, 427; CSM I, 50). For the role of *communes notiones* as links (*veluti vincula quaedam*), see *Rule XII* (AT X, 419; CSM I, 45) and Marion, *Cartesian Questions*, p. 48.
42 Regulae, p. 48 (AT 425).
43 Regulae, p. 49 (AT 427).
44 Regulae, pp. 44–5 (AT 419–20). The reader will have already noticed our debt to Marion's scholarship in general, and in particular to his essay on the simple natures as they appear in the Cartesian corpus ("What is the Method in the Metaphysics?" in *Cartesian Questions*, pp. 43–66). Two minor points of correction are in order. First, although the simple natures receive their fullest explication in *Rule XII*—as one would expect, since *Rule XII* presents itself as the summary of the previous eleven *regulae* as they bear on *propositiones simplices*)—they are not "introduced" in this rule, as Marion claims (*Cartesian Questions*, pp. 46–7). The *natura pura & simplex* is introduced by name in *Rule VI*'s discussion of the absolute (see AT X, 381; CSM I, 21) and anticipated by *Rule III*'s list of the objects of intuition (AT X, 368; CSM I, 14; Marion himself cites this list at *Cartesian Questions*, p. 51). Second, Marion characterizes *Rule XII*'s list of simple natures as "grouped under three headings," but neglects the "corresponding privations and negations" that Descartes says "it is as well to count among the simple natures" (AT X, 420; CSM I, 45). Arguably, there are *four* headings, not three—although one may perhaps group the privations with the common notional simple natures. (Later Marion detects "four types of simple natures" [p. 57], but the increase derives from conceiving real common natures and notional common natures as distinct types.)

45 Since the purely intellectual simple natures appear to play no role in the construction of composite bodies, the *Regulae* mentions them as a category but does not employ them. Marion cogently argues that Descartes does make full use of them in the *Meditations*. See *Cartesian Questions*, pp. 53–66.
46 *Rule V* (AT X, 379; CSM I, 20).
47 *Rule VI* (AT X, 381; CSM I, 21). CSM misleadingly renders *ars* as "method." Marion calls attention to the importance of the phrase *artis secretum in Rule VI* and emphasizes that it "sums up the entire *Regulae*." See Marion, *On Descartes' Metaphysical Prism* (Chicago and London: The University of Chicago Press, 1999), p. 62. Another place where Descartes identifies *scientia* as a mode of art or skill may be found in Letter to Hogelande, February 8, 1640 (AT III, 722; CSMK 144).
48 *Rule VI* (AT X, 381; CSM I, 21).
49 This is, of course, what Marion has called the *Regulae's l'ontologie grise*, which he describes in summary terms as "the counter-ontology that alone allows the mind to disqualify the *ousia* of beings so that they might be reduced to the rank of objects." See Marion, *On Descartes' Metaphysical Prism*, p. 5. As to the precise sense in which this counter-ontology ought to be termed a new "metaphysics," see the subtle and lengthy discussion in *On Descartes' Metaphysical Prism*, pp. 9–66.
50 *Rule VI* (AT X, 381–2; CSM I, 21).
51 *Rule VI* (AT X, 381; CSM I, 21).
52 That the simplicity in question "is an epistemological, not an ontological one" is well argued by Marion. See *Cartesian Questions*, p. 47 and p. 54.
53 *Rule X* (AT X, 404; CSM I, 35), emphasis mine. In the third rule of method as given in the *Discours*, Descartes explicitly licenses the habit of "supposing some order even among objects that have no natural order of precedence" (AT VI, 18–19; CSM I, 120).
54 *Rule X* (AT X, 404; CSM I, 35).
55 *Rule X* (AT X, 404–5; CSM I, 35–6).
56 *Rule X* (AT X, 405; CSM I, 36).
57 *Rule XII* (AT X, 412; CSM I, 40). In his Letter to Morin, 13 July 1638, Descartes similarly advises that his readers are not "obliged to believe" everything he writes (AT II, 201; CSMK 108).
58 *Rule XII* (AT X, 412; CSM I, 40). In commenting on *Rule V*, which introduces the importance of order, Catherine Pickstock writes: "This structuration of objects does not reflect the order in which reality arrives for everyday, confused passional perception, but subsists only within the abstract realm of mathematics, or else in the region where mathematics corresponds to reality, which is in physics" (*After Writing: On the Liturgical Consummation of Philosophy* [Oxford: Blackwell, 1998], p. 65). Her reading concurs with my own, insofar as "structuration" is imposed on things rather than merely observed.
59 *Rule III* (AT X, 369; CSM I, 14).
60 See *Rule IX* (AT X, 401; CSM I, 33).
61 *Rule XII* (AT X, 418; CSM I, 44).
62 *Cartesian Questions*, p. 47.
63 That they *do* so appear as a thread (perhaps even *the* thread) connecting the moments of Cartesian philosophy is the main point of Marion's essay.
64 *Cartesian Questions*, p. 61. Another potent source for the suggestion that simple natures may be constructed is the famous doctrine of the creation of mathematical truths. Mathematical truths such as "things that are the same as a third thing are the same as each other" (AT X, 419; CSM I, 45) seem to be considered as both common simple natures and creations of divine power. See Marion, *Cartesian Questions*, p. 52.

NOTES

65 CSM consistently translates *quaestio* as "problem." Descartes himself provides a certain justification for this rendering when he speaks of the "problèmes de Géométrie" in the *Géométrie* of 1637 and a "question de géométrie" in his Letter to Elisabeth from 1643 (AT IV, 38, quoted in Lachterman, *Ethics of Geometry*, p. 150).
66 For the important passage indicating this transition, see *Rule XII* (AT X, 428–9; CSM I, 50–1).
67 *Rule XIII* (AT X, 430; CSM I, 51–2).
68 *Rule XIII* (AT X, 431; CSM I, 52).
69 Contrary to what Murdoch seems to imply in his introduction to his translation (see CSM I, 7).
70 *Rule XIII* (AT X, 431; CSM I, 52).
71 *Rule XIV* (AT X, 439; CSM I, 56).
72 *Rule XIV* (AT X, 441; CSM I, 58).
73 *Rule XIV* (AT X, 441; CSM I, 58). I borrow the phrase "figurate extension" from the very useful treatment of the *Regulae* found in Jacob Klein, *Greek Mathematical Thought and the Origin of Algebra*, trans. Eva Brann (Cambridge, Mass. and London: The M.I.T. Press, 1968), pp. 197–211.
74 *Rule XIV* (AT X, 442; CSM I, 59).
75 *Rule XIV* (AT X, 445–6; CSM I, 61).
76 *Rule XIV* (AT X, 447; CSM I, 62).
77 *Rule XIV* (AT X, 440; CSM I, 57). Cf. *Rule XIV* (AT X, 449; CSM I, 63).
78 *Rule XIV* (AT X, 440; CSM I, 58).
79 *Rule XIV* (AT X, 447; CSM I, 62).
80 *Rule XIV* (AT X, 447; CSM I, 62).
81 *Rule XIV* (AT X, 448; CSM I, 63).
82 *Rule XIV* (AT X, 448; CSM I, 63).
83 *Rule XIV* (AT X, 450; CSM I, 63), emphasis mine.
84 *Rule XIV* (AT X, 453; CSM I, 65).
85 *Rule XVI* (AT X, 455; CSM I, 67).
86 *Rule XVI* (AT X, 456; CSM I, 68).
87 *Rule XVI* (AT X, 457; CSM I, 68).
88 *Rule XVI* (AT X, 455; CSM I, 67).
89 *Rule XVII* (AT X, 459; CSM I, 70).
90 *Rule XVII* (AT X, 459; CSM I, 70).
91 *Rule XVII* (AT X, 460; CSM I, 71).
92 For such readings, see Louis E. Loeb, "Is There Radical Dissimulation in Descartes' Meditations?" in Amélie Oksenberg Rorty (ed.), *Essays on Descartes' Meditations* (Berkeley, Los Angeles and London: The University of California Press, 1986), pp. 243–70 and Hiram Caton, "The Problem of Descartes's Sincerity," pp. 22–35 in Georges J.D. Moyal (ed.), *René Descartes: Critical Assessments*, vol. II (London and New York: Routledge, 1991).
93 For the Cartesian doctrine of continuous creation, see *Meditatio III* (AT VII, 49–51; CSM II, 33–5) and *Principia Philosophiae* (AT IX–A, 13; CSM I, 200).
94 For the earliest and most straightforward expression of Descartes's eternal truths doctrine, see the two letters to Mersenne written in the spring of 1630: Letter to Mersenne, 15 April 1630 (AT I, 135–50; CSMK 20–5), 27 May 1630 (AT I, 151–4). Recent French commentary has emphasized the persistence of the eternal truths doctrine throughout the Cartesian corpus. See Genevieve Rodis-Lewis, *L'Oeuvre de Descartes* (Paris: Vrin, 1959), pp. 125–40 and the table of references in Jean-Luc Marion, *Sur la théologie blanche de Descartes* (Paris: Presses Universitaires de France, 1981), pp. 270–1.
95 Rorty, *Philosophy and the Mirror of Nature*, p. 110.

96 Peirce, "Some Consequences of Four Incapacities," p. 28 in *The Essential Peirce*, vol. 1, ed. Nathan Houser and Christian Kloesel (Bloomington and Indianapolis: Indianapolis University Press, 1992).
97 Letter to Elizabeth, 28 June 1643 (AT III, 695; CSMK 228).
98 Conversation with Burman, 16 April 1648 (AT V, 165; CSMK 347).
99 Letter to Elizabeth, 28 June 1643 (AT III, 695; CSMK 228).
100 Descartes, Preface to the French edition of the *Principia* (AT IX–B, 11; CSM I, 184).
101 It is revealing to compare what the texts actually say with Stephen Toulmin's interpretation: "Using our understanding of Nature to increase comfort, or to reduce pain, was secondary to the central spiritual goal of Science. Rejecting in both method and spirit Bacon's vision of a humanly fruitful science, Descartes and Newton set out to build mathematical structures, and looked to Science for theological, not technological, dividends" (Toulmin, *Cosmopolis* [Chicago: The University of Chicago Press, 1990], p. 105). In a letter to Hogelande from August 1638, Descartes criticizes Comenius on the ground that his aphorisms "contain only such generalities that he seems to have a long way to reach particular truths—and it is the latter alone which are required for practice" (AT II, 347; CSMK 119).
102 *Discours* I (AT VI, 7; CSM I, 114).
103 Letter to Plempius for Fromondus, 3 October 1637 (AT I, 421; CSMK 64).
104 Letter to Plempius for Fromondus, 3 October 1637 (AT I, 421; CSMK 64).
105 Pascal, *Pensées* §84.
106 Descartes, Preface to the French edition of the *Principia* (AT IX–B, 18; CSM I, 189).
107 Peirce, "Some Consequences of Four Incapacities," p. 51. Some will be surprised by the fact that the founder of pragmatism criticizes others on the ground that they are unable to know the very realities of things. The puzzlement results from a widespread but impoverished understanding of pragmatism, an understanding that identifies it exclusively with its Deweyean/Rortyan wing and neglects the unashamedly "metaphysical" aims of Peirce and Royce.

5 THOMAS HOBBES

1 Thomas Hobbes, *Six Lessons to the Savilian Professors of the Mathematics*, in W. Molesworth (ed.), *The English Works of Thomas Hobbes*, vol. 7 (London: Longman, Brown, Green and Longmans, 1845), p. 184.
2 *Six Lessons*, p. 184. Hobbes asserts the hypothetical nature of physics throughout his writings. For example, see *Six Lessons*, p. 212, *Seven Philosophical Problems*, p. 4 (in *English Works*, vol. 7), *De corpore*, p. xi and p. 388 (in *English Works*, vol. 1), *Decameron Physiologicum*, p. 88 (in *English Works* vol. 7), *De Homine* 10.5 (in B. Gert, ed., *Man and Citizen* [Garden City, N.Y.: Doubleday, 1972], p. 42).
3 Leo Strauss, *Natural Right and History* (Chicago and London: The University of Chicago Press, 1953), pp. 174–5. See also his essay "On the Basis of Hobbes's Political Philosophy," in *What is Political Philosophy?* (New York: The Free Press, 1959), p. 174.
4 Strauss, *Natural Right and History*, p. 173.
5 Michael Oakeshott, *Rationalism in Politics and Other Essays* (Indianapolis: Liberty Fund, 1991), p. 243.
6 Oakeshott, *Rationalism in Politics*, p. 245.
7 This point is often missed. For example, Arthur Child takes Hobbes to think that "the geometer knows these first causes, whose names he defines, in virtue of having drawn and described them himself" (*Making and Knowing in Hobbes*,

Vico, and Dewey [Berkeley and Los Angeles: The University of California Press, 1953], p. 280).

8. Hobbes is quite adamant on this point. "But teaching of language is not mathematic, nor logic, nor physics, nor any other science; and therefore to call a definition, as you do, mathematical, or physical, is a mark of ignorance, in a professor inexcusable" (*Six Lessons*, p. 225). And a few paragraphs later: "When a geometrician prefixeth before his demonstrations a definition, he doth it not as a part of his geometry, but of natural evidence, not to be demonstrated by argument, but to be understood in understanding the language wherein it is set down" (*Six Lessons*, p. 229).
9. Hobbes, *Elements of Philosophy, The First Section, Concerning Body*, chapter 25, section 1, in *English Works*, vol. 1, p. 388. Hereafter we cite this work as *De corpore*, providing chapter and section number, along with a page reference to the English text.
10. *De corpore* 12.2 (*EW* 139).
11. *De corpore* 6.15 (*EW* 84–6).
12. "Author's Epistle to the Reader" (placed in introduction to *De corpore* in *English Works*, vol. 1), before page numbers begin).
13. *De corpore* 6.15 (*EW* 85).
14. *De corpore* 6.13 (*EW* 81–2).
15. *De corpore* 6.6 (*EW* 70).
16. *De corpore* 8.12 (*EW* 111). See also *Six Lessons*, p. 213.
17. Oakeshott, *Rationalism in Politics*, pp. 244–5.
18. See *De corpore* 1.5 (*EW* 6).
19. *Six Lessons*, pp. 249–50.
20. *Six Lessons*, p. 250.
21. *Six Lessons*, p. 250.
22. *Six Lessons*, p. 250.
23. *Six Lessons*, p. 214. Throughout the *Six Lessons*, Hobbes defends Euclid's definitions, not hesitating to use them against Wallis when useful. In an otherwise extremely useful essay on Hobbes and Wallis, Alexander Bird goes wrong when he speaks of "Hobbes's rejection of Euclid's definitions." Hobbes himself has this to say about the Euclidean definitions: "some, very few, you see are faulty; the rest either accurate, or good enough if well interpreted" (*Six Lessons*, 210). See Alexander Bird, "Squaring the Circle: Hobbes on Philosophy and Geometry," *Journal of the History of Ideas* 57.2 (1996), p. 224.
24. *Six Lessons*, p. 212.
25. Contrary to Richard Peters, who writes that "Hobbes, like Descartes, seems to have thought that if postulates are self-evident, they are true" (Peters, *Hobbes* [Baltimore: Penguin Books, 1956], p. 73).
26. *Six Lessons*, p. 184.
27. *Six Lessons*, pp. 184–5 (emphasis mine).
28. *Six Lessons*, p. 212.
29. *Six Lessons*, p. 212.
30. *Six Lessons*, p. 188.
31. *Six Lessons*, p. 188.
32. *Six Lessons*, p. 200.
33. *Six Lessons*, p. 199.
34. *Six Lessons*, p. 205.
35. *Six Lessons*, p. 205.
36. *Six Lessons*, p. 212.
37. *De corpore* 6.2 (*EW* 67).
38. *De corpore* 6.2 (*EW* 67).

39 *De corpore* 6.4 (*EW* 68).
40 *De corpore* 6.4 (*EW* 69).
41 *De corpore* 6.5 (*EW* 69).
42 *De corpore* 6.6 (*EW* 70).
43 Strauss, *Natural Right and History*, pp. 174–5.
44 *De corpore* 6.5 (*EW* 70).
45 *De corpore* 6.12 (*EW* 80–1).
46 *De corpore* 6.6 (*EW* 70).
47 *De corpore* 6.14 (*EW* 83).
48 *De corpore* 6.13 (*EW* 81).
49 *De corpore* 6.13 (*EW* 81).
50 De homine 10.4 (*Man and Citizen*, p. 41).
51 *De corpore* 6.6 (*EW* 71). See also *De corpore* 6.17 (*EW* 87), which speaks of "those things which may be demonstrated by simple motion (in which geometry consists)."
52 George Steiner, *Grammars of Creation* (New Haven and London: Yale University Press, 2001), p. 52.
53 For Hobbes on synthesis, see *De corpore* 1.2–1.5 (*EW* 3–6), 6.1 (*EW* 66), 6.6–6.10 (*EW* 70–9).
54 Bird valuably makes the point that Hobbes considers any refusal to accept his definitions as "a refusal to be taught—implying that a definition should have an educative content." See Bird, "Squaring the Circle," p. 221 and *De corpore* 6.15 (*EW* 84).
55 *Leviathan* 17.13 (Curley, p. 109)
56 Leo Strauss, "On the Basis of Hobbes's Political Philosophy," pp. 174 and 175.
57 *Elements of Law* 1.1, p. 2 in F. Tönnies (ed.), *The Elements of Law: Natural and Politic* (London: Frank Cass, 1969).
58 *De cive* 1.1, in *Man and Citizen*, p. 109.
59 *Leviathan*, chapter 9 (Curley, p. 48).
60 *Leviathan*, chapter 9 (Curley, p. 48).
61 *De corpore* 1.9 (*EW* 11).
62 Strauss, "On the Basis of Hobbes's Political Philosophy," p. 175. For a reading of Hobbes that places him in substantial continuity with Grotius, see Richard Tuck, *Philosophy and Government 1572–1651* (Cambridge: Cambridge University Press, 1993), particularly pp. 303–14.
63 *De corpore* 6.7 (*EW* 73).
64 *De corpore* 6.5 (*EW* 70).
65 "Author's Epistle to the Reader" of *De corpore*.
66 "Author's Epistle to the Reader."
67 "Author's Epistle to the Reader."
68 "Author's Epistle to the Reader."
69 Strauss, *Natural Right and History*, p. 174; "On the Basis of Hobbes's Political Philosophy," p. 182.
70 See Hobbes's Introduction to *Leviathan* (Curley, p. 4).
71 *De corpore* 1.6 (*EW* 7).
72 *Six Lessons*, p. 199.
73 *De corpore* 1.6 (*EW* 7).
74 *Leviathan* 31.41 (Curley, p. 243–4).
75 *Leviathan* 18.1 (Curley, p. 110).
76 David Gauthier, "Hobbes on Demonstration and Construction," *Journal of the History of Philosophy* 35.4 (1997), p. 521.
77 Gauthier, "Hobbes on Demonstration and Construction," p. 520.
78 See *Elements of Law*, Epist. Ded. and 1.1 (Tönnies, pp. xv–xvi, 1).

79 *Decameron Physiologicum*, in *EW*, vol. 7, p. 82.

6 GIAMBATTISTA VICO

1 *De antiquissima* 1.1 (Cristofolini *OF* 63).
2 Second Article, *Giornale de' letterati d'Italia*, 8.10 (1711): 308–38, trans. L.M. Palmer in *On the Most Ancient Wisdom of the Italians*, p. 139.
3 *De antiquissima* 1.1 (Cristofolini *OF* 63).
4 *De antiquissima* 1.1 (Cristofolini *OF* 63).
5 *De antiquissima* 1.1 (Cristofolini *OF* 63).
6 *De antiquissima* 1.1 (Cristofolini *OF* 63).
7 *De antiquissima* 1.1 (Cristofolini *OF* 63).
8 *De antiquissima* 1.1 (Cristofolini *OF* 63).
9 *De antiquissima* 1.1 (Cristofolini *OF* 63).
10 *De antiquissima* 4.2 (Cristofolini *OF* 93). Cf. *Prima Risposta* 2 (Cristofolini *OF* 135) "non comprende l'infinito, ma bene il può andar raccogliendo."
11 *De antiquissima* 1.1 (Cristofolini *OF* 63).
12 *De antiquissima* 1.1 (Cristofolini *OF* 63).
13 *De antiquissima* 1.1 (Cristofolini *OF* 63).
14 *De antiquissima* 1.1 (Cristofolini *OF* 63).
15 *De antiquissima* 1.1 (Cristofolini *OF* 63).
16 *De antiquissima* 1.1 (Cristofolini *OF* 63).
17 *De antiquissima* 1.1 (Cristofolini *OF* 63).
18 *De antiquissima* 1.1 (Cristofolini *OF* 63).
19 *De antiquissima* 1.1 (Cristofolini *OF* 63).
20 *De antiquissima* 1.1 (Cristofolini *OF* 63–5).
21 *De antiquissima* 1.1 (Cristofolini *OF* 65).
22 *De antiquissima* 1.1 (Cristofolini *OF* 65).
23 *De antiquissima* 1.1 (Cristofolini *OF* 65).
24 *De antiquissima* 1.1 (Cristofolini *OF* 65).
25 *Prima Risposta* 2 (Cristofolini *OF* 136).
26 *De antiquissima* 1.2 (Cristofolini *OF* 65).
27 *De antiquissima* 1.2 (Cristofolini *OF* 65).
28 *De antiquissima* 1.2 (Cristofolini *OF* 67).
29 *De antiquissima* 1.2 (Cristofolini *OF* 67).
30 *De antiquissima* 1.2 (Cristofolini *OF* 67).
31 *De antiquissima* 1.2 (Cristofolini *OF* 67).
32 *De antiquissima* 1.2 (Cristofolini *OF* 67).
33 *De antiquissima* 1.2 (Cristofolini *OF* 67). I wish to thank Jason Taylor for pointing out this and other allusions by Vico to Lucretius. It does not, of course, follow that Vico means to identify his own perspective with that of Lucretius, contrary to the argument of Gino Bedani, *Vico Revisited*.
34 Vico considers *brevitas* as a vice of thinking, since it prevents comprehension of the whole, but he also understands it as a virtue of discourse about the mind. See *Seconda Risposta* 2 (Cristofolini *OF* 151).
35 *De antiquissima* 1.2 (Cristofolini *OF* 67).
36 *Prima Risposta* 2 (Cristofolini *OF* 135).
37 *De antiquissima* 1.2 (Cristofolini *OF* 69).
38 *De antiquissima* 1.2 (Cristofolini *OF* 67).
39 *De antiquissima* 1.2 (Cristofolini *OF* 69).
40 *De antiquissima* 1.2 (Cristofolini *OF* 67).
41 *Prima Risposta* 2 (Cristofolini *OF* 135). And see *Seconda Risposta* 1 (Cristofolini *OF* 148), "io investigato i nostri antichissimi filosofi aver nelle lor massime che

NOTES

l'uom talmente opera nel mondo dell'astrazioni, quale opera Iddio nel mondo delle realitadi. E così il modo più proprio di concepire la generazion delle cose s'apprenda dalla geometria e dall'aritmetica."

42 *De antiquissima* 1.2 (Cristofolini *OF* 69).
43 *De antiquissima* 1.2 (Cristofolini *OF* 67).
44 *De antiquissima* 1.2 (Cristofolini *OF* 69).
45 *De antiquissima* 1.2 (Cristofolini *OF* 69).
46 *De antiquissima* 1.2 (Cristofolini *OF* 69).
47 *De antiquissima* 1.2 (Cristofolini *OF* 69).
48 *De antiquissima* 3 (Cristofolini *OF* 83). Cf. *Seconda Risposta* 4 (*OF* p. 167, where Vico says that "nelle mathematiche conosco il vero col farlo; nelle fisiche e nelle altre va la cosa altrimenti."
49 *De antiquissima* 1.2 (Cristofolini *OF* 69).
50 *De nostri temporis studiorum ratione* 6, pp. 126–8 in Vico, *Opere*, vol. 1, ed. A. Battistini.
51 See *De antiquissima* 2 (Cristofolini *OF* 77).
52 *De antiquissima* 1.2 (Cristofolini *OF* 69).
53 *De antiquissima* 1.2 (Cristofolini *OF* 69).
54 *De antiquissima* 1.3 (Cristofolini *OF* 73). For a more detailed analysis of Vico's critique of the *cogito*, see my *Vico, Genealogist of Modernity*, pp. 13–19.
55 *De antiquissima*, conclusio (Cristofolini *OF* 131).
56 Such debates continue to rage, *pace* cognitive scientists who claim an authoritative teaching about how the mind works, or who take themselves to have explained consciousness.
57 *De ratione* 10, p. 154.
58 See *De antiquissima* 3 (Cristofolini *OF* 81) and *Seconda Risposta* 4 (*OF* 156), "il pruovare dalla causa sia il farla."
59 *De antiquissima* 3 (Cristofolini *OF* 83).
60 *De antiquissima* 4.2 (Cristofolini *OF* 87).
61 *Prima Risposta* 3 (Cristofolini *OF* 143). This perspective is retained in the later work; see *Scienza nuova* §367: "metaphysics is the sublime science which distributes their certain subject matters to all the 'subaltern sciences.'"
62 *De antiquissima* 4.1 (Cristofolini *OF* 85).
63 *De antiquissima* 4.2 (Cristofolini *OF* 87).
64 *De antiquissima* 4.2 (Cristofolini *OF* 87).
65 *De antiquissima* 4.2 (Cristofolini *OF* 87).
66 *De antiquissima* 4.2 (Cristofolini *OF* 87).
67 *Seconda Risposta* 4 (Cristofolini *OF* 157).
68 A particularly lucid formulation of this point may be found in Lachterman, "Mathematics and Nominalism in Vico's *Liber Metaphysicus*," p. 53.
69 *De antiquissima* 4.2 (Cristofolini *OF* 87).
70 Descartes, Letter to Mersenne, 27 July 1638, in *The Philosophical Writings of Descartes*, vol. 3, p. 119 (AT 268).
71 *De antiquissima* 4.2 (Cristofolini *OF* 87).
72 *De antiquissima* 4.2 (Cristofolini *OF* 93).
73 *Autobiography*, p. 127.
74 Lachterman, "Mathematics and Nominalism in Vico's *Liber Metaphysicus*," p. 57.
75 Milbank, *The Religious Dimension of the Thought of Giambattista Vico 1668–1744*, vol. 1, p. 173.
76 Lachterman, "Mathematics and Nominalism in Vico's *Liber Metaphysicus*," p. 68.
77 Letter to Msgr. Muzio Gaeta, 1737 (no date), p. 105 in *Opere di Giambattista Vico*, vol. 6, ed. Giuseppe Ferrari.
78 *Scienza nuova* §199.

NOTES

79 *Scienza nuova* §375.
80 *Scienza nuova* §402.
81 *Scienza nuova* §213. Cf. §822.
82 *Scienza nuova* §374.
83 *Scienza nuova* §375.
84 *Scienza nuova* §186.
85 *Scienza nuova* §186.
86 That Vico describes Axiom 37 of the Elements as a "degnità filologico-filosofica" (*Scienza nuova* §187), a privileged point of intersection between philosophy and philology, may be important. In any case, we cannot accept Bedani's view that Vico's comparisons between children and early man are "analogical and illustrative devices" without "any serious theoretical or epistemological function" (*Vico Revisited*, p. 189).
87 *Scienza nuova* §340; cf. §182, §506.
88 *Scienza nuova* §375.
89 *Scienza nuova* §916.
90 *Scienza nuova* §385.
91 *Scienza nuova* §385.
92 *Scienza nuova* §383.
93 *Scienza nuova* §591. On Vico's characteristic use of the "sintagma alliterativa," see Battistini's note in Vico, *Opere*, vol. 2, p. 1481.
94 *Scienza nuova* §518. The critique of the empty "conceit of the learned" in this passage is an example of his "genealogical" approach to secular modernity. For an interpretation of Vico's work as a whole in this manner, see my study *Vico, Genealogist of Modernity*.
95 *Scienza nuova* §838.
96 Vico, *Autobiography*, p. 166.
97 This lack of kindness is also reflected at the end of Vico's denial that Homer possessed any esoteric wisdom. There he declares that, far from being philosophers, Homer's men are "like children in the weakness of their minds, like women in the vigor of their imaginations (*fantasie*), and like violent youths in the turbulence of their passions" (*Scienza nuova* §787). One might also mention the "mal regolata fantasia" at §330, or Vico's letter to Estevan of 12 January 1729, in which he complains that "the majority are all memory and *fantasia*, for which reason they have spoken evil of the New Science" (trans. Giorgio Pinton, *New Vico Studies* 16: 1998, p. 48).
98 *Scienza nuova* §916.
99 *Scienza nuova* §376.
100 *Scienza nuova* §377.
101 *Scienza nuova* §379.
102 David Lachterman, "Vico and Marx: Notes on a Precursory Reading," p. 51. Decisive confirmation that *fingere* is the proper act of *fantasia* may be had in the ninth philosophical proof of the true Homer, in which Vico notes that in Terence we often find *comminisci* for *fingere*, "ch'è propio della fantasia, ond'è '*commentum*', ch'è un ritruovato finto" (*Scienza nuova* §819).
103 *Scienza nuova* §402.
104 *Scienza nuova* §498. Cf. Aristotle's *Poetics* 1448b and Giuseppe Mazzotta, *The New Map of the World*, p. 158.
105 *Scienza nuova* §215.
106 *Scienza nuova* §216.
107 *Scienza nuova* §349.
108 *Scienza nuova* §331.
109 *Scienza nuova* §331.

110 *Scienza nuova* §331.
111 Lachterman, "Vico and Marx," p. 56.
112 Vico, *Autobiography*, p. 127.
113 *Scienza nuova* §331.
114 Vico, *Autobiography*, p. 138.
115 Vico, *Autobiography*, p. 139.
116 Vico, *Autobiography*, p. 139.
117 *Scienza nuova* §121.
118 *Scienza nuova* §183.
119 *Scienza nuova* §376.
120 *Scienza nuova* §379.
121 Arnaldo Momigliano, "Vico's *Scienza nuova*: Roman 'Bestioni' and Roman 'Eroi,'" *History and Theory*, p. 8. "In practice Vico made little use of Plato and Tacitus: they remained pieces of classical scenery, the one contemplating man as he should be, the other as he is."
122 *Scienza nuova* §2.
123 *Scienza nuova* prima §47, in Vico, *Opere*, vol. 2, ed. A. Battistini, p. 1009.
124 Eric Voegelin, *History of Political Ideas*, vol. VI, p. 109.
125 *Scienza nuova* §40.
126 *Scienza nuova* §630.
127 *Scienza nuova* §163.
128 *Scienza nuova* §691.
129 See *Scienza nuova* §7 and §97.
130 *Scienza nuova* §357.
131 *Scienza nuova* §147.
132 *Scienza nuova* §177. I thank Jason Taylor for pointing out the Livonic origins of the language of this passage.
133 *Scienza nuova* §178.
134 *Scienza nuova* §338. Cf. *Scienza nuova* §523: "such and so much divine force was needed to reduce these giants, as wild as they were gross, to human duties."
135 *Scienza nuova* §191.
136 *Scienza nuova* §191.
137 *Scienza nuova* §178.
138 *Scienza nuova* §181. Cf. §120.
139 *Scienza nuova* §193 and §144.
140 Milbank, *The Religious Dimension of the Thought of Giambattista Vico 1668–1744*, vol. 2, p. 37.
141 *Scienza nuova* §473.
142 *Scienza nuova* §473.
143 See *De constantia iurisprudentia: Liber alter, De constantia philologiae*, in *Opere giuridiche*, ed. P. Cristofolini, pp. 401–3.
144 See *Scienza nuova* §369.
145 *Scienza nuova* §349.
146 *Scienza nuova* §2. Cf. §42.
147 *Scienza nuova* §179.
148 *Scienza nuova* §165.
149 *Scienza nuova* §505.
150 *Scienza nuova* §13.
151 *Scienza nuova* §504.
152 *Scienza nuova* §248.
153 *Scienza nuova* §555.
154 *Scienza nuova* §555.
155 *Scienza nuova* §552.

NOTES

156 *Scienza nuova* §553.
157 *Scienza nuova* §263.
158 *Scienza nuova* §552.
159 *Scienza nuova* §347.
160 *Scienza nuova seconda* §1132. Cf. *Vico: Selected Writings*, edited and translated by Leon Pompa, p. 269.
161 *Scienza nuova seconda* §1132. Cf. *Vico: Selected Writings*, p. 269.
162 Berlin is not correct to ascribe to Vico the view that "it is almost, but not quite, impossible to work back from the present, think away society and civilization, and imagine what it must have been like to be a primitive savage wandering in the 'vast forest of the earth'" (*Vico and Herder*, p. 29).
163 *Scienza nuova* §338. It is relevant that in the Idea of the Work, Vico says that it is *metaphysics* that enables him to descend into the crude minds of the first founders of the gentile nations, "all robust sense and vast imagination" (§6). One might notice possible exemplars of the descent, such as Vergil, whose epic is described as "made by divination" (§721). Is Vico emulating the descent of Aeneas, using a quasi-divinatory process to go down to the world of the first humans? A positive answer to this question would force the equation of Vico's own metaphysics, by which he makes the descent, with divination, an equation which in my view cannot be sustained. For another viewpoint, see Verene, *Vico's Science of Imagination*, p. 151.
164 *Scienza nuova* §338.
165 *Scienza nuova* §378. Goetsch's contention that Vico uses "*fantasia*" for the poetic mind and "*immaginazione*" to denote "a faculty of the age of rational abstraction" (*Vico's Axioms*, p. 39) contains a double error: (1) Vico never, at least in the *Scienza nuova*, uses "*immaginazione*"; the noun is *immaginativa*; (2) Vico does use *immaginativa*, and not just *fantasia*, to describe the poetic mind, as for example when he writes that "è naturalmente niegato di poter entrare nella vasta immaginativa di que primi uomini" (§378).
166 *Scienza nuova* §34.
167 *Scienza nuova* §338, §378, §700.
168 *Scienza nuova* §700.
169 Vico, *Autobiography*, p. 123–4. Clearly Vico conceives a type of *ingenium* that is possible only for the abstractive mind of the third age, and that is trained by synthetic geometry. But it does not follow that earlier ages utterly lack *ingenium*: Vico describes the heroic age as one of "vigorosa memoria, della robusta fantasia e del sublime ingegno" (*Scienza nuova* §896; cf. §819, which also credits the *fanciulli delle nazioni* with "acuto ingegno nel rapportargli a' loro generi fantastici"). Though sublime, *ingegno* is not necessarily true: one thinks of the *Vita*'s description of Bacon's *De sapientia veterum* as "più ingegnoso e dotto che vero" (*Autobiography*, p. 148). (One of Vico's early critics uses this same line against him, claiming that he "magis ingenio indulgere quam veritati." See the *Vici vindiciae* 11 [Cristofolini *OF* 349].)
170 *Scienza nuova* §794. Additional proof that Vico conceives a type of *ingenium* distinct from and irreducible to *fantasia* is found in the ninth philosophical proof for the true Homer, where Vico holds in the heroic age, "'fantasia' altresì prendesi per l'ingegno (come ne' tempi barbari ritornati si disse 'uomo fantastico' per significar 'uomo d'ingegno'" (*Scienza nuova* §819).
171 See *Scienza nuova* §185.
172 *Scienza nuova* §819.
173 *Scienza nuova* §819.
174 *Prima Risposta* 2 (Cristofolini *OF* 138). Just before this passage, Vico claims *memoria* and *fantasia* are "una medesima facultà," in order to distinguish them

NOTES

from *l'ingegno*, which is "la particolar facultà del sapere," since it is that by which "l'uomo compone le cose, le quali a coloro che pregio d'ingegno non hanno, sembravano non aver tra loro nessun rapporto" (*OF* 138).

175 *De antiquissima* 7.5 (Cristofolini *OF* 123).
176 *De antiquissima* 7.4 (Cristofolini *OF* 117). See Lachterman, "Vico and Marx," p. 56.
177 *De antiquissima* 7.4 (Cristofolini *OF* 117).
178 Nietzsche, *On the Use and Abuse of History for Life*, §9.
179 *Scienza nuova* §345.
180 Vico, *De mente heroica*, in *Opere*, vol. 1, ed. A. Battistini, p. 378.
181 *Scienza nuova* §334.
182 *Scienza nuova* §349.
183 *Scienza nuova* §5.
184 *Prima Risposta* 3 (Cristofolini *OF* 142).
185 *De antiquissima* 6 (Cristofolini *OF* 111).
186 Christian Moevs, "Self-Knowledge and the Totality of Learning in Vico," p. 7 (unpublished paper).
187 *Scienza nuova* §31.
188 *De antiquissima* 1.2 (Cristofolini *OF* 67).
189 *De mente heroica*, in *Opere*, vol. 1, ed. Battistini, p. 378. Vico opens and closes the *De mente heroica* with reference to the near-divine nature of the mind (compare p. 372 and p. 398). The *Scienza nuova* speaks of the mind in the same terms: the poetic mind attempts "celebrare la sua presso che divina natura" with the enlargement of particulars by imagination (*Scienza nuova* §816).
190 This is the title of Book IV of the *Scienza nuova*. Bergin and Fisch's "The Course the Nations Run" misses the important reference to *fare/facere*.
191 *De uno universi iuris uno principio et fine uno* X, in Vico, *Opere giuridiche*, ed. Cristofolini, p. 45. Cf. *Sinopsi del diritto universale*, in *Opere giuridiche*, p. 5.
192 *Scienza nuova* §1111.
193 *Scienza nuova* §2. Vico speaks of "la metafisica in atto di estatica." Bergin and Fisch's "attitude of ecstasy" is too weak.

EPILOGUE

1 James J. O'Donnell, introduction to his edition of Augustine, *Confessions*, vol. 1, p. xvii. O'Donnell also draws attention to parallel usages at Ephesians 4:15, "veritatem autem facientes in caritate augeamur il illo per omnia, qui est caput Christus" and 1 John 1:6, "si dixerimus quoniam societatem habemus cum eo et in tenebris ambulamus, mentimur et non facimus veritatem." See O'Donnell, vol. 3, pp. 156–7.
2 Augustine, *Confessiones* 10.5 (O'Donnell, vol. 1, p. 121).
3 See O'Donnell, introduction to his edition of Augustine, *Confessions*, vol. 1, p. xxx.
4 See *Faith and Political Philosophy: the Correspondence Between Leo Strauss and Eric Voegelin*, p. 94.
5 See *Fides et Ratio* §47.
6 Bacon, *Novum Organum* 1.93.
7 Samuel Coleridge, *Essays on Principles of Method* in *The Friend*, in *The Collected Works of Samuel Taylor Coleridge*, ed. B.E. Rooke (Princeton, 1969), IV/1, 491, quoted in Charles Whitney, *Francis Bacon and Modernity*, p. 39.
8 Bacon, *Distributio Operis*, p. 23.
9 Bacon, *The Advancement of Learning*, p. 83.
10 Bacon, *Novum Organum* 1.129. Cf. Preface to *Instauratio Magna*, p. 15 and the parallel passage in *The Advancement of Learning*, p. 38.

NOTES

11 Bacon, *Novum Organum* 1.129.
12 Bacon, *Novum Organum* 1.129. The expression is attributed to Caecilius Comicus, according to Fowler's edition of the *Novum Organum*.
13 Nietzsche, *Ecce Homo*, trans. Walter Kaufmann (New York: Vintage Books, 1967), 246.
14 Stanley Rosen, *The Ancients and the Moderns*, pp. 219–20.
15 On the spatialized character of the secular order and its characteristic suppression of time, cf. Catherine Pickstock, *After Writing: On the Liturgical Consummation of Philosophy*, pp. 47–100.

BIBLIOGRAPHY

Ames, William (1979) *Technometria*, trans. Lee W. Gibbs, Philadelphia: University of Philadelphia Press.
Anderson, James (1949) *The Bond of Being: An Essay on Analogy and Existence*, New York: Greenwood Press.
Aquinas, Thomas (1912–36), *Summa Theologiae*, trans. Fathers of the Dominican Province, London: Burns, Oates and Washbourne.
—— (1952) *De Veritate*, vol. 1, trans. R.W. Mulligan, S.J. Chicago: Henry Regnery.
Bacon, Francis (1889) *Novum Organum*, ed. Thomas Fowler, Oxford: Clarendon Press.
—— (2001) *The Advancement of Learning*, ed. G.W. Kitchin, Philadelphia: Paul Dry Books.
—— (1994) *Novum Organum, with other parts of the Great Instauration*, eds. Peter Urbach and John Gibson, Chicago: Open Court.
Beck, Lewis (1969) *Early German Philosophy: Kant and His Predecessors*, Cambridge, Mass.: Belknap Press of Harvard University Press.
Bedani, Gino (1989) *Vico Revisited: Orthodoxy, Naturalism and Science in the* Scienza nuova, Oxford and New York: St. Martin's Press.
Berlin, Isaiah (1976) *Vico and Herder*, London: Hogarth.
Bird, Alexander (1996) 'Squaring the Circle: Hobbes on Philosophy and Geometry', in *Journal of the History of Ideas*, 57.2, pp. 217–31.
Brann, Eva (1984) 'The Roots of Modernity', in *St. John's Review*, Spring 1984, pp. 66–9.
Burrell, David (1973) *Analogy and Philosophical Language*, New Haven: Yale University Press.
Caton, Hiram (1991) 'The Problem of Descartes's Sincerity', in *René Descartes: Critical Assessments*, vol. II, ed. Georges J.D. Moyal, London and New York: Routledge, pp. 22–35.
Child, Arthur (1953) *Making and Knowing in Hobbes, Vico, and Dewey*, Berkeley and Los Angeles: The University of California Press.
Coleridge, Samuel (1969) *The Collected Works of Samuel Taylor Coleridge*, ed. B.E. Rooke, Princeton University Press.
Collingwood, R.G. (1938) *The Principles of Art*, Oxford: Clarendon Press.
—— (1939) *An Autobiography*, Oxford: Oxford University Press.
—— (1942) *The New Leviathan*, Oxford: Clarendon Press.
Cusanus, Nicolaus (1936) *De coniecturis*, vol. 3 of *Nicolai de Cusa opera omnia*, eds. E. Hoffmann, R. Kilbansky and H. Liebmann, Leipzig: R. Meiner.

—— (1979) *Idiota de mente*, trans. Clyde Lee Miller, *The Idiot, about Mind*, New York: Abaris Books.
—— (1986) *De ludo globi*, trans. Pauline Moffitt Watts, *The Game of Spheres*, New York: Abaris Books.
—— (1989) *Idiota de sapientia*, trans. M.L. Führer, *The Layman on Wisdom and the Mind*, Ottawa: Dovehouse Editions.
Davenport, Anne (1999) *Measure of a Different Greatness: The Intensive Infinite, 1250–1650*, Leiden and Boston: Brill.
Descartes, René (1985–91) *The Philosophical Writings of Descartes*, 3 vols., eds. John Cottingham, Robert Stoothoff and Dugald Murdoch, Cambridge: Cambridge University Press.
Dunne, Joseph (1993), *Back to the Rough Ground: 'Phronesis' and 'Techne' in Modern Philosophy and in Aristotle*, Notre Dame: University of Notre Dame Press.
Faith and Political Philosophy: The Correspondence Between Leo Strauss and Eric Voegelin, 1934–1964 (1993), eds. and trans. Peter Emberley and Barry Cooper, University Park, Penn.: The Pennsylvania State University Press.
Gadamer, Hans-Georg (1989), *Truth and Method*, 2nd edn., trans. Joel Weinsheimer and Donald G. Marshall, New York: Continuum.
Gauthier, David (1997), "Hobbes on Demonstration and Construction", in *Journal of the History of Philosophy*, 35.4, pp. 509–22.
Goetch, James (1995) *Vico's Axioms*, New Haven: Yale University Press.
Grene, Marjorie (1998) *Descartes*, Indianapolis: Hackett Publishing.
Hacking, Ian (1993) *Representing and Intervening*, Cambridge and New York: Cambridge University Press.
—— (1999) *The Social Construction of What?* Cambridge, Mass.: Harvard University Press.
Harries, Karsten (2001) *Infinity and Perspective*, Cambridge, Mass.: MIT Press.
Hemming, Laurence Paul (2000) "*Quod Impossible Est!* Aquinas and Radical Orthodoxy" in *Radical Orthodoxy?: A Catholic Enquiry*, ed. L.P. Hemming, Aldershot, UK. and Burlingate, Vt.: Ashgate, pp. 76–93.
Hesse, Mary (1968) "Francis Bacon's Philosophy of Science", in *Essential Articles for the Study of Francis Bacon*, ed. B. Vickers, Hamden, Ct.: Archon Books, pp. 114–39.
Hobbes, Thomas (1840) *The English Works of Thomas Hobbes*, ed. William Molesworth, London: John Bohn.
——. *The Elements of Law: Natural and Politic* (1969), ed. F. Tönnies, London: Frank Cass.
——. *Leviathan* (1994), ed. Edwin Curley, Indianapolis: Hackett Publishing.
John Paul II (1998), *Fides et Ratio: On the Relationship between Faith and Reason*, Boston: Pauline Books and Media.
Jordan, Mark (1977) 'Creation and Intelligibility in Aquinas: A Reading in the Contra Gentiles', unpublished thesis, University of Texas-Austin.
Kennington, Richard (1998), "The Reform of Nature", in *Modern Enlightenment and the Rule of Reason*, ed. John C. McCarthy, Washington, D.C.: The Catholic University of America Press, pp. 40–54.
Kenny, Anthony (1968) "Descartes on Ideas", in *Descartes: A Collection of Critical Essays*, ed. Willis Doney, Notre Dame: University Of Notre Dame Press, pp. 227–49.
Kerr, Fergus (2002) *After Aquinas: Versions of Thomism*, Malden, Mass.: Blackwell Publishing.

Klein, Jacob (1968) *Greek Mathematical Thought and the Origin of Alegebra*, trans. Eva Brann, Cambridge, Mass.: MIT Press.
Kusukawa, Sachiko (1996) "Bacon's Classification of Knowledge", in *The Cambridge Companion to Bacon*, ed. Markku Peltonen, Cambridge and New York: Cambridge University Press, pp. 47–74.
Lachterman, David (1983) "Vico and Marx: Notes on a Precursory Reading", in *Vico and Marx: Affinities and Contrasts*, ed. Giorgio Tagliacozzo, Atlantic Highlands, N.J.: Humanities Press, pp. 38–61.
—— (1985) "Mathematics and Nominalism in Vico's Liber Metaphysicus", in *Sachkommentar zu Giambattista Vicos Liber Metaphysicus*, eds. Stephan Otto and Helmut Viechtbauer, Munich: Fink, pp. 47–97.
—— (1989) *The Ethics of Geometry: A Genealogy of Modernity*, New York: Routledge.
Le Doeuff, Michèle (1990) "Man and Nature in the Gardens of Science", in *Francis Bacon's Legacy of Texts*, ed. William A. Sessions, New York: AMS Press, pp. 119–38.
Loeb, Louis E. (1986) "Is There Radical Dissimulation in Descartes' Meditations?" in *Essays on Descartes' Meditations*, ed. A.O. Rorty, Berkeley, Los Angeles and London: The University of California Press, pp. 243–70.
Malherbe, Michel (1996) "Bacon's Method of Science", in *The Cambridge Companion to Bacon*, ed. Markku Peltonen, Cambridge and New York: Cambridge University Press, pp. 75–98.
Marion, Jean-Luc (1981) *Sur la théologie blanche de Descartes: analogie, création des vérités éternelles et fondement*, Paris: Presses Universitaires de France.
—— (1999a) *Cartesian Questions*, Chicago and London: The University of Chicago Press.
—— (1999b) *On Descartes' Metaphysical Prism*, Chicago and London: The University of Chicago Press.
Maritain, Jacques (1953) *Creative Intuition in Art and Poetry*, New York: Pantheon.
——. (1962) *Art and Scholasticism and the Frontiers of Poetry*, New York: Scribner.
Mascall, E.L. (1949) *Existence and Analogy*, New York: Longmans, 1949.
Mazzotta, Giuseppe (1999) *The New Map of the World: The Poetic Philosophy of Giambattista Vico*, Princeton: Princeton University Press.
—— (2001) *Cosmopoiesis: The Renaissance Experiment*, Toronto and Buffalo: University of Toronto Press.
McInerny, Ralph (1996) *Aquinas and Analogy*, Washington, D.C.: Catholic University of America Press.
Milbank, John (1991) *The Religious Dimension of the Thought of Giambattista Vico: Part 1, The Early Metaphysics*, Lewiston, N.Y.: Edwin Mellen Press.
—— (1992) *The Religious Dimension of the Thought of Giambattista Vico: Part 2, Language, Law, and History*, Lewiston, N.Y.: Edwin Mellen Press.
—— (1997) *The Word Made Strange: Theology, Language and Culture*, Cambridge, Mass.: Blackwell.
Milbank, John and Pickstock, Catherine (1991) *Truth in Aquinas*, London: Routledge.
Mill, John Stuart (1969) *Autobiography*, ed. J. Stillinger, Boston: Houghton Mifflin.
Miner, Robert (2002) *Vico, Genealogist of Modernity*, Notre Dame: University of Notre Dame Press.
Moevs, Christian (1996) 'Self-Knowledge and the Totality of Learning in Vico', unpublished paper.

Momigliano, Arnaldo (1966) 'Vico's Scienza nuova: Roman "Bestoni" and Roman "Eroi"', in *History and Theory*, 5.1, pp. 3–23.
Nietzsche, Friedrich (1967) *Ecce Homo*, in *On the Genealogy of Morals* and *Ecce Homo*, trans. W. Kaufmann and R.J. Hollingdale, New York: Vintage Books.
—— (1980) *On the Advantages and Disadvantages of History for Life*, trans. Peter Preuss, Indianpolis: Hackett Publishing.
Oakeshott, Michael (1991) *Rationalism in Politics and Other Essays*, Indianapolis: Liberty Fund.
O'Donnell, James J. (1992) *Augustine's Confessions*, text and commentary, Oxford and New York: Oxford University Press.
Pascal, Blaise (1995) *Pensées*, trans. A.J. Krailsheimer, London and New York: Penguin.
Peirce, C.S. (1992) 'Some Consequences of Four Incapacities,' in *The Essential Peirce: Selected Philosophical Writings*, vol. 1, eds. Nathan Houser and Christian Kloesel, Bloomington and Indianapolis: Indiana University Press, pp. 28–55.
—— (1998) 'An Essay Toward Improving our Reasoning in Security and in Uberty', in *The Essential Peirce: Selected Philosophical Writings. Volume 2 (1893–1913)*, ed. Peirce Edition Project, Bloomington and Indianapolis: Indiana University Press, pp. 463–74.
Pérez-Ramos, Antonio (1988) *Francis Bacon's Idea of Science and the Maker's Knowledge Tradition*, Oxford: Oxford University Press.
—— (1996a) "Bacon's Forms and the Maker's Knowledge Tradition", in *The Cambridge Companion to Bacon*, ed. Markku Peltonen, Cambridge and New York: Cambridge University Press, pp. 99–120.
—— (1996b) "Bacon's Legacy", in *The Cambridge Companion to Bacon*, ed. Markku Peltonen, Cambridge and New York: Cambridge University Press, pp. 311–34.
Peters, Richard (1979) *Hobbes*, Westport, Conn.: Greenwood Press.
Pickstock, Catherine (1998) *After Writing: On the Liturgical Consummation of Philosophy*, Oxford: Blackwell.
Pieper, Josef (1999) *The Silence of St. Thomas*, trans. John Murray, S.J. and Daniel O'Connor, South Bend, Ind.: St. Augustine's Press.
Quinton, Anthony (1980) *Francis Bacon*, Oxford and New York: Oxford University Press.
Raiger, Michael (1999) 'Coleridge's Metaphysics and the Method of Deconstruction from Bacon to Heidegger', in *The Coleridge Bulletin* 14, pp. 16–25.
Rees, Graham (1980) 'Atomism and "Subtlety" in Francis Bacon's Philosophy', in *Annals of Science* 37, pp. 549–71.
Rodis-Lewis, Genevieve (1959) *L'Oeuvre de Descartes*, Paris: Vrin.
Rorty, Richard (1979) *Philosophy and the Mirror of Nature*, Princeton: Princeton University Press.
Rosen, Stanley (1989) *The Ancients and the Moderns: Rethinking Modernity*, New Haven: Yale University Press.
—— (1993) *The Question of Being: A Reversal of Heidegger*, New Haven: Yale University Press.
Rossi, Paolo (1968) *Francis Bacon: From Magic to Science*, trans. Sacha Rabinovitch, London: Routledge and Kegan Paul.
—— (1984) 'Ants, Spiders, Epistemologists', in *Francis Bacon, terminologia e fortuna nel XVII secolo*, ed. Marta Fattori, Rome: Edizioni dell'Ateneo, pp. 245–60.

Rousseau, Jean-Jacques (1987) *Discourse on the Sciences and the Arts*, trans. Donald Cress in *Basic Political Writings of Jean-Jacques Rousseau*, Indianapolis and Cambridge, Mass.: Hackett Publishing.
Sayers, Dorothy (1941) *The Mind of the Maker*, London: Metheuen.
Sepper, Dennis (1996) *Descartes's Imagination*, Berkeley: University of California Press.
Steiner, George (2001) *Grammars of Creation*, New Haven and London: Yale University Press.
Strauss, Leo (1953) *Natural Right and History*, Chicago and London: The University of Chicago Press.
—— (1959) 'On the Basis of Hobbes's Political Philosophy', in Leo Strauss, *What is Political Philosophy?* New York: The Free Press, pp. 170–96.
Taylor, Charles (1989) *Sources of the Self: The Making of the Modern Identity*, Cambridge, Mass.: Harvard University Press.
—— (1995) *Philosophical Arguments*, Cambridge, Mass.: Harvard University Press.
Toulmin, Stephen (1990) *Cosmopolis*, Chicago: The University of Chicago Press.
Trinkaus, Charles (1995) *In Our Image and Likeness: Humanity and Divinity in Italian Humanist Thought*, Notre Dame: University of Notre Dame Press.
Tuck, Richard (1993) *Philosophy and Government 1572–1651*, Cambridge: Cambridge University Press.
Urbach, Peter (1987) *Francis Bacon's Philosophy of Science*, La Salle, Ill.: Open Court.
Velde, Rudi A. te (1995) *Participation and Substantiality in Thomas Aquinas*, Leiden and New York: E.J. Brill.
Verene, Donald Phillip (1981), *Vico's Science of Imagination*, Ithaca: Cornell University Press.
Vickers, Brian (1992), 'Francis Bacon and the Progress of Knowledge', in *Journal of the History of Ideas*, 53.3, pp. 495–518.
Vico, Giambattista (1852–54) *Opere di Giambattista Vico*, ed. Giuseppe Ferrari, Milano: Società tipog. de'classici italiani.
—— (1971) *Opere filosofiche*, ed. Paolo Cristofolini, Firenze: Sansoni.
—— (1974) *Opere giuridiche*, ed. Paolo Cristofolini, Firenze: Sansoni.
—— (1982) *Vico: Selected Writings*, ed. and trans. Leon Pompa, Cambridge: Cambridge University Press.
—— (1990) *Opere*, 2 vols., ed. Andrea Battistini, Milano: Mondadori.
—— (1998) "Four Letters of Giambattista Vico," trans. Giorgio Pinton, in *New Vico Studies* 16, pp. 31–58.
Voegelin, Eric (1999) *History of Political Ideas, vol. vi: Revolution and the New Science*, ed. Barry Cooper, Columbia, Mo.: University of Missouri Press.
Whitney, Charles (1986) *Francis Bacon and Modernity*, New Haven and London: Yale University Press.
Yolton, John (1990) 'Mirrors and Veils, Thoughts and Things: The Epistemological Problematic', in *Reading Rorty*, ed. Alan Malachowski, Oxford: Blackwell, pp. 58–73.

INDEX

abstractions: dividing 101; mathematics 32, 102, 105; metaphysics 100–1; mind 30; presuppositions 101–2; Vico 100–3
abstractive model 7–8, 153n169
actual/possible 31
algebra 72
American Indians 109
Ames, William 58
analogy: Aristotle 12; attribution 12, 13, 15; being 13, 14–15; Cajetan 11–12; inequality 12, 16; metaphysics 11–12; presuppositions 12; proportionality 12, 13–15, 132n62
anatomy 53
Anderson, James 13–14, 16
ant example 45, 46
anvil example 42
Aquinas, Saint Thomas: creation xiv, 2–11, 18, 19, 131n36; *esse* 14, 15–16; generation 7, 8–9; God's creation 2–7, 131n36; healthy example 12–13; human creation xiii–xiv, 7–11, 18, 19; metaphysics analogy 11–12; substantiality 16; *Summa Theologiae* 3; technical making 2–3; truth 11; *verbum mentis* doctrine 9
Aristotle: *analogia* 12; categories 46; form 24–5; healthy example 12–13; induction 136n19; knowledge 51; reason 23–4; *techne* 131–2n47
arithmetic 101, 106
ars/techne 1–2
art 4; artifact xiii; craft xiii; creation 9, 18; divine 22, 37–8; function 20–1; image 21–2
artifact xiii, 1, 22–3
artifice 41, 88–9

assimilation 27–8, 29–30
assimilationes/notiones 31
atheism 111
atomism 50, 54, 140n111
attribution analogy 12, 13, 15
Augustine of Hippo, Saint xiii, 58, 126–7, 154n1
axioms, Bacon 40, 43; light 44, 46; literate experience 47–8; science 46; sense/memory/reason 47; transformation 53; true 44; works 40, 49–50

Bacon, Francis xii–xiii; atomism 50, 54, 140n111; axioms 40, 43, 44, 46, 47, 49–50, 53; charity 56–7, 59; contemplation 55–6, 136n25; creation 47; desacralized world 58–9; experience 46–7; forms 50–1, 52, 53, 140n100; human/divine learning 57; human/divine mind 54–5; human making 40; induction 41–2, 45–6; knowledge 128–9; light 127–8; limited objective principle 49; mathematics 54, 140–1n113; modernity xiv, xv–xvi, 38–9, 127; moral knowledge 137n29; natural philosophy 57–8; *Novum Organum* 40, 51, 139–40n94; *opus* 44–5; schematism 53; scholasticism 55–6; science 42; subtlety of nature 40–1; theology 59
Barth, Karl 15–16
Bedani, Gino 151n86
bee example 45, 46, 47–8
being analogy 13, 14–15; *see also esse*
Berlin, Isaiah 153n162
blacksmith example 61

161

body/motion 106
body politic 87–8
Boethius, Anicius 16
Boulnois, Olivier 16
Brann, Eva 137n29
bridge example 8
Burrell, David 14

Cajetan 11–12, 13
Carnap, Rudolf xi
Cartesian: *see* Descartes
Cassirer, Ernst 34–5
categories 46
causes/knowledge 51, 139–40n94
charity 55–7, 59
Child, Arthur 146–7n7
children 109–10, 113, 151n86
circle 30, 80–1
civil philosophy: creation 88–90; geometry 78, 93–4; rules 86–7; technical making 85–6, 88–9
civil world 116, 123–4
cogitare/intelligere 99, 107
cogitatio 98
cognition 97–8
cognitive value 60
Coleridge, Samuel 128
Collingwood, R. G.: art/artifact xiii; bridge example 8; craft 3; limited objective principle 49; technical making xii, 1–2, 4, 86, 87, 89
commonwealth: generative definition 93; technical making 85–91
complicatio/explicatio 33–4
comprehension 36–7; *see also* knowing; understanding
concept xv, 8, 60
conceptio 27
concipere/intelligere 31
Condillac, Étienne Bonnot de 118
conjecture 21, 24
construction xi–xii, xvi, 60, 63
contemplation 20, 34, 55–6, 136n25
craft xiii, 3
craftsman 1–2, 4–6, 8, 11
creatio 27
creation xiii; Aquinas xiv, 2–11, 18, 19, 131n36; art 9, 18; artifice 88–9; Bacon 47; civil philosophy 88–90; Descartes 73–4; dividing 100; generation 6, 7, 8–9, 11; geometry 113–14; God 2–7, 9, 18, 19, 43–4, 88, 112; Hobbes 88, 89–90; law-maker 10–11; mathematics 105; nature 76–7, 129; plan 8; poetry 5–6, 112, 113; technical making 2, 4; *see also* human creation; making
creativity xiv, 5–6, 7–11, 113
Croce, Benedetto 121
Cusanus, Nicolaus 18; actuality 31; assimilation 27–8, 29–30; Cassirer 34–5; human creativity 38–9; *Idiota de Mente* xiv, 19, 20–1, 133n30; *Idiota de Sapientia* 20; making 37–8; *mens* 37; mirroring power 28–9; philosopher 20–1; reason 23–6; *res* 37; rhetoric 25–6; secular space 35–6; solidity 32; unfoldings/enfoldings 33–4

Davenport, Anne 16, 17, 18
deduction 60, 65–6
definitions 80; generative 80–1, 93; geometry 79–80; Hobbes 79–83, 85, 91; non-generative 82; propositions 79; truth 83
demiurge 1, 4, 99
demonstration, rules of 82
desacralized world 58–9, 115–16
Descartes, René xii–xiii; anvil example 42; composite natures 65–6; construction 60, 63; creation 73–4; deduction 60, 65–6; dimension 71–2; *Discours de la Méthode* 60, 61; *Géométrie* 60; geometry xv, 72; God 74–5; human creation 74; ideas 62–3; imagination 71; making 63; mathematics 67, 75–6; metaphysics 75; modernity xiv, xv–xvi, 38–9, 127; painting 63; physics 65, 75; *quaestiones* 70–3; *Regulae ad directionem ingenii* 61; representation 61–3, 64, 65–6; *scientia* 66, 68; simple natures 66, 67–9
dialectic 41
difference 37
dimension 71–2
dissection 43, 50, 54, 100
dividing 100, 101
Dunne, Joseph 131–2n47

eidos 128
empiricism xvi, 45–6
enfoldings/unfoldings 33–4
Enlightenment xvi
Epicureans 124

esse 14, 15–16; *see also* being analogy
ethics 101, 103, 104
Euclid 81, 83, 147n23
exemplars 24–5, 26, 30, 131n33
experience 46–8
explicatio 27, 33–4
extension 71

faith/reason xvi, 57, 128
false inference 82
family 120–1
fantasia: children 109–10; imagination 109, 111–12; Lachterman 151n102; mythopoesis 108–9; science 122; Vico 108–12
fear 118
Ficino, Marsilio xiv
figure 71, 72
form: Aristotle 24–5; artifact 22–3; Bacon 50–1, 52, 53, 140n100; latent process 53; making 22–3; mathematics 25–6; matter 1; metaphysics 54; Plato 50
Freud, Sigmund 129

Gadamer, Hans-Georg 133n3
Gassendi, Pierre 61, 62
Gauthier, David 93, 94
generation 6, 7, 8–9, 11
Genesis, Book of 19
genus 24, 25, 37
geometry: civil philosophy 78, 93–4; creation 113–14; definitions 79–80; Descartes xv, 72; Hobbes 78, 81–2, 84–5, 146–7n7; metaphysics 107–8; point 119; quantity 68; truth 106; Vico 101, 106–8
Gilbert, William 70
God: *artifex* 4; craftsman 4–5, 100; creation 2–7, 9, 18, 19, 43–4, 88, 112, 131n36; Descartes 74–5; divine art 22, 37–8; Freud 129; light 43, 44, 127–8; loss of faith in 57; making 99, 108; metaphysics 125; philosophy 124–5; *scientia* 104; self-knowledge 5, 6; singulars 3; speaking/making 131n36
gods 110
gold example 51, 53
Goodman, Nelson xi
grace 127
Grene, Marjorie 142n21
Grotius, Hugo 119, 121

Hacking, Ian xi–xii, 63
happiness 127
Harries, Karsten 135n113
healthy example 12–13
Heidegger, Martin xii, xiii, xvi
Hobbes, Thomas: civil philosophy 85–91; creation 88, 89–90; definitions 79–83, 85, 91; *Elements of Law* 87, 89, 90, 94; geometry 78, 81–2, 84–5, 146–7n7; human nature 90–1; intuition 83–4, 92; knowing/making xii–xiii, 78–9; knowledge 79; language 147n8; *Leviathan* 82, 86, 87, 89, 90, 92, 93, 112; modernity xiv, xv–xvi, 38–9, 127; nature 119–20; passions 109; physics 78; practical philosophy 92–3; rules of demonstration 82; technical making 91; teleology 94–5; *verum-factum* principle 92, 95; violent men 121
Homer 123, 151n97
human beings/nature 42
human creation: Aquinas xiii–xiv, 7–11, 18, 19; Bacon 40; Cusanus 37–9; Descartes 74; and God's 88; Renaissance xiv; *see also* making, human
human nature 90–1
humanism 108–9
hylomorphism 37

ideas: absolute perfection 97; adventitious 62; Descartes 62–3; humanly constructed 62–3; innate 62; knowledge 5; representation 61–2
ignorance 118
image: art 21–2; divine art 37–8; example 23; exemplars 26; mind 38; solid/plane 98–9
imagination: Descartes 71; *fantasia* 109, 111–12; gods 110; intellect 71, 73; memory 123; understanding 122–3
imitatio/perfectio 31
imitation 31, 113
induction: Aristotle 136n19; Bacon 41–2, 45–6; Plato 42
inequality analogy 12, 16
ingenium 122–3, 153n169
instruments 40
intellect/imagination 71, 73
intelligentia 98

intelligere: cogitare 99, 107; cognition 97–8; *concipere* 31; *similitudo* 37
intuition 29, 83–4, 92

Jacobi, F. H. xii
John's Gospel 126
Jordan, Mark 11
Jove 110

Kant, Immanuel xi–xii, xv
Kennington, Richard 136n25
Kenny, Anthony 142n10
Kierkegaard, Søren xi
knowing: making xi, xii–xiii, 2, 78–9; seeing 1
knowledge: Aristotle 51; Bacon 128–9; causes 51, 139–40n94; charity 55; Hobbes 79; ideas 5; maker's xii; moral 137n29; poetic 11; power 93
Kusukawa, Sachiko 139–40n94

Lachterman, David: construction xiv–xv, 60; *fantasia* 151n102; *ingenium* 123; mathematics 108; self-deception 112; Vico 114
Lactantius 109
language 147n8
latent process 53, 54
law-maker 10–11
laws/nature 51–2; *see also* natural law
layman 20, 21–2, 25, 28–9
learning, human/divine 57
Leibniz, Gottfried xv, 25, 74, 76
light: axioms 44, 46; Bacon 127–8; God 43, 44, 127–8
limited objective principle 49
line 32, 80, 81, 84–5, 106
literate experience 47–8
Locke, John 76
logic 101, 103
Logos 126, 127
Lucretius 3, 101, 149n33

McInerny, Ralph 14
making xii–xiii; civil philosophy 85–6, 88–9; cognition 97; comprehension 36–7; contemplation 20; Descartes xii–xiii, 63; form 22–3; God 99, 108; human xiv, 37–8, 40, 99, 108; knowing xi, xii–xiii, 2, 78–9; mimetic xiii, 113; modernity xiv; seeing 29; *see also* creation; technical making
Malherbe, Michel 41–2

Manicheans 58
Marion, Jean-Luc 65–6, 67, 69, 143n44
Maritain, Jacques 5–6, 8, 9, 11, 131n33
marriage 120
Mascall, Eric 14–15, 16
mathematics xv; abstractions 32, 102, 105; Bacon 54, 140–1n113; creation 105; Descartes 67, 75–6; form 25–6; Lachterman 108; mind 25–6; Pérez-Ramos 141n113; truth 103, 106, 107, 144n64; Vico 101–2
matter 1, 7
measuring 21, 32, 34, 72
mechanics 101, 103
medicine 101, 103
memory/imagination 123
mens 26–7, 37; *see also* mind
mensurae 34; *see also* measuring
Mersenne, Marin 63
metaphysics: abstractions 100–1; Aquinas 11–12; body/motion 106; Descartes 75; forms 54; geometry 107–8; God 125; Heidegger xii; power 45; Vico 105–6
Milbank, John 15, 108, 118, 132n62
Mill, John Stuart 138n54
mimetic making xiii, 113; *see also* imitation
mind: abstractions 30; conjecture 21; human/divine 26–7, 29, 54–5; image 38; mathematics 25–6; measuring 21, 32; mirroring 28–9; modernity xv; modifications 114–15, 116–17; power 28, 34, 45; primitive 117–18; reality 33; truth 99; unfolding 27; universe 40; *see also mens*
mirroring 28–9, 63, 143n28
modernity: Bacon xiv, xv–xvi, 38–9, 127; construction xvi; Descartes xiv, xv–xvi, 38–9, 127; Hobbes xiv, xv–xvi, 38–9, 127; making xiv; mind xv; nihilism xi; secular 129
Moevs, Christian 124
Momigliano, Arnaldo 115
mondo civile 116, 119, 121
moral knowledge 137n29
moral philosophy 87, 94, 104
motion 84, 103, 106
mythopoesis 108–9, 110, 112–13

naming 23, 24–5
natural history 48
natural law 10, 121

INDEX

natural philosophy 43–4, 57–8, 59, 76
nature: creation 76–7, 129; dissection 43, 54; Hobbes 119–20; human beings 42; laws 51–2; mirroring 143n28; savage 122; subtlety 40–1; Vico 114, 119–20
natures: complex 54, 65–6; Descartes 66, 67–9; representation 65–6; simple 53, 65–6, 68–9, 144n45
Nietzsche, Friedrich 55, 123, 128–9
nihilism xi, 77
notiones 28, 29, 30, 31, 34
number 71

Oakeshott, Michael 79, 81, 88
Ockham, William of 31
O'Donnell, James 126, 154n1
Olivi, Peter 16–17, 18
operatio 51–3
opinion 24
opus 44–5

paganism 99
painting 7–8, 20, 63
Paracelsus 57
participation 16–17
particularism 3
Pascal, Blaise 64, 74, 76, 104
passions 109
Peirce, C. S. 40, 74–5, 77, 138n66, 146n107
Pérez-Ramos, Antonio 51, 52, 136n19, 140n100, 141n113
perfectio/imitatio 31
philology 12, 116–17, 121
philosopher 20–1, 25
philosophy: God 124–5; philology 116–17, 121; practical 64, 76, 92–3; *see also* natural philosophy
physics 101; Descartes 65, 75; Hobbes 78; latent process 54; motion 103, 106; quantity 68; works 45
Pickstock, Catherine 144n58
Pieper, Josef 9
plan 8
Plato: demiurge 1, 4, 99; forms 50; induction 42; painting 20; *Timaeus* 1; wisdom 124
Platonism 24–5, 107, 108, 128
Plutarch 111
poetry 5–6, 11, 112, 113; theological 110, 112
poiesis xii, xiii

point 32–3, 34, 106, 119
Popper, Karl 48, 49
posse facere 36
posse fieri 36
power: active/passive 36; constructive 34; knowledge 93; of mind 45; mirroring 28, 63, 143n28
precepts 52–3, 61
preconceptions xiii
presumptions, negative 49
presuppositions 12, 36, 48, 101–2
principia 36
Proclus xiv
productio 27
proportionality analogy 12, 13–15, 132n62
propositions 79
providence 9, 18, 118–19
Pufendorf, Samuel 121
Pythagoreans 107

quaestiones 70–3
qualities 70–1
quantity 68
Quinton, Anthony 140–1n113

ratio 28, 97, 127
rationalism xvi, 45–6; *see also* reason
reality 33
reason 23–6; faith xvi, 57, 128; *see also ratio;* rationalism
religion 116, 118, 120
Renaissance xiv, 12
representation: accurate 62–3, 64; Descartes 61–3, 64, 65–6; as *factum* 64; ideas 61–2; mirroring power 63; simple natures 65–6
res 37
rhetoric 25–6
Rorty, Richard 28, 62–3, 74
Rosen, Stanley xiii, 129
Russell, Bertrand xi

Sayers, Dorothy 19
scepticism 104
schematism 53
scholasticism 55–6
science: axioms 46; Bacon 42; *fantasia* 122; religion 116; Vico 116–17
scientia: assimilation 30; Descartes 66, 68; God 104; latent process 53; Vico 98–9
Scotus, John Duns xiii, 16, 17–18, 31

INDEX

scripture 100
secular space 35–6, 129
seeing 1, 29
self-contemplation 30
self-deception 112
self-knowledge 5, 6, 126–7
Sepper, Dennis 63, 64
shame 118–19
similitudo 36, 37, 98
singulars 3
solidity 32
Solomon 128
speaking/making 131n36
species 24, 25, 37
spider 45, 46
Spinoza, Baruch 16, 76
spirit 5–6
spoon-making example 20–3, 28–9, 31, 35
Steiner, George 85
Stoicism 106, 124
Strauss, Leo 79, 84, 89, 92, 127
Suarez, Francisco de 15
substantiality 16–17
superinduction 54
superstition 111
surface 32, 106
syllogism 41

Tacitus 109, 115
Taylor, Charles 56–7, 63
techne 1–2, 4, 131–2n47
technical making: Aquinas 2–3; artifice 88–9; civil philosophy 85–6, 88–9; Collingwood xiii, 1–2, 4, 86, 87, 89; commonwealth 85–91; creation 2, 4; Hobbes 91
teleology 94–5
theological poets 110, 112
theology 38, 58, 59
theurgy xiv
thinking 63; *see also cogitare*
Toulmin, Stephen 146n101
transformation 7, 48, 53, 86–7
translation 126
triangularity 26
Trinity 6, 7, 16–18, 35–6
truth 97–8, 108; Aquinas 11; definition 83; geometry 106; human/divine 98; mathematics 103, 106, 107, 144n64; mind 99

type, concept 58

understanding 97, 122–3
unfoldings/enfoldings 27, 33–4
universalism 3
universe 40
univocity 16, 18

Vattimo, Gianni 129
Velde, Rudi te 16
Verbum 126
verbum mentis doctrine 9
verum-factum principle: Augustine 126; Hobbes 92, 95; paganism 99; Vico xii, xvi, 96–7, 105
Vickers, Brian 48
Vico, Giambattista xiii; abstractions 100–3; American Indians 109; arithmetic 106; *Autobiography* 96, 111, 114, 115, 123; *De antiquissima* 96, 99–100, 100, 102–4, 105, 108, 113, 123, 124; *De mente heroica* 124; desacralized world 115–16; dissection 100; family 120–1; *fantasia* 108–12; geometry 101, 106–8; humanism 108–9; *Idea of the Work* 122; *ingenium* 153n169; Lachterman 114; mathematics 101–2; metaphysics 105–6; mind/image 38; mythopoesis 109, 110; natural law 121; nature 114, 119–20; Poetic Morals 111; point 34; *Prima Risposta* 100, 101, 105, 123; science 116–17; *scientia* 98–9; *Scienza nuova* 105, 108, 109, 111, 113, 116–17, 119, 123, 124, 153n163; *Seconda Risposta* 106; superstition 111; theological poets 112; thinking 63; *verum-factum* principle xii, xvi, 96–7, 105
visibility example 27–8
Voegelin, Eric 116, 127

Wallis, John 79, 81, 82, 83, 147n23
William of Ware 17
wisdom 124
works from axioms 40, 45, 49–50

Yolton, John 63

Zenonians 106, 108

eBooks – at www.eBookstore.tandf.co.uk

A library at your fingertips!

eBooks are electronic versions of printed books. You can store them on your PC/laptop or browse them online.

They have advantages for anyone needing rapid access to a wide variety of published, copyright information.

eBooks can help your research by enabling you to bookmark chapters, annotate text and use instant searches to find specific words or phrases. Several eBook files would fit on even a small laptop or PDA.

NEW: Save money by eSubscribing: cheap, online access to any eBook for as long as you need it.

Annual subscription packages

We now offer special low-cost bulk subscriptions to packages of eBooks in certain subject areas. These are available to libraries or to individuals.

For more information please contact webmaster.ebooks@tandf.co.uk

We're continually developing the eBook concept, so keep up to date by visiting the website.

www.eBookstore.tandf.co.uk